SOTHEBY'S

ART AT AUCTION 1990–91

SOTHEBY'S
ART AT AUCTION 1990–91

SOTHEBY'S PUBLICATIONS

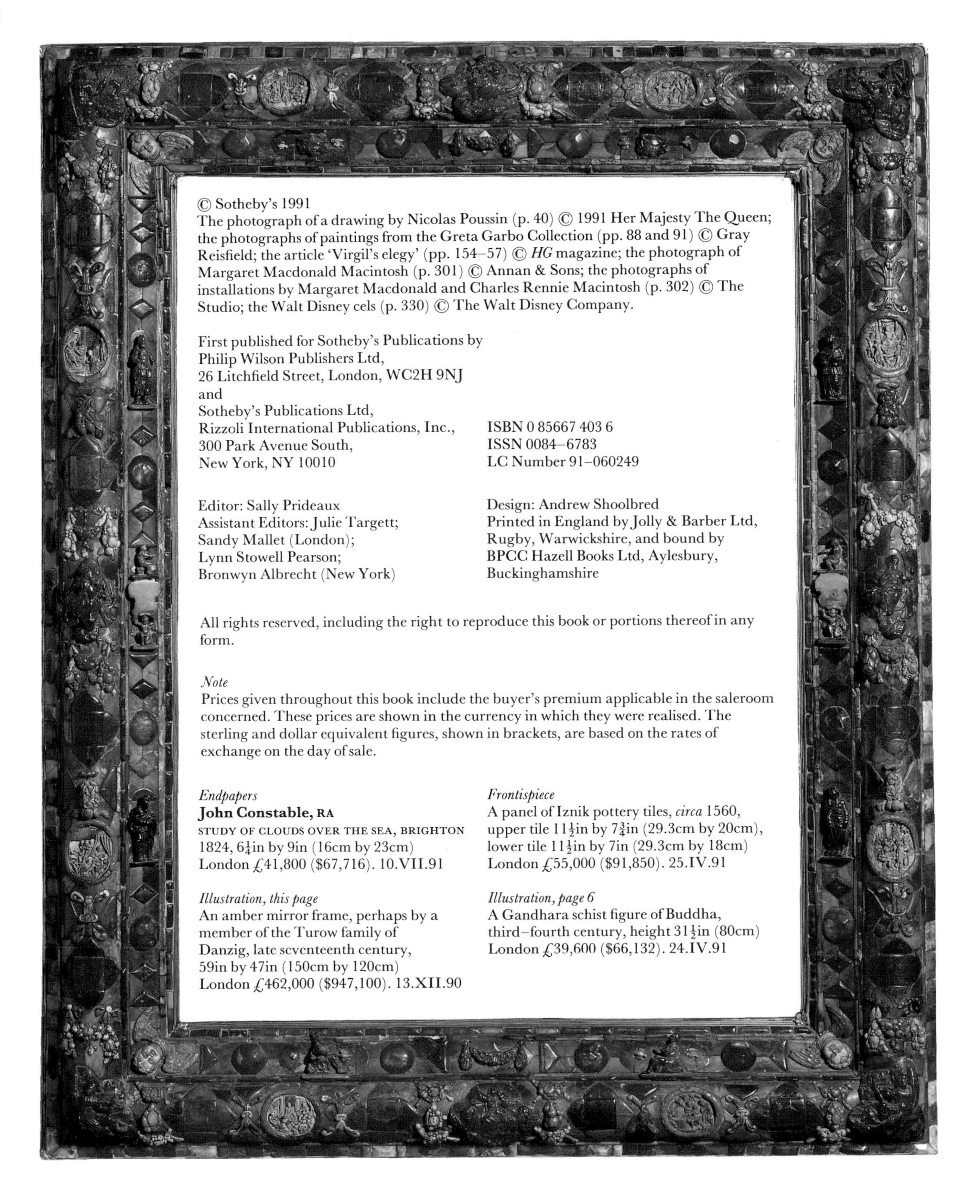

First published for Sotheby's Publications by
Philip Wilson Publishers Ltd,
26 Litchfield Street, London, WC2H 9NJ
and
Sotheby's Publications Ltd,
Rizzoli International Publications, Inc.,
300 Park Avenue South,
New York, NY 10010

ISBN 0 85667 403 6
ISSN 0084–6783
LC Number 91–060249

Editor: Sally Prideaux
Assistant Editors: Julie Targett;
Sandy Mallet (London);
Lynn Stowell Pearson;
Bronwyn Albrecht (New York)

Design: Andrew Shoolbred
Printed in England by Jolly & Barber Ltd, Rugby, Warwickshire, and bound by BPCC Hazell Books Ltd, Aylesbury, Buckinghamshire

Note
Prices given throughout this book include the buyer's premium applicable in the saleroom concerned. These prices are shown in the currency in which they were realised. The sterling and dollar equivalent figures, shown in brackets, are based on the rates of exchange on the day of sale.

Endpapers
John Constable, RA
STUDY OF CLOUDS OVER THE SEA, BRIGHTON
1824, 6¼in by 9in (16cm by 23cm)
London £41,800 ($67,716). 10.VII.91

Illustration, this page
An amber mirror frame, perhaps by a member of the Turow family of Danzig, late seventeenth century,
59in by 47in (150cm by 120cm)
London £462,000 ($947,100). 13.XII.90

Frontispiece
A panel of Iznik pottery tiles, *circa* 1560,
upper tile 11½in by 7¾in (29.3cm by 20cm),
lower tile 11½in by 7in (29.3cm by 18cm)
London £55,000 ($91,850). 25.IV.91

Illustration, page 6
A Gandhara schist figure of Buddha,
third–fourth century, height 31½in (80cm)
London £39,600 ($66,132). 24.IV.91

Contents

Preface

A. Alfred Taubman

Chairman, Sotheby's Holdings, Inc.

Francisco José de Goya y Lucientes
A MAJA AND CELESTINA
Carbon black; touched with red wash, heightened with graffito on ivory, 2⅛in by 2⅛in (5.4cm by 5.4cm)
New York $550,000 (£321,637). 30.V.91
From the collection of Mr Andrew Clark, by descent from Lord Kenneth Clark

Winds of change swept through the 1990–91 auction season. Worldwide economic recession and the Gulf war significantly affected the activity of both buyers and sellers at auction. Nevertheless, many collecting fields continued to show strength and growth.

We saw strong sales results in French furniture, books and manuscripts, jewellery, antiquities, European works of art, coins, American furniture, folk art, photographs, Japanese art and tribal art. In fact, many of the individual highlights of the season came from the decorative arts areas. Consequently, at Sotheby's we have seen a return to the more traditional division of the market between fine and decorative arts.

Highlights of the season included Robert Rauschenberg's *Rebus* which sold for $7.3 million. This price surpassed the painting's previous record of $6.3 million achieved only two and a half years earlier. Other notable sales were Constable's *The Lock* which established an auction record for any British picture, Renoir's *La Tasse de Chocolat* from the Ford Family Collection, a first printing of *The Declaration of Independence* which brought the record for any printed Americana at auction and a Senufo female rhythm pounder, one of the finest works of African art ever sold by Sotheby's.

Opposite
Honoré Daumier
LES TROIS COMMERES
Pen and indian ink and watercolour heightened with gouache over charcoal, signed, *circa* 1855, 10¼in by 7⅛in
(26cm by 18cm)
London £319,000
($644,380). 5.XII.90

Outstanding collections also distinguished the season. Among these were those of Greta Garbo, the Ford Family, Irene Mayer Selznick, Ava Gardner, Barbara Hutton and Chester Beatty. In addition, the last of the nine sales of antiquities and ancient coins from Nelson Bunker Hunt and William Herbert Hunt were completed this season, setting records in both categories.

We continued our international expansion by opening three new European offices: Lugano, Basel and Berlin, where we held the first international sale of twentieth-century German art. In Tokyo this spring, we held the first public auction of Japanese prints by a Western auction house. Sotheby's will continue to develop relationships in markets around the world to fulfil our ongoing commitment to providing the best possible service to our clients.

In this period of change, we would like to recognise the outstanding support and contributions of the dedicated people in our offices around the world. On behalf of the Board of Directors of Sotheby's Holdings, Inc., I congratulate the senior management of Sotheby's worldwide.

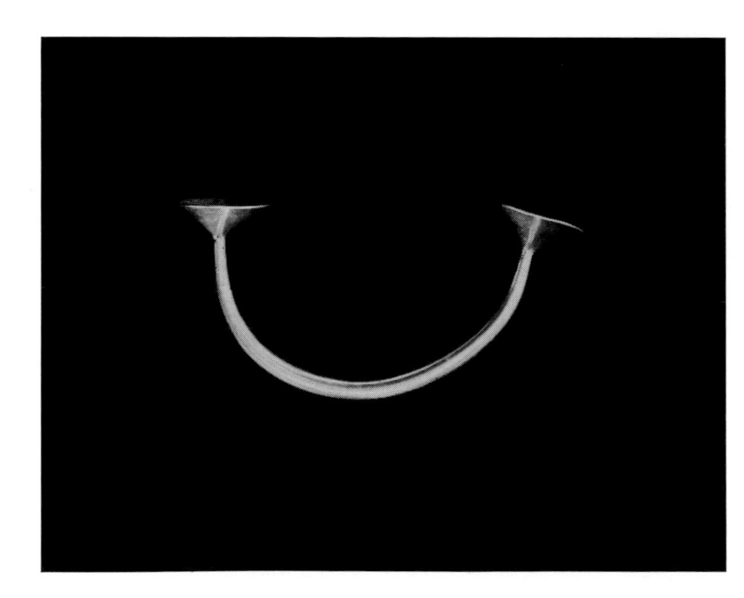

A gold garment clasp, *circa* 800–500 BC, width 4¾in (12cm)
One of thirteen pieces of Irish Bronze age gold jewellery, from the collection of the Dukes of Northumberland, sold through Sotheby's to the National Museum of Ireland.

A sheet-gold lunula, said to be from County Galway, Early Second Millennium BC, 7¾in (19.7cm)
A gold ribbon torc, said to be from County Sligo, *circa* 1500–800 BC, diameter 4in (10.2cm)
Two gold dress fasteners, 800–600 BC, widths 1in (2.4cm)
This group of Irish Bronze age gold jewellery, from the collection of the Dukes of Northumberland, was sold through Sotheby's to the National Museum of Ireland. The jewellery had been discovered in Ireland in the last century.

Heritage sales: trusts and estates

Timothy Sammons

Peter Tillemans
LITTLE HAUGH HALL, SUFFOLK
33in by 59in (83.8cm by 149.8cm)
The Patteson Collection was sold by private treaty through Sotheby's, with an acceptance in lieu of tax, to Norwich Castle Museum.

Sotheby's trusts and estates department has again been working successfully with owners to assist in the planning of the ownership and disposition of their works of art. One of the many avenues that can be explored in any planning discussion is that of 'heritage sales'. The undeniable advantage of such a 'sale' is that the owner will only incur 75% of his tax liabilities. This used to mean either a sale with concessions to one of the National institutions or an acceptance by the Treasury in lieu of tax due. These alternatives did not always cover certain situations, but the flexibility of the system has now been reinforced and Sotheby's has been involved in pioneering new approaches to deal with problems as they arise. For example, there now exists a hybrid arrangement, which is a mixture of a private treaty sale to an institution and an acceptance in lieu of tax. This precedent was set when the nation received Picasso's *Weeping Woman* from Sir Roland Penrose (see *Art at Auction* 1987–88, pages 23–25), and has now been successfully employed again in the Patteson Collection. The diversity of objects covered by heritage negotiations can be seen by looking at some of the successful transactions of the past season.

One of the most extensive collections of documents for the British side of Naval operations in the American War of Independence was sold to the National Maritime Museum. Referred to as the Sandwich Papers, this is the personal and state archive

Opposite
John Zoffany, RA
JOHN WILKES AND HIS DAUGHTER POLLY
Circa 1779, 49¾in by 39¼in (126cm by 100cm)
Sold by private treaty through Sotheby's to the National Portrait Gallery.

Sir Thomas Lawrence, PRA
PORTRAIT OF LYDIA, LADY ACLAND, WITH HER TWO SONS THOMAS AND ARTHUR
60in by 46in (152.4cm by 116.8cm)
Sold by private treaty through Sotheby's to the National Trust.

A Roman gold ring, third – second century BC
This ring, from the collection of the Dukes of Northumberland, was sold by private treaty through Sotheby's to the University of Newcastle.

Opposite
One of two Florentine *pietre dure* cabinets, seventeenth century, overall heights approximately 4ft 10in (147cm)
Sold by private treaty through Sotheby's to the National Trust; to remain in situ at Chirk Castle.

of John Montagu, 4th Earl of Sandwich and first Lord of the Admiralty. John Montagu (1718–1792) was the most senior official in the British Navy at the time and the events covered are some of the most significant in a crucial period of Anglo-American relations.

The C. H. Brackenbury Memorial Collection of early wind instruments was accepted in lieu of tax, and is currently on display at Edinburgh University. Private treaty sales were arranged for several pieces from the Duke of Northumberland's collection including a group of early Egyptian papyri, sold to the British Museum, two early Roman gold rings sold to the University of Newcastle, and a carnelian intaglio from High Rochester sold to English Heritage. A bed designed by Charles Rennie Mackintosh was sold to the National Trust for Scotland to remain in The Hill House at Helensburgh, for which it was made. Two superb Florentine cabinets were sold to the National Trust, which will remain at Chirk Castle in Wales where they have been for many years.

As usual the majority of activity was to do with pictures and of particular interest was the portrait *John Wilkes and his daughter Polly* by John Zoffany, which was sold to the National Portrait Gallery, and the portrait of Lady Acland and her children by Thomas Lawrence, which was sold to the National Trust to hang at Killerton in Devon. Originally an Acland estate, Killerton was given to the National Trust by Sir Richard Acland, who died this year.

A group of pictures known as the Patteson Collection, assembled by Dr Cox Macro in the late seventeenth and early eighteenth centuries, was transferred to the Norwich Castle Museum by means of the 'hybrid' arrangement mentioned above. This is the single most important acquisition of paintings made by the Castle Museum since 1946 and includes works by various artists including Peter Tillemans. Dr Macro, an ancestor through marriage of the Patteson family, had been a patron and close associate of Tillemans throughout the artist's life.

The court plate of James I

Philippa Glanville

Detail of Fig. 1, showing the arms of James I.

King James consumed that mighty mass of Treasure left by Queen Elizabeth without bettering any man except a few beggerlye Scots.
(Simonds D'Ewes, *Diary*, 1620)

James I has attracted a consistently bad press for almost 400 years. His sexual tastes, his physical attributes (or lack of them), his Scottish favourites, his hounding of Sir Walter Raleigh and his perceived indifference to the artistic sensibilities of Anne of Denmark and Prince Henry are all held against him. He has certainly never been credited with an informed interest in the decorative arts. However, there is strong evidence to modify and even to reverse this judgment, at least as far as an interest in the work of the goldsmith is concerned.

Fig. 1
One of a pair of silver-gilt flagons, maker's mark *FT*, London, 1580–81, height 17¼in (44cm) (Reproduced by courtesy of the Moscow Kremlin Armoury Museum).

This flagon was presented to Tsar Boris Godunov by James I's ambassador to Moscow, Sir Thomas Smith, in 1604–1605.

The evidence for James's interest in his silver is partly buried in Jewel House documents in the Public Record Office and partly visible in the English silver preserved in the Kremlin. It shows that he took great care to direct the court goldsmiths and spent heavily on this most costly of the crafts in the first decade of his reign. As was customary, he showed off the precious and historic contents of the Jewel House to his princely visitors and recognised their significance for the crown, declaring the Imperial Crown and other regalia 'to be among the Roiall and Princely Jewells and ornaments' which were inalienable from the monarchy.

In 1603 he had taken over a Jewel House whose contents were already greatly depleted from their 1559 level. Because of the poor state of the English economy in the 1590s, largely caused by a long and draining war with Spain and a series of bad harvests, Elizabeth had been forced to despatch more than a fifth of her silver-gilt plate to the Mint to be turned into coin.

In order to restore normal relations with Spain and the Spanish Netherlands, James was faced immediately after his accession with a demanding and expensive diplomatic visit from a distinguished group of noble envoys, led by the Constable of Castile. By tradition, all envoys expected to be presented with generous gifts – at the very least, gold chains, and often a complete 'cupboard' (set) of plate in silver gilt or even gold. Negotiating a peace treaty ranked with arranging a royal marriage in terms of the expectations of the envoys. These 'exceptional occasions of state' were always costly to the host country; in 1559 after the ratification of the Treaty of Cateau-Cambresis Elizabeth's Lord Chamberlain, Lord Howard of Effingham received 'a very large and honorable present of very fair and stately plate' amounting to 4,140 ounces.

Given the short notice of these obligations, new plate of the appropriate splendour and quantity simply could not be made in time for the presentations after the signing of the Treaty of London in August 1604. Thus existing royal plate was drawn on heavily. The Constable of Castile, Don Juan Fernandez de Velasco, the Duke of Villamediana and their four colleagues shared between them 28,000 ounces of silver gilt. What makes the 1604 diplomatic gifts memorable was the inclusion (inevitable given the lack of choice available to James) of plate associated with Henry VIII, Cardinal Wolsey, Catherine of Aragon and the Duke of Northumberland.

The 1574 Jewel House inventory had described around a thousand sets of objects, but only a handful of these are preserved today. The best known, and the only object to have survived from the medieval Jewel House, is the fourteenth-century enamelled Royal Gold Cup, now in the British Museum. One of Henry VIII's surviving pieces could recently be seen at the National Maritime Museum: the Goldsmiths Company's French clock salt; another is the rock crystal and gold cup from the Munich Residenz. At the Victoria and Albert Museum are two objects emanating directly from the court, the Howard Grace Cup, probably commissioned by Catherine of Aragon, and a pair of snuffers made for the use of the Privy Council of Edward VI.

In fact, very little silver survives from the period after the 1574 inventory. With so few extant examples, the collection of Tudor and Stuart pieces now housed in the Kremlin has a special significance, well understood by such plate historians as Wilfred Cripps, who visited Moscow in 1880 and arranged for Elkingtons to make electrotype copies (see Fig. 2), and Charles Oman, who published his study of the Kremlin silver in 1961. Some of the most important pieces from after 1574 in the Kremlin include a pair of 1580–81 flagons, one of which was exhibited at the successful and much talked of Sotheby's exhibition in January 1991 (Fig. 1). The leopard flagon (Fig. 5), also included in the Victoria and Albert's Russian exhibition in 1967, attracted interest because of its sheer size and animal appeal, and the questions raised as to its purpose. Other pieces, such as the flagons with chains (see Fig. 4), are impressive because of their rarity, although the type was common enough in the sixteenth century, as the royal inventories demonstrate.

The Constable was presented in 1604 with buffet plate, three pairs of great gilt pots (at least one pair from Wolsey's collection), layers and flagons including an Antwerp pair purchased by Henry VIII, and the most recently made piece, a basin

Fig. 2
An electrotype of a silver-gilt water pot, maker's mark *RB*, London, 1615–16, made by Elkington & Co., *circa* 1885, height 24¼in (61.5cm) (Reproduced by courtesy of the Board of Trustees of the Victoria & Albert Museum).

A Jacobean version of an early sixteenth-century Spanish object, formerly in the Tudor Jewel House.

Opposite
Fig. 3
One of a pair of silver-gilt water pots, maker's mark *WI*, London, 1604–1605, height 25⅛in (64cm) (Reproduced by courtesy of the Moscow Kremlin Armoury Museum).

Sold by Charles I in 1626, this water pot was exported to Russia and purchased by Tsar Mikhail Romanov in 1629.

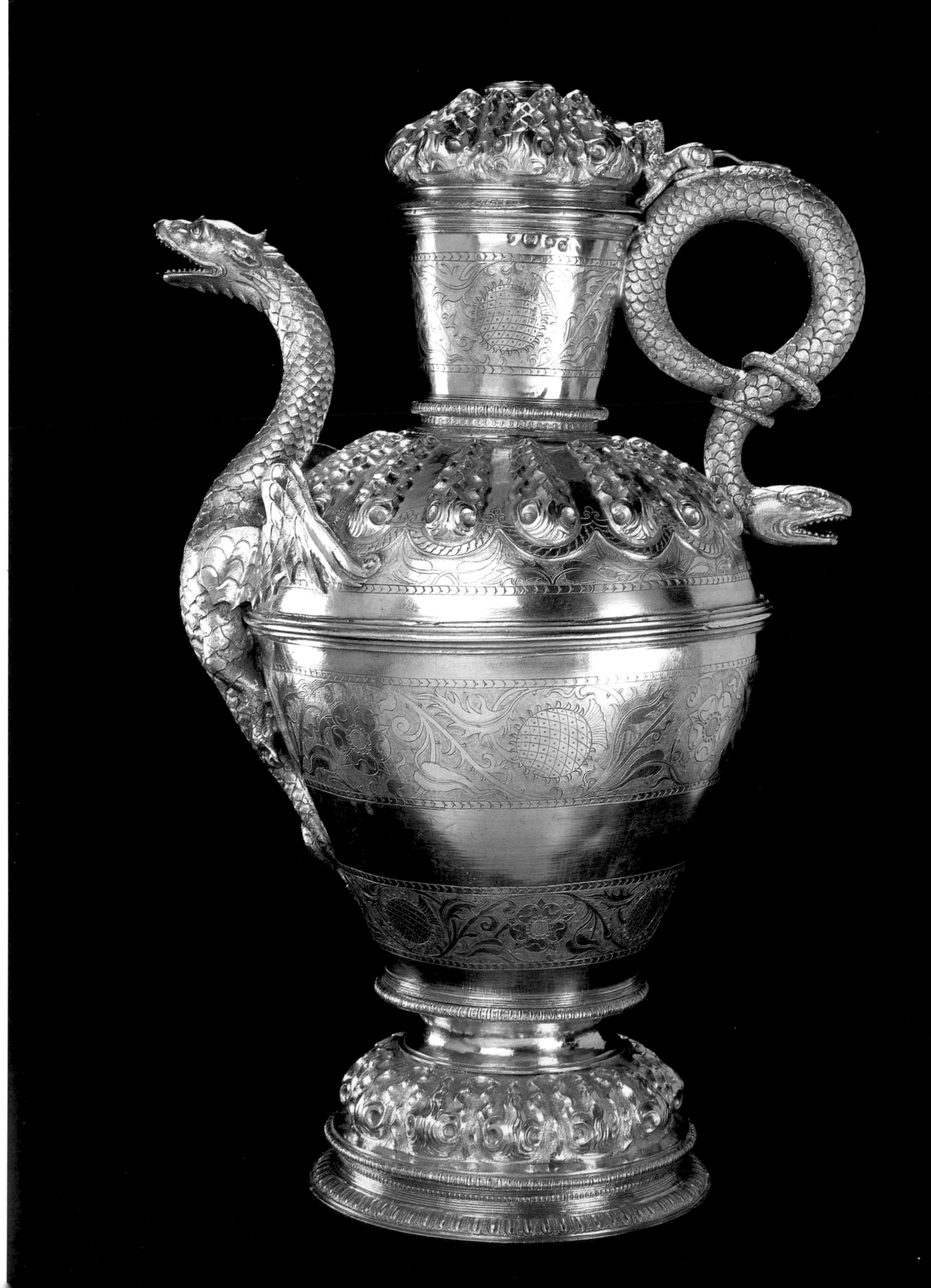

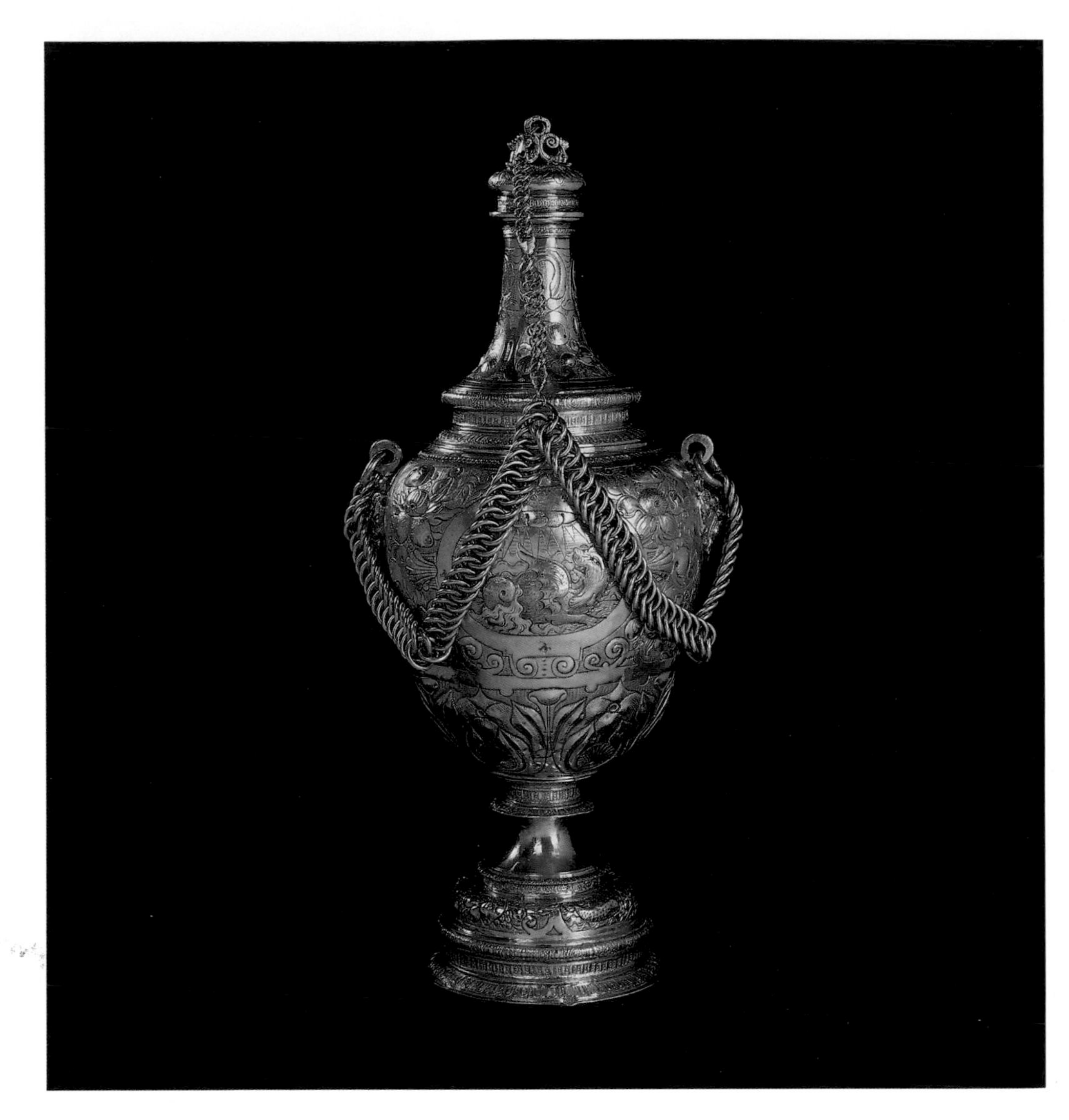

Fig. 4
A silver-gilt flagon, maker's mark *IS*, London, 1619–20, height 19in (48.5cm)
(Reproduced by courtesy of the Moscow Kremlin Armoury Museum).

This flagon was a gift of James I to Tsar Mikhail Romanov in 1620.

and ewer which Lord Lumley had presented to Elizabeth at Nonsuch in 1584. He also received the splendid gold ewer and basin made for Queen Jane Seymour (probably to Holbein's design), the Royal Gold Cup and another gold piece. The Duke of Villamediana was given seven sets of plate, made half a century before, including double Almain cups. Among the representatives of the Spanish Netherlands, Count Arenberg had two pairs of great pots, at least one of which had been in the Royal Collection by 1521, and Richardot received, among other gifts, four cups with antique work, another pair of early Tudor flagons and a fountain belonging to Henry VIII. Because the descriptions of pieces given away are sufficiently detailed in the inventories taken in 1521, 1532, 1547, 1550, 1559 and 1574, their history and eventual fate can be reconstructed. This would be so much enjoyable but pointless antiquarianism, were it not for James's determination to replenish the Jewel House with exact copies of the plate which he had to give away in August 1604. Because of this decision, at least one set of water pots in Russia (and probably two) reproduce the early sixteenth-century originals.

The King's intention, forcibly expressed in a warrant to Sir Edward Carey, Treasurer of the Jewels and Plate, issued on 2 September within 10 days of the presentation to the Spanish envoys, specified that all the replacement pieces were to be 'answerable in weights and fashion according to the several patterns thereof taken'.

The concept of making an exact copy of an object was relatively novel, but was part of the growing spirit of antiquarianism which characterised the late sixteenth and early seventeenth centuries. In 1579 the Master and Fellows of Corpus Christi College, Cambridge, commissioned a copy of their Swan Mazer to present to Sir Nicholas Bacon, and a generation later Bishop Lancelot Andrewes ordered copies to be made for himself of three ancient pieces belonging to his college, Pembroke. James's policy in 1604 was therefore less bizarre than it may seem. He wanted exact copies of the Tudor plate that was given away, and required his Master of the Jewel House that 'Nothinge be omitted either in the curiousnesse of the workmanship or qualitie of the pieces that maye add either grace or beawtie unto them'. In the event the first warrant was modified twice and the objects delivered between 1604 and 1607 were not exact copies. One pair of great gilt pots made in 1604 was chased both with the Stuart thistles and with early Tudor marigolds, and an inscription referring to Henry's union of the two roses (York and Lancaster) and James's union of the two kingdoms.

Analysing the twenty-four sets of replacement plate ordered in 1604, few can be linked precisely to their originals, as described in the 1574 and other inventories. However, the first warrant had specified a new gold ewer and basin as a replacement for the Seymour set. That warrant had also mentioned two flagons 'laide in couloures' (presumably enamelled, an unusual form of decoration on English plate), and weighing 1,265 ounces. These massive vases, with their antique handles chased with 'personages in roundells', recall Giustinian's description of the great vases displayed at Wolsey's lavish entertainment of the French legates at Westminster Hall in 1518.

A great gilt fountain supplied in 1604 was intended as a replacement for 'A Bason gilte well chased with a woman holding above hir handes with a gilte fountaine having vi pillars and a gilte pipe', which is recorded in 1574 as weighing 737 ounces. This was given to Jean Grusset Richardot, President of the Privy Council of the Netherlands. The replacement fountain weighed almost the same (753 ounces) and was 'well chased with sundry devices to make water runne'.

James's policy of replacement also provided the pair of great gilt water pots of 1604–1605 that are now in the Kremlin (Fig. 3). The one brought to London struck many visitors to the Sotheby's exhibition as quite uncharacteristic of Stuart plate. Its shape, the dragon spout and scaly handles, the encrustations around the cover, body and foot, seem almost barbaric and from another age. The originals of these water pots, described as 'two water pottes of silver guilte chased with flames of fyer and borders of Roses and thistles, the handles like snakes, the spout like dragons winged,' probably came from Spain as part of Catherine of Aragon's dowry (see Fig. 2).

In wishing to see copies of the plate of his Tudor predecessors, James's motives were no doubt a mixture of two well-known characteristics, his respect for royal tradition and his antiquarian zeal. Perhaps he also felt an admiration for the Renaissance forms and decoration of Wolsey and Henry VIII's plate. All but one of the pieces given away in 1604 had come into the Royal Collection before the accession of Elizabeth, and some already belonged to her father Henry VIII in 1521. These early sixteenth-century pieces, balanced and elegant with their applied busts in roundels and antique work, were distinctly different from the Mannerist plate of the late sixteenth century, crammed with disproportionate figures, fish and 'frutage'. Perhaps James's appreciation of the old plate had a strong aesthetic element too. Since no silver commissioned by him, apart from the pieces in Russia, now survives this can only be suggested.

Certainly James recognised the historic significance of the royal plate; as part of the long and convivial visit to England in 1606 of Christian IV of Denmark, James gave his brother-in-law a personally conducted tour of the Tower. Christian was shown the Mint, the 'Armorie for warlike provision', the Menagerie with its lions, and the Wardrobe. The highlight of their visit was the Jewel House 'where the most rare jewels and beautiful plate were shown to him'.

The spirit of antiquarianism and respect for ancient ceremony ran strongly in James, and from the time of his accession to the English throne he consciously sought to bolster his dynastic legitimacy. Even in death, he left orders to have himself interred in Westminster Abbey not with his wife or his mother, but on top of the coffins in the vault of Henry VII and Elizabeth of York.

The plate eventually supplied to carry out James's wishes did not conform precisely to the original 1604 warrant. None of the twenty-three silver-gilt cups and bowls were made, presumably because there was a greater need for handsome large buffet plate. As a result the additional metal was incorporated into the flagons, ewers, and pots, which were far heavier than their predecessors. (The new works ranged from 1,263 to 506 ounces; whereas very few buffet pieces listed in the 1521 and 1574 inventories weighed more than 500 ounces.) Such objects would have had very little practical use, since they were far too heavy and bulky to manipulate when full. A kind of giganticism seems to have seized the royal goldsmiths.

After his expenditure on the replacement sets James still had an inadequately stocked Jewel House, and he was never able to make up all the deficiencies he had inherited. Indeed when Christian IV visited again in 1614 he was not presented with a princely gift of old silver as before. In 1623 a warrant concerning the Jewel House regretfully noted 'There is a greate defect and want of necessaire store of plate . . . whereby the King's service many times and especially at festivall times and for entertainement of ambassadors suffers much dishonour'. But the King had no money. Within three years his son was to sell 20,000 ounces of plate, including the costly replacement pieces, to the court goldsmith, John Acton. Some, including the copies of the Spanish water pots, ended up in Russia, purchased by the agents of the Tsar, who presumably recognised the appeal of these large, elaborate pieces. It is likely that their secondhand value bore very little relation to their initial cost.

Fig. 5
A silver-gilt leopard flagon, maker's mark a triangle intersected, London, 1600–1601, height 38½in (98cm)
(Reproduced by courtesy of the Moscow Kremlin Armoury Museum).

Sold by Charles I in 1626, this flagon was exported to Russia and purchased by Tsar Mikhail Romanov in 1629.

Above
Fig. 1
Giuseppe Vasi
THE PYRAMID OF CESTIUS AND PORTA SAN PAOLO (LE MAGNIFICENZE DI ROMA)
Etching, 5½in by 8½in (14cm by 21.5cm)
(Reproduced by courtesy of the British Library).

Left
Fig. 2
Giovanni Battista Piranesi
THE PYRAMID OF CESTIUS (VARIE VEDUTE)
Etching, 5½in by 9in (14cm by 23cm)
(Reproduced by courtesy of the British Library).

Piranesi, the Pyramid and the 'Vedute di Roma'

John Wilton-Ely

Piranesi is universally recognised as being among the greatest interpreters of Rome through his series of magnificent etched views – the *Vedute di Roma*. These 135 images, produced throughout the thirty years of his active career, not only provided souvenirs for eighteenth-century visitors to the Eternal City, but over the centuries have continued to dominate conceptions of Roman grandeur. Piranesi would never have achieved this reputation if he had simply been a 'vedutista' or topographical artist. The power of these particular etched views stems from the unique connection with his parallel activities as an archaeologist as well as an architectural theorist and polemicist. The plates of the *Vedute*, by plotting his changing attitudes to certain monuments, can be seen as reflecting Piranesi's aesthetic and intellectual development.

Hardly a year passes without early states of these graphic masterpieces fetching steadily increasing prices on the market. Until recently, however, few people had ever seen displayed the complete range of the *Vedute di Roma*. This exceptional opportunity was provided in the spring of 1991 through the generosity of the Arthur Ross Foundation when an exhibition of the *Vedute* was held, under the sponsorship of the Fondazione Donatella Flick, at the Royal Institute of British Architects in London. This collection, accumulated with dedication and discernment over many years by Arthur Ross, had also been shown in turn in Philadelphia, New York, Rome, Florence (at Sotheby's galleries in Palazzo Capponi) and in Paris.

By the time of Piranesi's arrival in Rome as a trained architect from his native Venice in 1740, the growing market in engraved views for travellers on the Grand Tour was dominated by the Sicilian, Giuseppe Vasi. Since he needed a means of financial support in the absence of architectural commissions, Piranesi soon learnt the rudiments of etching from Vasi and set up business in the Via del Corso, opposite the French Academy. Within a short time he had swiftly out-distanced his master with some fifty small views produced for assorted guidebooks, known today as the *Varie Vedute*. These modest plates, measuring about 14cm by 23cm, already reveal Piranesi's genius for dramatising the remains of classical antiquity and investing the decaying fragments with emotions, both of pathos and of enduring grandeur. Piranesi's early training in stage design with its contrived perspectives, as well as his painterly sense of light (in this he was a true Venetian), was to transform a conventional souvenir into a potent image, capable of conveying archaeological facts, symbolic ideas and a profound sense of historical change.

A prominent monument which Piranesi was to record on four separate occasions is the Pyramid of Cestius, incorporated into the walls of Rome next to Porta San Paolo. This tomb of the wealthy magistrate Gaius Cestius, who died in 12 BC, is celebrated today for casting its shade over the grave of John Keats in the nearby Protestant Cemetery. Compared with Vasi's relatively objective if uninspired statement in his series *Le Magnificenze di Roma* (Fig. 1), his former pupil's interpretation must have appeared disturbingly summary, especially in the illusionistic effect of clipping off the apex of the pyramid with the plate edge (Fig. 2). Despite the symmetrical placing of the tomb at the centre of the composition, its full volume is effectively described by the play of light enlivening the ascending planes of the two visible surfaces. Nothing of significance is omitted, whether it be the battlements of the adjacent Porta San Paolo or the two solitary Doric columns. The careful positioning of a sinuous foliate tree to the right completes the design and reinforces the stern dignity of this funerial geometry.

Piranesi's growing prosperity, his preoccupation with archaeology as a means to stimulate the torpid imagination of contemporary architects, and the need for a greater plate area to do justice to his subject matter, led him, shortly before 1748, to adopt the large etchings inaugurating the *Vedute di Roma*. While many of the initial plates show evidence of frequent reworking, mainly in terms of lighting and the clarification of minor details, none shows such striking evidence of revision as his first large *veduta* of the Pyramid, measuring 41cm by 54cm (Fig. 3). In its first state Piranesi adopts a similar viewpoint to that used in the small plate, although the angle of the monument's apex is less acute, being in fact close to the 60-degree angle of the actual tomb. Generous space is now given to conveying the wildness of the natural setting with its deeply rutted receding road as well as the prosaic buildings of the nearby gatehouse.

Not long after, however, Piranesi appears to have decided to alter the same copper plate radically, re-etching the pyramid on a larger scale (Fig. 4). The apex is now raised to within a few centimetres of the margin and its angle altered to 55 degrees, bringing the work still closer to the first small plate. Moreover, a prominent tree is inserted on the right achieving the earlier compositional effect. Much of the pyramid's surface is 'stripped' of its picturesque foliage and weeds, both to produce a clearer profile as well as to reveal the inscriptions. Significantly, the Pyramid was

Below, left
Fig. 3
Giovanni Battista Piranesi
THE PYRAMID OF CESTIUS AND PORTA SAN PAOLO (VEDUTE DI ROMA)
Etching, first state, 16$\frac{1}{8}$in by 21$\frac{1}{4}$in (41cm by 54cm) (Reproduced by courtesy of the British Architectural Library).

Right
Fig. 4
Giovanni Battista Piranesi
THE PYRAMID OF CESTIUS AND PORTA SAN PAOLO (VEDUTE DI ROMA)
Etching, second state, 16$\frac{1}{8}$in by 21$\frac{1}{4}$in (41cm by 54cm) (Reproduced by courtesy of Eileen Tweedy).

Fig. 5
Giovanni Battista Piranesi
THE PYRAMID OF CESTIUS
(VEDUTE DI ROMA)
Etching, 15$\frac{3}{8}$in by 21in
(39cm by 53.5cm)
(Reproduced by courtesy of the British Architectural Library).

also illustrated at this time in Piranesi's magisterial treatise, *Le Antichità Romane* of 1756, in a somewhat clinical *veduta*.

Some four years later, around 1760, with over 86 of the *Vedute di Roma* behind him, Piranesi returned to the Pyramid for the last time. He was now deeply embroiled in a bitter controversy provoked by scathing attacks on the achievements of Roman antiquity by scholars and architects who exalted the creative superiority of Greece. This time Piranesi exploited topography for polemical effect. The resulting *veduta* is among his finest works where compositional drama, etching skills and intellectual rhetoric are combined in an image of compelling force (Fig. 5). Ancient Rome has become a mythic world of superhuman feats, and Piranesi develops to its maximum potential the compositional formula of his earliest version of the Pyramid, enhancing the subject through the use of powerful tonal contrasts. He extends the Pyramid's apex to touch the upper margin of the plate and, at the same time, seeks the lowest possible view-point in order to throw into vertiginous contrast the open sky on one side and the crumbling escarpment of the Aurelian Wall on the other. The sheer violence of the tomb's perspective is echoed by the apparent assault of gnarled, predatory trees which appear to tear at the antique masonry. All of this throws into insignificance the minute forms of the human beings, scratching about in the shadows or dwarfed by the large illusionistic scroll. Fact and vision have become fused into a triumphant dream of Roman achievement. As Horace Walpole was to write a few years later: 'study the sublime dreams of Piranesi who seems to have conceived visions of Rome beyond what it boasted even in the meridian of its splendour'.

Old master paintings

Benvenuto Tisi, called Garofalo
CHRIST WASHING THE FEET OF THE APOSTLES
Oil on panel, 14⅛in by 20½in (36cm by 52cm)
Monte Carlo FF3,774,000 (£381,212:$740,000). 7.XII.90

Opposite
Bernardo Daddi
ST CATHERINE OF ALEXANDRIA
Tempera on panel, gold ground, 30in by 16¾in (76.5cm by 42.5cm)
London £352,000 ($718,080). 12.XII.90
From the Locko Park Collection

Previous page, left
Jan Brueghel the Younger
STILL LIFE OF FLOWERS IN A BLUE AND WHITE PORCELAIN VASE
Oil on panel, 19in by 14in (48cm by 35.5cm)
New York $1,100,000 (£575,916). 10.I.91

Previous page, right
Philip de Marlier and Frans Francken the Younger
STILL LIFE OF FLOWERS IN A METAL VASE PAINTED WITH THE RAPE OF DEIJANARA
Oil on panel, 23¾in by 19in (60.5cm by 48.5cm)
London £462,000 ($942,480). 12.XII.90

Jan de Bray
PORTRAIT OF A BOY HOLDING A BASKET OF FRUIT
Oil on panel, signed and dated *1658*, 26⅜in by 21⅝in (67cm by 55cm)
Amsterdam Dfl1,035,000 (£313,636:$522,727). 14.XI.90
From the collection of Mrs P. van Aalst

Jean-Baptiste Le Prince
FEMME ALLONGEE SUR UN CANAPE
Signed and dated *1772*,
28¾in by 35⅞in
(73cm by 91cm)
Monte Carlo FF5,661,000
(£568,945:$920,488).
21.VI.91
From the Peyriague Collection

Willem Claesz. Heda
STILL LIFE WITH A PLATE OF OYSTERS
Oil on panel, signed and dated *1635*, 23¼in by 31in
(59cm by 79cm)
New York $1,430,000
(£748,691). 10.I.91

Tomás Hiepes
STILL LIFE WITH FLOWERS, FRUIT AND DOVES
$34\frac{1}{4}$in by $49\frac{5}{8}$in
(87cm by 126cm)
Madrid Ptas29,680,000
(£161,304:$276,608).
21.V.91

Below
Filippo Falciatore
CONCERTO DEI CONTADINI; CONCERTO DEI SIGNORI
Each $23\frac{3}{4}$in by 17in
(60.3cm by 43cm)
Milan L192,100,000
(£87,041:$151,140).
21.V.91

Above
Giovanni Antonio Canal, called Il Canaletto
THE GRAND CANAL, VENICE, FROM SANTA MARIA DELLA CARITA TO THE BACINO DI SAN MARCO
Circa 1726–30, 18¼in by 25in (46.5cm by 63.5cm)
New York $990,000 (£578,947). 30.V.90

Antoine Watteau
LA PORTE DE VALENCIENNES
12¾in by 16in (32.5cm by 40.5cm)
London £638,000 ($1,301,520). 12.XII.90

Old master drawings

Guido Reni
HEAD OF A BEARDED MAN LOOKING DOWN TO THE RIGHT
Red chalk heightened with white chalk, 5½in by 4in (14cm by 10cm)
London £9,240 ($18,110). 18.II.91

This drawing is a preparatory study for Reni's *Head of St Joseph* in the Galleria Nazionale di Arte Antica, Rome.

Ludovico Cardi, called Il Cigoli
POPE SIXTUS V AT HIS DESK, INSPIRED BY ANGELS
Pen and brown ink and watercolour over traces of black chalk, with touches of white heightening, 10½in by 8⅞in (26.7cm by 22.5cm)
New York $63,800 (£33,403). 8.I.91

This is a newly discovered drawing which can be connected with Cigoli's designs for tapestries, commissioned by Cardinal Montalto but apparently never executed.

Giuseppe Maria Crespi
A YOUNG MAN TEACHING A BIRD TO SING
Red chalk, 9⅜in by 15¼in (24cm by 38.8cm)
London £30,800 ($49,588). 1.VII.91

Giulio Romano

Opposite, above
Giulio Pippi, called Giulio Romano
A STUDY FOR A LUNETTE: JUPITER'S EAGLE BRINGS PSYCHE WATER FROM THE STYX
Pen and brown ink, 8in by $15\frac{3}{8}$in (20.5cm by 38.9cm)
London £44,000 ($70,840). 1.VII.91
From the collection of the British Rail Pension Fund

This is a preliminary study for one of the twelve lunettes in the Sala di Psyche at the Palazzo del Te, Mantua, painted in 1528.

Below
Jacques de Gheyn II
THE FISHERMAN'S WIFE
Pen and brown ink and grey wash, $4\frac{7}{8}$in by $6\frac{7}{8}$in (12.4cm by 17.5cm)
London £42,900 ($69,069). 1.VII.91

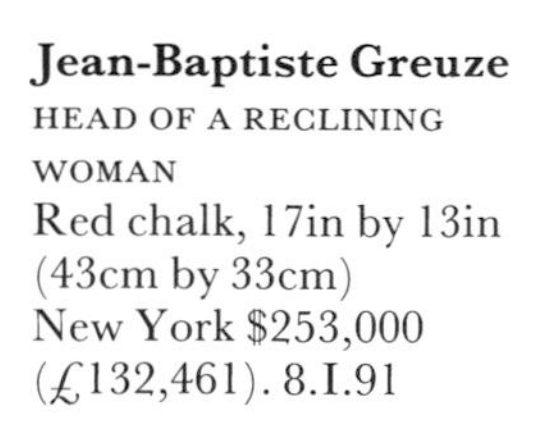

Jean-Baptiste Greuze
HEAD OF A RECLINING WOMAN
Red chalk, 17in by 13in (43cm by 33cm)
New York $253,000 (£132,461). 8.I.91

Poussin drawings: a postscript to the Ashmolean exhibition

Hugh Brigstocke

The bitter controversies that have surrounded the connoisseurship of Nicolas Poussin's drawings in recent years reflect a more general failure to appreciate the nature and function of his activity as a draughtsman, and the extent to which his working methods set him apart from his own contemporaries in Paris and Rome. Most seventeenth-century artists working in the grand manner furiously competed for large scale decorative projects and major altarpieces in Roman churches and French palaces, and those who were successful quickly built up a team of studio assistants to help in the execution of their designs. Most of their creative energy was devoted to the preparatory stages of the commission, academic life drawings for individual figures, and large scale cartoons and elaborate oil sketches for the complete design. Poussin, on the other hand, generally avoided working on a large scale, and apparently did not entrust any part of the execution of his oil paintings to assistants. For him, the transfer of his initial ideas onto canvas was an integral part of the creative process, for only then were many essential details, such as the facial expressions and precise gestures of individual figures, fully resolved. It is hardly surprising that in his early paintings one frequently finds *pentimenti* (visible both with the naked eye and by X-ray), although in his maturity he appears to have worked with a more decisive assurance. Consequently Poussin's drawings fulfil a very different function from those of many of his contemporaries.

The drawings range from fully executed sketches, in chalk and/or pen and ink, in which an initial idea or *concetto*, inspired from a literary source, was first visualised, to highly finished studies almost but never quite identical to the finished pictures in which all the intricacies of the designs are fully resolved. However, by far the most impressive and exciting drawings lie between these extremes: elaborate compositional studies, often executed with brush and wash over a spare linear framework of chalk or pen and ink, in which the overall design and focal point of the narrative would be fully explored with much freedom and vigour, and the relationship of the figures to the architectural or landscape background would be tested.

The central core of the Oxford exhibition was devoted to such compositional drawings, which reveal all the dynamics of Poussin's creative procedures but which, from the connoisseur's point of view, comprise the least controversial aspect of the master's oeuvre. Drawings for the celebrated Richelieu *Bacchanals*, notable for their intricate abstract designs, were juxtaposed with elaborate studies for some of the most moving and dramatic history and religious pictures, including *The Death of Germanicus, The Saving of Pyrrhus, The Rape of the Sabines, Confirmation, The Finding of Queen Zenobia* and a magnificent late work (rare in British collections) showing *The*

Opposite, above
Fig. 1
Nicolas Poussin
THE BIRTH OF ADONIS
Pen and brown ink and grey wash, 7¼in by 12¾in (18.3cm by 32.5cm) (Reproduced by courtesy of the Royal Library Windsor Castle).

Below
Fig. 2
Nicolas Poussin
CEPHALUS AND AURORA
Pen and brown ink and wash, 8in by 13⅜in (20.3cm by 34.1cm) (Reproduced by courtesy of the Trustees of the British Museum).

Raising of Lazarus, which as Jeremy Wood pointed out (*Apollo*, April 1991) I dated far too early in the exhibition catalogue, although I had already changed my mind by the opening day. These drawings are notable above all for Poussin's confident use of broad brown washes, applied without regard for line or contour, to establish the source of light which he might then adjust, at a later stage, in order to integrate a group of figures, or to isolate individual forms, and thereby produce carefully modulated stage effects. At the same time he would also consciously create a more general pattern of light and shade across the entire picture surface so as to establish more abstract compositional rhythms and a wholly unified pictorial image.

Compared with the almost proto-baroque energy invested in many such drawings, Poussin's more highly finished and more fully resolved compositional drawings are often regarded as dry and lifeless. In fact many have been condemned by modern critics as copies after connected paintings: most recently, the series of illustrations of scenes from Ovid, for long identified as those described by Bellori, which Poussin made at the outset of his career in Paris for the Italian poet, Marino (see Fig. 1). Notwithstanding their subsequent provenance, from the collection of the artist's close Roman friend, Cardinal Massimi, the Austrian scholar Konrad Oberhuber, at a recent exhibition 'Poussin. The Early Years in Rome' (Fort Worth, 1988), downgraded them as mid seventeenth-century Roman copies after lost original drawings, and thus provoked a furious controversy. For while his opinion was accepted by many highly regarded scholars, it was also questioned by Anne Harris (*Art Bulletin*, March 1990) and myself (*Times Literary Supplement*, October 1988, and again in the exhibition catalogue). Happily the question has now been satisfactorily resolved, following an investigation of the watermarks on all the Windsor drawings which allowed Martin Clayton to demonstrate that they are on French paper produced at Sancey, near Troyes, by Jean Nivelle before 1621 (*Burlington Magazine*, April 1991).

The rehabilitation of the Marino drawings as early book illustrations by Poussin, made in Paris *circa* 1622–23, should have created a favourable climate for reassessing other disputed drawings in a similar style. Two drawings, connected with early Roman paintings by Poussin, were exhibited at Oxford as highly finished preparatory studies by Poussin himself: *Joshua's victory over the Amorites* in the Fitzwilliam Museum, which connects with a picture in Moscow, and *Cephalus and Aurora* (Fig. 2), which connects with a picture in an English private collection. However resistance to the acceptance of these drawings persists, most notably in the exhibition review by Pierre Rosenberg (*Burlington Magazine*, March 1991) which was written after the Marino drawings' watermarks had been identified.

A far more intriguing dispute surrounds a large group of closely related but widely scattered drawings, many of which were formerly in the Crozat Collection, with a traditional attribution to Poussin, and which are executed in a fluid Italianate manner reminiscent of Roman artists from Poussin's immediate circle such as Pietro Testa and Pier Francesco Mola. Friedlaender and Blunt, in their catalogue raisonné, rejected them as the work of Italian imitators, but Oberhuber has attempted to reverse the position and give them all back to Poussin. Although most critics probably now agree that Oberhuber has been too expansive (of the 192 drawings in his list for the period up to 1630, only 28 were previously accepted), I believe that at least some of these drawings are indeed quick exploratory sketches by Poussin dating

Fig. 3
Nicolas Poussin
APOLLO AND HYACINTH
Pen and brown ink and wash, heightened with white, 7⅞in by 10½in (19.9cm by 26.6cm)
(Reproduced by courtesy of the Trustees of the British Museum).

from his early years in Rome. In the Oxford exhibition I confined the debate to only three sheets: *Cephalus and Aurora*, and *Rinaldo and Armida*, both from the British Museum, and a previously unpublished *Tancred and Erminia* from a private collection, bearing an old inscription with the name of Pietro Testa. I also exhibited, but consigned to limbo, ex catalogue, a drawing of *Apollo and Hyacinth* (Fig. 3), which in the course of the Oxford show I came to accept as by the same hand as the other three, a view also shared by Nicholas Turner. All of these drawings have the same distinctive handwriting, a decorative preoccupation with filling the entire picture space, and an unusually vivid sense of the way light and shade can be manipulated to enrich the atmosphere of the original poetic concept. By their very nature these drawings cannot be connected directly with Poussin's finished paintings, and although I am well aware that Oberhuber only felt able to admit them after first wrongly excluding the more mannered Marino drawings, and although I am also mindful of Rosenberg's objections (*loc. cit.*) that they are 'far too elegantly drawn and superficial to be by Poussin', I am also encouraged by the sensitive and authoritative observations of the great eighteenth-century French connoisseur Pierre-Jean Mariette, who remarked:

There are very few finished drawings by Poussin. When he was drawing his only aim was to get his ideas down on paper, and they came out in such abundance that a single theme would stimulate in his mind an incredible number of different sketches. With a simple line, sometimes with the addition of a few brush strokes of wash, he was able to express clearly what his imagination had conceived. At this stage he was not concerned with correctness of drawing or with the truth of the expressions or with effects of chiaroscuro. It was when he was working on the canvas itself, brush in hand, that he attended to these matters. He was of the opinion that any other method merely held back his genius and slowed up his work . . . for Poussin's genius was in the highest degree poetical.

British paintings

William Hogarth
THE EDWARDS HAMILTON FAMILY ON THEIR TERRACE IN KENSINGTON
27in by 33¾in (68.5cm by 86cm)
London £401,500 ($650,430). 10.VII.91

This important conversation piece, painted in 1733, was a commission from Mary Edwards, one of the greatest heiresses in the country and an early patron of Hogarth. It was painted looking south from the terrace of the family's house in Kensington which was close to Kensington Palace and the largest private house in the area. Mary Edwards holds a copy of the *Spectator* containing an essay extolling the virtuous rearing of children, whilst gesturing towards her son.

William Hogarth and George Lambert
CHISWICK HOUSE, MIDDLESEX
Signed and dated *G.Lambert/1741*, 30½in by 40½in (77.5cm by 103cm)
London £220,000 ($453,200). 14.XI.90
From the collection of Mr and Mrs John E. Treleaven

This painting probably belongs to the set of views of Chiswick by Lambert and Hogarth which were commissioned by Lord Burlington. Lambert often called upon Hogarth for help with figure painting.

JAMES STEWART.
B.1742 . D.1821.

George Stubbs, ARA
A DARK BAY HUNTER HELD BY A GROOM, THE PROPERTY OF GEORGE, 4TH DUKE OF MARLBOROUGH
40in by 50in (101.6cm by 127cm)
New York $990,000 (£592,814). 7.VI.91

Stubbs painted this hunter in the late 1760s as a commission from George, 4th Duke of Marlborough, an influential early patron who also commissioned from the artist *The Tiger*, a painting which still hangs at Blenheim Palace.

Opposite
Pompeo Batoni
PORTRAIT OF JAMES STEWART
54in by 39in (137cm by 99cm)
London £242,000 ($392,040). 10.VII.91

Batoni painted this portrait in Rome in 1767 whilst the sitter was in Italy on the Grand Tour. The Stewart family lived in Ireland and James probably reached Rome with an introduction to Batoni, whose earliest patrons had been a group of Irishmen who went to Rome in the 1740s.

Constable's *Lock* of 1824

Ian Fleming-Williams

In his Suffolk years, before settling down in London with his young wife in 1817, Constable had drawn and painted the stretch of the canalised Stour above and below Flatford Lock a great many times. His main works at the annual Academy show at Somerset House in 1812 and 1813 had both been views from beside the lock, and the largest and most ambitious picture he ever attempted to paint before the motif, the Tate Gallery's *Flatford Mill*, again depicted the lock, only this time from further away, from a spot by the footbridge a short distance upstream.

For several years after 1817 the river at Flatford and its traffic continued to provide Constable with subjects for his major exhibition works. This is understandable. Tracing his association with the river back to his 'careless boyhood', he attributed his making as a painter to all that lay 'on the banks of the Stour', (spelt 'Stower' in the minutes of the meetings of the Stour Navigation Proprietors and Commissioners, and presumably pronounced so). But he was also indebted materially to the river, a river with which his family had been connected since the middle of the eighteenth century. Never having to rely solely upon an income derived from the sale of his work, Constable had been dependent in his early years upon an allowance from his father and subsequently very largely upon his share of the profits from the family business. This was primarily a trade in corn and coal, and relied heavily for its success on the availability of river transport. The business provided an income that enabled Constable to maintain his integrity as an artist, to work without thought of others, to work – as he told his friend Fisher – turning his head neither to left or right, but always keeping it 'straight forward – thinking of himself alone', like, he said, 'a friend of mine in the battle of Waterloo'.

In 1819, 1821 and 1822 his main exhibits, his first six-foot canvases, were all of scenes around Flatford: *The White Horse* (Frick Collection, New York), *The Hay Wain* (National Gallery, London) and *View of the Stour* (Huntington Library and Art Gallery, San Marino). For the subject of his exhibit at the Academy in 1824, Constable again chose a scene at Flatford, this time a view of the lower gates of the lock, a close-up from just across the mill-pool. This, his sole exhibit, was titled *A boat passing a lock* in that year's exhibition catalogue. Now known just as *The Lock* (Fig. 1), the painting sold on the opening day of the show, an event unique in Constable's whole career. The purchaser was James Morrison, a wealthy manufacturer, then still in his thirties.

Fig. 1
John Constable, RA
THE LOCK
1824, 56in by 47½in
(142cm by 121cm)
London £10,780,000
($22,206,800). 14.XI.90

The canalised Stour, that is the lower part of the river, is twenty-three and a half miles in length. Between the quays at Mistley Thorn (the estuary port where coastal vessels and the river traffic could load and unload their cargoes) and the river-basin

Fig. 2
John Constable, RA
BARGES ON THE STOUR
Oil on paper laid on canvas, *circa* 1811, 10¼in by 12¼in (26cm by 31cm)
(Reproduced by courtesy of the Board of Trustees of the Victoria and Albert Museum, London).

Fig. 3
John Constable, RA
SKETCH FOR THE LOCK
Circa 1823, 56in by 48in (142cm by 122cm)
(Reproduced by courtesy of the Philadelphia Museum of Art, John Howard McFadden Collection).

Fig. 4
John Constable, RA
A BOAT PASSING A LOCK
Circa 1823–26, 40¾in by 51⅛in (103.5cm by 129.9cm)
(Reproduced by courtesy of the National Gallery of Victoria, Melbourne, Felton Bequest, 1951).

Fig. 5
John Constable, RA
A BOAT PASSING A LOCK
1826, 40in by 50in (101.6cm by 127cm)
(Reproduced by courtesy of the Royal Academy of Arts, London).

at Sudbury, there were thirteen locks to be negotiated. Brantham was the first, Flatford the second. Next came Dedham and then Stratford-St-Mary, both of which provided Constable with subjects for major paintings. At Brantham there were two mills – a windmill and a tide-mill. To work the latter the incoming tide was allowed to fill the reach of river as far as Flatford. At the turn, the gates were shut and the resultant head of sea water employed to turn the wheel. An early oil sketch by Constable of Flatford Lock (Fig. 2), from a viewpoint near to the one from which he envisaged the scene painted in 1824, shows the level of the river at high tide, when the gates at Brantham would be shut. In this often reproduced little painting Constable has depicted the posts and overreaching lintels that ran the length of the lock, part of the box-frame structure, characteristic of the locks along this waterway. When it came to painting a picture of the subject, these presented a problem – awkwardly aligned as they were with the distant horizontals – after a couple of attempts to include the nearest lintel on its supports in the composition, Constable decided it was better without, and none of his paintings of this scene feature the upper framework of the lock.

In all, there are five paintings of the subject: a full-size sketch in the Philadelphia Museum of Art (Fig. 3); the painting Morrison bought in 1824 (Fig. 1); an horizontal, unfinished painting in the National Gallery of Victoria, Melbourne (Fig. 4); a replica of the Morrison *Lock*, painted in 1825, partly by Constable's assistant Johnny Dunthorne, now in a private collection; and, another horizontal, Constable's Diploma work, at the Royal Academy of Arts (Fig. 5).

For his Academy picture of 1813, a view from the upper gates at Flatford looking upstream known as *Boys Fishing*, Constable had worked from two compositional oil sketches and two drawings, one of which was of the main group of trees (Fig. 6), the other of the lock gates (Fig. 7), both, presumably, studies drawn the previous year (1812). After experimenting on his full-size sketch for *The Lock* (Fig. 3), Constable used the pencil study of trees as a skeletal basis for the massive trunks and branches of the trees in the Morrison picture (Fig. 1) and in the copy painted in 1825. The replication in almost every detail of the same timbers of the lock entrance and many of the plants on the foreground bank in all but the Philadelphia sketch, suggests that for this area Constable worked on these later canvases from a single study. No such drawing or oil sketch is known, but it is possible that this was also a pencil study of 1812, a companion to the one of the upper gates (Fig. 7). Constable never hesitated to re-use and use again earlier material. In fact, after 1817 he very largely depended on the store of sketches and studies he had amassed during his Suffolk years. A tree in the well-known *Cornfield* in the National Gallery, a work of 1826, was taken from a painting exhibited in 1802, and his great series of paintings of Helmingham Dell (1823–30) was based on a large pen and wash drawing he had made while working there in solitude in 1800.

When he came to paint *The Lock*, Constable was fully aware that for a major painting he required some incident around which to build the composition. In his big river scenes, his six-footers, he had so far represented the ferrying of a tow-horse across to the further bank of the river (*The White Horse*, Frick Collection, New York), children fishing beside a lock entrance (*Stratford Mill*, National Gallery, London), and the strenuous manoevering of a pair of barges past a sailing boat (*View on the*

Stour, Huntington Library and Art Gallery, San Marino). In the first of these a man in the barge on the extreme left is leaning heavily on a pole to keep the vessel with its load away from the bank, but otherwise the scene is one of undisturbed tranquillity. This mood prevails in both *Stratford Mill* and *The Hay Wain*. In *View on the Stour*, however, while the landscape is serene enough, the central incident depicts physical endeavour – three men straining to bring a pair of barges out into midstream and avoid a boat moored against the further bank. This theme, man exercising his strength to the full, was brought even more to the fore in *The Lock*.

In the beautifully detailed paintings of Dedham lock and mill (the first of which was exhibited in 1818), a lock-keeper in a red-fronted waistcoat and black hat is seen in the distance at work, lowering the water in the lock for a barge making its way downstream. This, plainly, was the nucleus of the idea for *The Lock*. In the Philadelphia sketch (Fig. 3), the lock-keeper is in much the same attitude, inserting his crow-bar in the windlass. (It was by turning the windlass that the underwater 'paddle' on the end of its chain was raised, and the water in the lock-basin released.) Requiring a more powerful and immediate image, in *The Lock* Constable placed his figure in an heroic attitude, muscles tensed, with one knee bent to prevent the windlass from unwinding, a pose possibly derived from a study he had made when a student in the life-class at the Academy Schools. As a counter balance he has a boatman in the barge pulling hard on a rope to check the vessel's momentum. In contrast to the earlier canal paintings, this is 'full of the Bustle incident to such a scene' – a quote from Constable's description of his next six-footer, the even more dynamic *Leaping Horse*.

Not a great deal is known about the men employed by the Stour Navigation Commissioners to operate the locks and oversee the traffic on the river. One of the Stour Commissioners' resolutions concerned the appointments of three 'Lock-gate Keepers' to Dedham and two of the upper locks, to 'attend to the General Works on the River, and be also appointed as Constables'. There was a need, it seems, for the river to be policed. In 1798, for example, 'by reason of Bargemen, Boatmen, & Servants and other Persons, taking away or otherwise removing Staunch Boards' (that is, the boards that controlled the level of the river between locks), severe penalties were threatened 'in case any Staunch Board or Boards shall be found in or upon any Barge, Boat, Keel, Lighter or other Vessell navigating on the said River'. Besides operating the lock and keeping an eye on the traffic, one of the duties of the lock-gate keeper would presumably have been to receive the tolls from the barge or boatmen passing through, sums of money that varied according to the type of goods carried and the length of the river to be used: eight shillings for wheat carried the full distance downstream from Sudbury, one shilling from Flatford. For malt, four shillings at Sudbury, sixpence at Flatford. Nails (in 'Baggs'), firkins of butter, glass (in crates), tallow and paper (one shilling per hundred bundles) were among other goods listed in the toll-tables.

Although managing the locks was a constant duty, there must have been times when there was little for the lock-keeper to do. In an age when game-laws were strict and offenders severely punished, fishing around the locks seems to have been permitted, and the rod with its line dangling in the water in the Philadelphia sketch (Fig. 3), evidently laid down by the man at the windlass, suggests that for him, the

Above, left
Fig. 6
John Constable, RA
STUDY OF TREES AT FLATFORD
Pencil on wove paper, *circa* 1812, 18½in by 11½in (47cm by 29.1cm)
(Reproduced by courtesy of the Fondazione Horne, Florence).

Right
Fig. 7
John Constable, RA
FLATFORD LOCK: THE UPPER GATES
Pencil on wove paper, *circa* 1812, 10¾in by 17¾in (27cm by 45cm)
(Private collection).

lock-keeper, fishing was one way of passing the time. But it is possible that at Flatford the lock-keeper also acted in another capacity. In a number of Constable's oil sketches and in two of his exhibited works – *The Ferry* of 1814 in a private collection and the Tate Gallery's *The Valley Farm* – we see a man in a black hat and red waistcoat poling a small rowing-boat through a gap to the bank on the far side of the mill-stream by Willy Lott's house. The progress of the barges up and down the river was slow – the journey between Sudbury and Brantham normally took two days – and the lock-keeper would have seen vessels approaching Flatford from up or downstream long before their arrival at the gates. There would have been time enough between arrivals for him to ferry anyone wanting to cross the river, and combine his duties as lock-keeper with those of ferryman.

Although Willy Lott does not figure in any of Constable's paintings, as the owner of a house the artist depicted so often the eccentric old farmer's name lives on. While remaining nameless, it is perhaps time that the lock-keeper at Flatford, so frequently and so vividly portrayed by Constable, should receive equal recognition for the part he played in the artist's story.

Joseph Mallord William Turner, RA
OLD MARGATE PIER
Oil on panel, $10\frac{3}{4}$in by 16in (27.5cm by 40.5cm)
London £220,000 ($356,400). 10.VII.91
From the collection of Mrs Gaskell

This seascape was exhibited by Turner at his gallery in Harley Street in 1804 and given by him to his friend and patron Samuel Dobree.

Opposite, above
Thomas Gainsborough, RA
WOODED LANDSCAPE WITH FIGURES, BRIDGE, DONKEYS, DISTANT BUILDINGS AND MOUNTAIN
Signed with intials, 14in by $17\frac{1}{2}$in (35.5cm by 44.5cm)
London £231,000 ($374,220). 10.VII.91

A characteristic example of Gainsborough's early Bath period, this landscape dates from *circa* 1763–64, and was painted for the Warre family who lived near Taunton.

Below
Thomas Gainsborough, RA
WOODED LANDSCAPE WITH A DROVER AND CATTLE AND A DISTANT MANSION
$47\frac{1}{2}$in by $57\frac{1}{2}$in (121cm by 146cm)
London £209,000 ($338,580). 10.VII.91

Painted *circa* 1768–71, this ambitious large landscape belonged to Edward Pleydell-Bouverie whose ancestor, Lord Radnor, was an important patron of Gainsborough.

British watercolours

Joseph Mallord William Turner, RA
CONWAY CASTLE, NORTH WALES
Watercolour over pencil with scratching out and stopping out, 21$\frac{1}{8}$in by 30$\frac{1}{8}$in (53.5cm by 76.5cm)
London £280,500 ($499,290). 11.IV.91

This view shows Conway Castle from the east and is the largest of four recorded views of this subject. It is based upon sketches in the Hereford Court Sketchbook of 1798 but was commissioned about two years later.

Right
Joseph Mallord William Turner, RA
FLORENCE, FROM THE CHIESA AL MONTE
Watercolour over pencil heightened with bodycolour and scratching out, signed and dated *1818*, $5\frac{1}{4}$in by $8\frac{1}{2}$in (13.5cm by 21.5cm)
London £82,500 ($146,850). 11.IV.91

Below
John Robert Cozens
CETARA ON THE GULF OF SALERNO
Watercolour over pencil, signed and dated *1790*, $14\frac{3}{8}$in by $20\frac{5}{8}$in (36.5cm by 52.5cm)
London £110,000 ($195,800). 11.IV.91
From the collection of Tom Girtin

Above
Office of Sir Jeffry Wyatville
DESIGN FOR THE DECORATION OF THE EAST WALL OF THE GREAT DRAWING ROOM, WINDSOR CASTLE
Watercolour over pencil heightened with bodycolour, initialled by George IV on the mount, 12¼in by 35½in (31cm by 90cm)
London £35,200 ($72,512). 15.XI.90

This room is now called the Crimson Drawing Room, and is at the northern end of the East range. It still contains the suite of furniture shown here.

Francis Wheatley, RA
MRS WHEATLEY ASLEEP
Pen and grey ink and watercolour over traces of pencil, signed, diameter 7½in (19cm)
London £26,400 ($42,240). 11.VII.91
From the collection of Colin Hunter

John Martin
THE DESTRUCTION OF PHARAOH'S HOST
Watercolour and bodycolour with scratching out and gum arabic, signed and dated *1836*,
22⅝in by 33½in (57.5cm by 85cm)
London £107,800 ($172,480). 11.VII.91

In one of his most dramatic biblical watercolours, Martin here depicts Moses and the Israelites watching the destruction of the Egyptian army as the passage through the Red Sea closes.

Nineteenth-century European paintings

Jean-Louis-André-Théodore Gericault
LE COLONEL BRO A SAINT DOMINGUE
Pen and ink, signed and inscribed *à son voisin M. Braut*, 8½in by 12⅛in (21.5cm by 30.9cm)
Monte Carlo FF3,330,000 (£336,364:$652,941). 8.XII.90

Below
Carl Rottmann
THE TEMPLE OF APOLLO AT AEGINA
Signed and dated *1835*, 19½in by 24¾in (49.5cm by 62.9cm)
Munich DM264,000 (£90,102:$145,966). 12.VI.91

Opposite
Jean-Léon Gérôme
A BASHI-BAZOUK AND HIS DOG
Oil on panel, signed, 1865, 14in by 9⅞in (35.6cm by 25.1cm)
New York $396,000 (£204,124). 23.X.90

Jean-Baptiste-Camille Corot
SOUVENIR DE L'ECLUZE, PRES DOUAI
Signed, *circa* 1868, 15$\frac{3}{4}$in by 20$\frac{7}{8}$in (40cm by 53cm)
London £269,500 ($560,560). 28.XI.90

Opposite
Jean-Baptiste-Camille Corot
LE CHEVRIER TRAVERSANT UN RUISSEAU. PAYSAGE ITALIEN
Signed, *circa* 1865–70, 22in by 17$\frac{3}{4}$in (56cm by 45cm)
London £242,000 ($389,620). 19.VI.91

Giuseppe Pellizza da Volpedo
MAMMINE
Signed and dated *1892*, $85\frac{3}{4}$in by $80\frac{3}{4}$in (218cm by 205cm)
London £517,000 ($832,370). 19.VI.91

Opposite
Giovanni Boldini
IN THE GARDEN
Oil on cradled panel, signed and dated *'74*, 16in by $11\frac{5}{8}$in (40.6cm by 29.5cm)
New York $330,000 (£190,751). 22.V.91
From the collection of Eulalie A. Hilts

Ferdinand Hodler
DAS WETTERHORN
Signed, $18\frac{7}{8}$in by $25\frac{5}{8}$in
(48cm by 65cm)
Zurich SF748,000
(£304,065:$598,400).
21.XI.90

Franz von Stuck
SPHINX
Oil on cradled panel, with original frame, signed, titled and dated *1901*, overall size 31in by 60in
(78.7cm by 152.4cm)
New York $242,000
(£139,884). 22.V.91

Joaquín Sorolla y Bastida
SALIDA DEL BAÑO (PLAYA DE VALENCIA)
Signed and dated *1908*, 32$\frac{1}{4}$in by 41$\frac{3}{4}$in (81.9cm by 106cm)
New York $2,640,000 (£1,526,012). 22.V.91

Victorian and modern British paintings

Sir John Everett Millais
CHILL OCTOBER
Signed with monogram and dated *1870*, 55½in by 73½in (141cm by 186.5cm)
London £407,000 ($655,270). 19.VI.91

This was the first of the Scottish landscapes of Millais' maturity. It was painted from a backwater of the Tay near Perth. Why Millais turned to landscape painting is not known, but he certainly enjoyed the experience: 'I do so delight in painting landscapes, so much more than portraiture! . . . you have only yourself to please'.

Dante Gabriel Rossetti
GIOTTO PAINTING THE PORTRAIT OF DANTE
Watercolour over pencil heightened with gum arabic, signed with initials and dated *Sept 1852*,
14¾in by 18½in (37.5cm by 47cm)
London £115,500 ($185,955). 19.VI.91

Originally intended as part of a triptych, this painting is an early example of Rossetti's fascination with the life of Dante. The model for the head of Dante appears to be the artist's brother, William Michael Rossetti. Beatrice was modelled by Elizabeth Siddall with her distinctive red hair.

Charles Rennie Mackintosh
ANEMONES
Watercolour and bodycolour over pencil on paper, signed, 19$\frac{1}{2}$in by 18$\frac{1}{2}$in (49.5cm by 47cm)
Glasgow £198,000 ($392,040). 5.II.91

Opposite
Louis Bosworth Hurt
SUNSHINE AND SHOWER
Signed and dated *1897*, 50$\frac{1}{2}$in by 40$\frac{1}{8}$in (128cm by 102cm)
Gleneagles £82,500 ($171,600). 28.VIII.90

Sir Alfred James Munnings, PRA
PONIES
Signed, 40in by 50in (101.6cm by 127cm)
New York $374,000 (£223,952). 7.VI.91

Opposite
Sir George Clausen, RA, RWS
A SCHOOLGIRL
Signed and dated *1889*; also signed and dated *1889* on the reverse, 22in by 16in (56cm by 40.5cm)
London £137,500 ($284,625). 7.XI.90

G. CLAUSEN
1889

Sir Stanley Spencer, RA
THE BAPTISM
30in by 50in (76cm by 127cm)
London £462,000 ($794,640). 1.V.91

Opposite
John Craxton
BOY, GIRL AND CAT
Signed and dated *48–49*, 80in by 46in (203cm by 117cm)
London £60,500 ($104,060). 1.V.91

The Chester Beatty Collection

Family tradition has it that Sir Alfred Chester Beatty made his first auction purchase – a piece of pink mineral calcite – at the age of ten. His schoolboy passion for rocks and minerals led the young Chester Beatty to study mining engineering at New York's Columbia School of Mines. His career started in Denver, Colorado, where he worked for $2 a day as a 'mucker', and – as he later recalled – rode the Rockies with a pistol in his boots and a Winchester on the saddle. He then worked for the Guggenheim brothers in Mexico's Sierra Madre territory, and, as their consultant, developed the copper mines that made the modern automobile industry possible. In 1911, after the death of his first wife, he moved to London. The company he formed there, Selection Trust, undertook mining projects all over the world, opening up the west coast of Africa for diamonds and discovering the copper belt of Zambia. In later years he occupied himself increasingly with his collections and projects of philanthropy, endowing many national and public institutions, particularly those connected with medical research.

Chester Beatty's love of collecting was to develop in many forms. A fascination with Arab calligraphy led to his collection of rare oriental and western manuscripts, which he was to bequeath to the Irish people. He also became one of the greatest collectors of Impressionist and modern art in England.

In 1928 he gave his second wife a cheque for £100,000 and advised her to concentrate on the Impressionists. The Beatty Collection was kept in their house in London, Baroda House, originally built for the Maharaja of Baroda. A. J. Wilson, in *The Life and Times of Sir Alfred Chester Beatty* (1985) described it, 'On the walls of the adjoining rooms, Edith Beatty displayed her collection of Impressionist paintings which at various times included some very famous ones: Manets; Utrillos; five van Goghs; several Cézannes, including *Boy with the red Waistcoat*; and two smaller versions of Renoir's *Bathers*.'

The paintings sold at Sotheby's on 25 June 1991 included two works by Toulouse-Lautrec: *La Toilette: Madame Fabre* (Fig. 1), an early portrait of the mother of Emile Fabre, a popular Parisian playwright of the early 1900s, and *Le Lit*. Dating from about 1886 is *Femmes accoudées à une Balustrade* (Fig. 2) by Degas, an intimate and confidential group, similar in feeling to the *Chez la Modiste* series of 1885. Renoir's *Portrait de Monsieur Lestringuez* is an affectionate portrait of a friend, a civil servant who accompanied the painter to Algeria in 1881, and who also appears in *Au Moulin de la Galette* and *Le Déjeuner des Canotiers*.

Chester Beatty's son continued the tradition of collecting, and it was he who bought the contemporary paintings in the 1950s that were sold on 27 June. These included works by Josef Albers and Jean Dubuffet, and four late works by Nicolas de Staël (see page 106).

Fig. 1
Henri de Toulouse-Lautrec
LA TOILETTE: MADAME FABRE
Oil on board, signed, 1891, $28\frac{3}{8}$in by $25\frac{1}{4}$in
(72cm by 64cm)
London £2,420,000
($3,944,600). 25.VI.91
From the Chester Beatty Collection

Fig. 2
Edgar Degas
FEMMES ACCOUDEES A UNE BALUSTRADE (SUR LE BATEAU)
Pastel, *circa* 1886, 22⅜in by 32⅝in (57cm by 83cm)
London £1,430,000 ($2,330,900). 25.VI.91
From the Chester Beatty Collection

Renoir's *La Tasse de Chocolat*

After showing in the first three Impressionist exhibitions of 1874, 1876 and 1877, Renoir's frustration with unfavourable press and poor sales led him to submit *La Tasse de Chocolat* to the Salon of 1878, where he received his first acceptance since 1870. Renoir wrote to Durand-Ruel, justifying his defection from the Impressionist group and his decision to make a concerted effort at becoming a portraitist to rich Parisians by exhibiting at the highly acclaimed Salon as follows:

There are in Paris scarcely fifteen art lovers capable of liking a painting without Salon approval. There are 80,000 who won't buy an inch of canvas if the painter is not in the Salon . . . Furthermore, I don't want to descend to the folly of thinking that anything is good or bad according to the place where it is hung. In a word, I don't want to waste my time in resentment against the Salon: I don't want to even give that impression. I believe one must do the best painting possible. That's all . . . My submitting to the Salon is entirely a business matter. (John Rewald, *The History of Impressionism*, 1973)

In order to create a portrait which would appeal to the Salon jury, Renoir made the canvas large and rendered the figure clearly. Renoir's strategy for achieving official recognition was rewarded with a small but growing following of critics and patrons, and commissioned portraits comprised a significant portion of his output between 1878 and 1880. Aside from his commissioned portraits, most of Renoir's models between 1875 and 1883 were from the working class – seamstresses, flower sellers, milliners and dancers at the Moulin de la Galette, who agreed to pose in order to earn a little extra cash. Marguerite Legrand, called Margot, was one of the artist's favourites. In *La Tasse de Chocolat* she is seated in Renoir's studio at the rue St Georges. In 1921 Georges Rivière gave a description of Margot that contrasts vividly with the pretty young woman in Renoir's portrait:

. . . rather dull chestnut hair, she had sparse eyebrows, and her reddened eyelids were without lashes. Her rather large nose seemed to sit between her plump cheeks as if between two pillows, and her sensual mouth with thick, bleeding lips would at times crease into a disdainful smile . . . All in all she was typical of a coarse type of working-class girl. Nevertheless, through the magic of Renoir's art, she was made to look pretty, almost dignified. (Nicholas Wadley, *Renoir, A Retrospective*, 1987)

A frequent model for Renoir, Margot also posed for *Chez la Modiste* and *Au Moulin de la Galette*.

Pierre-Auguste Renoir
LA TASSE DE CHOCOLAT
Signed, *circa* 1878, 39⅜in by 31⅞in (100cm by 81cm)
New York $18,150,000 (£9,213,198). 12.XI.90
From the Henry Ford II Family Collection

manet

Degas

Previous page, left
Edouard Manet
BOUQUET DE PIVOINES
Signed, 1882, 22¼in by 17½in (56.5cm by 44.5cm)
New York $4,400,000 (£2,244,898). 13.XI.90

Previous page, right
Edgar Degas
DANSEUSES SUR LA SCENE
Pastel over monotype in black ink on paper, signed, *circa* 1878–80, 15in by 10⅝in (38cm by 27cm)
New York $2,530,000 (£1,290,816). 13.XI.90

Georges Seurat
VUE GENERALE AVEC CAVALIER DE LA FEMME AU SINGE, ETUDE POUR LA GRANDE JATTE
Oil on panel, *circa* 1884–85, 6in by 9¾in (15.2cm by 24.8cm)
New York $1,375,000 (£794,798). 7.V.91
From the estate of Irene Mayer Selznick

Opposite
Paul Cézanne
LE JAS DE BOUFFAN
Circa 1885–87, 29in by 21½in (74cm by 55cm)
New York $7,150,000 (£3,629,442). 12.XI.90
From the estate of Henry Ford II

The Greta Garbo Collection

Lynn Stowell Pearson

Fig. 1
Greta Garbo in the film *Queen Christina*, 1933.

Opposite
Fig. 2
Pierre Bonnard
LES COQUELICOTS
Signed, *circa* 1914–15,
27½in by 23in
(70cm by 58.5cm)
New York $3,190,000
(£1,627,551). 13.XI.90
From the Greta Garbo
Collection

'Her features were so photogenic. You could light her face in any manner possible; any angle; up, down. Her bone structure and her proportions – her forehead, her nose was just right, the distance between here and there was just right. And her eyes were set in such a way that you couldn't go wrong . . .' This description of Greta Garbo was made by George Hurrell, a studio photographer for MGM during the early 1930s, but it could have been made by just about anyone in Hollywood. Film directors, actors, actresses and critics alike have described her perfect instinct for doing the right thing before the camera, as well as her beauty, glamour and mystery. Ann Sheridan, a star during the 1940s, once said 'Dietrich *is* glamour. Like Garbo was, still is glamour. There is a mystery to them . . .'

It is the mystery of Garbo that fascinates most of us and her desire for privacy was legendary. Even before Garbo's abrupt departure from the silver screen, MGM's publicity department had already created an alluring image for her, and this undoubtedly helped to cultivate a certain mysteriousness. The studio regularly cast her for roles which entailed passionate romantic scenes, often as a lady with a past. In *Flesh and the Devil*, 1927, Garbo hungrily kisses John Gilbert – a scene which was considered sensational at the time. The two teamed up again in *Love*, 1927, and they swiftly became Hollywood's top romantic stars. As 'talkies' became popular, MGM kept Garbo in the silents, afraid that her accent might alienate audiences. It was not until *Anna Christie*, 1930, that Garbo was cast in a talkie. The film was heralded as 'Garbo talks!' Audiences loved it. Other box office hits followed, including *Mata Hari*, 1931, *Grand Hotel*, 1932, *Queen Christina*, 1933 (see Fig. 1), *Anna Karenina*, 1935, and *Camille*, 1937. In 1939 MGM again used a catchy headline, billing *Ninotchka* as 'Garbo laughs!' In 1941, at the age of thirty-six, she withdrew from the screen, retiring to a secluded life that, by its very privacy, only added to the Garbo mystique.

For nearly four decades Greta Garbo lived in a spacious apartment in New York overlooking the East River. There she created a refuge her great-niece Gray Horan has described as 'a sanctuary of peace and imagination . . . Inside there was colour – roses, salmons, greens . . . There were paintings everywhere, even behind the draperies, and beautiful furniture, carved, painted, inlaid.' Admittance to this sanctuary was permitted only to close friends and relatives and these visits were always prearranged. According to Gray Horan, 'you certainly did not drop in.'

The paintings, drawings, furniture and decorations in the Greta Garbo Collection were representative of her own unique vision and sensitivity to colour. Using her own collecting instincts, Miss Garbo regularly visited the New York galleries and auctions to find just the right painting or commode. Tallulah Bankhead once said, 'she loved to go antiquing . . . she loves to go into shops.' Gray Horan recounted an amusing anecdote of how Garbo came to acquire one of these decorations. 'One day she passed a decorator's shop in the neighbourhood and spied some handmade silk tulips. They were very unusual, just the right colour and shape for a pair of Ming jars she prized. She asked the proprietor if she could buy them. He said they were not for sale, but he would give them to her if she would sign one of her photographs. She said she never signed anything. He gave her the flowers anyway.'

The paintings she chose – works by Renoir, Bonnard, Jawlensky, Rouault – all harmonised perfectly with her colour scheme. Many of the paintings were still lifes – nosegays of wildflowers, overblown roses and peonies, and lush bouquets. Bonnard's colourful *Les Coquelicots* (Fig. 2) depicts red poppies in a pitcher. There were also many pictures of women and children. In 1942 Miss Garbo fell in love with Renoir's *Enfant assis en robe bleue (Portrait d'Edmond Renoir, Jr)* (Fig. 3) at Jacques Seligmann's gallery in New York – it had just the right shades of salmon and pink. Greta Garbo once told her niece, Gray Reisfield 'I love colour. I want the room to sing. How can one not understand? With me it's inborn. I just know. I didn't have to learn it. This room is my creation and I think it's pretty good.'

Each work of art Greta Garbo acquired was carefully considered and then just as carefully arranged in her apartment. As her friend Cecile de Rothschild observed, 'With the same sensitivity that characterised her work as an actress, she easily grasped and interpreted the artist's intentions. There was never a false note or an awkward juxtaposition in her arrangements.'

Fig. 3
Pierre-Auguste Renoir
ENFANT ASSIS EN ROBE BLEUE (PORTRAIT D'EDMOND RENOIR, JR)
Signed, 1889, 25½in by 21¼in (64.8cm by 54cm)
New York $7,040,000 (£3,591,837). 13.XI.90
From the Greta Garbo Collection

Opposite
Pablo Picasso
VERRE D'ABSINTHE
Painted bronze and perforated absinthe spoon, inscribed inside with raised letters *III KH*, 1914, height 9½in (24cm)
New York $2,530,000 (£1,284,264). 12.XI.90
From the estate of Henry Ford II

René Magritte
LES MENOTTES DE CUIVRE
Hand-painted plaster, 1936, height 14½in (37cm)
London £82,500 ($166,650). 5.XII.90

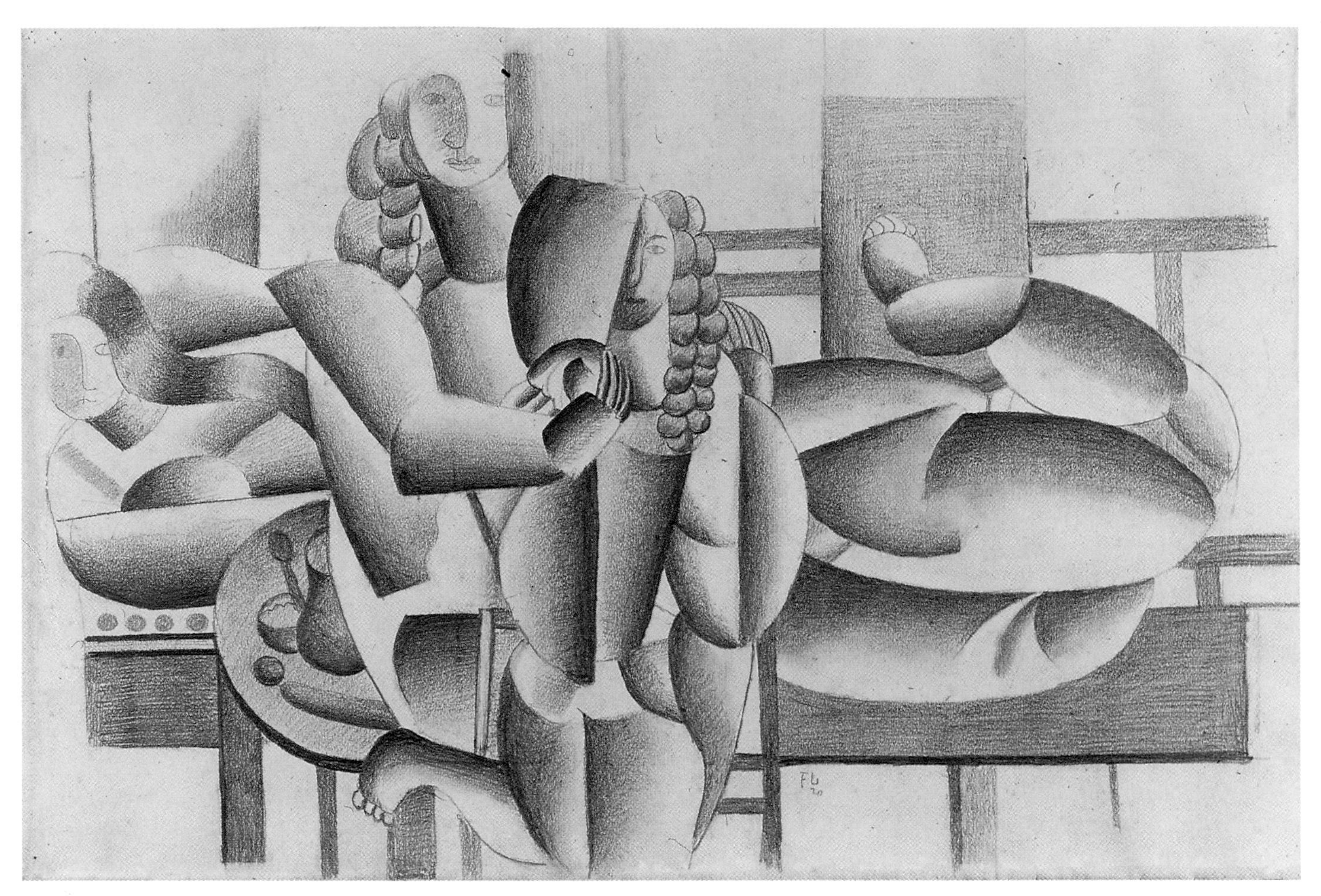

Fernand Léger
TROIS NUS
Pencil, signed with initials and dated *'20*, 16$\frac{3}{8}$in by 24$\frac{3}{8}$in (41.5cm by 62cm)
London £506,000 ($829,840). 26.VI.91
From the collection of Christian Berg

Opposite
Robert Delaunay
FORMES CIRCULAIRES – SOLEIL NO.3
Signed and dated *1912–1913*, 32in by 25$\frac{3}{4}$in (81.5cm by 65.5cm)
London £418,000 ($681,340). 25.VI.91

Max Ernst
FORET ET SOLEIL
Signed, 1927, 31⅞in by 39⅜in (81cm by 100cm)
London £528,000 ($860,640). 25.VI.91
From the estate of Alfred Hecht

Opposite
Joan Miró
DANSEUSE ESPAGNOLE
Signed, inscribed *danseuse espagnole* and dated *7–7–45* on the reverse, 57½in by 44⅞in (146cm by 114cm)
New York $5,940,000 (£3,030,612). 13.XI.90

Magritte

The Surrealist vision of René Magritte

John Tancock

Magritte is without doubt one of the most popular Surrealist painters. The huge quantity of posters and framed reproductions of the more familiar images of the 1950s and 1960s – the ubiquitous bowler-hatted men, for example – attest to Magritte's universal appeal. The clarity of his bizarre, humorous images and the unsurprising nature of his technique with its business-like application of paint succeed in persuading many of his admirers that he was a master of visual conundrums, a twentieth-century Belgian Douanier Rousseau perhaps, who had absorbed only what appealed to him in the writings of André Breton. Magritte did nothing to dispel this illusion. His uneventful life in a suburb of Brussels after three years in Paris from 1927 to 1930, and the absence of anything remotely 'bohemian' in his private life, found its aesthetic equivalent in his disdain for the methods of many of the Surrealists and in emphatic dismissal of abstract art. The mundane façade of the man concealed a rich inner life and the seemingly guileless charm of many of the painted images would not continue to fascinate without rich undercurrents of philosophical and poetic meditation.

Magritte started his professional career as a belated Futurist and Cubist, and it was not until the mid 1920s, after seeing a reproduction of *The Song of Love* by Giorgio de Chirico in *Valori Plastici*, that he began to paint works that he valued more for the expression of poetic ideas rather than for any formal interest they might have. In the earlier Surrealist works Magritte juxtaposed dissimilar objects in the manner indicated by the Comte de Lautréamont in his famous reference to 'the chance encounter of a sewing machine and an umbrella on a dissecting table'. Magritte listed some of these poetic ideas in a lecture given at the Musée Royal des Beaux Arts, Antwerp on 20 November 1938:

> the displacement of objects, for example: a Louis Philippe table on an ice floe, the flag on a dung heap . . . The creation of new objects; the transformation of known objects; the alteration of certain objects' substance – a wooden sky, for example; the use of words associated with images; the false labelling of an image; the realisation of ideas suggested by friends; the representation of certain day-dreaming visions – all these, in sum, were ways of forcing objects finally to become sensational.

Magritte soon discovered, however, that 'sensational' effects could be created more surreptitiously by looking for hidden affinities between objects:

> One night in 1936 I awoke in a room in which someone had put a cage with a sleeping bird. A wonderful aberration made me see the cage with the bird gone and replaced by an egg. There and then, I grasped a new and astonishing poetic secret, for the shock I felt had been

Fig. 1
René Magritte
LA PHILOSOPHIE DANS LE BOUDOIR
Signed, titled and dated *1947* on the reverse, 31in by 24⅛in (79cm by 61.3cm)
New York $1,925,000 (£982,143). 13.XI.90
From the estate of Catherine Schlumberger Jones

Fig. 2
René Magritte
PERSPECTIVE: MADAME RECAMIER DE DAVID
Signed, titled and dated *1951* on the reverse, 23¾in by 31½in (60.4cm by 80cm)
New York $742,000 (£378,571). 13.XI.90
From the estate of Catherine Schlumberger Jones

caused precisely by the affinity of the two objects, the cage and the egg, whereas previously this shock had been caused by the encounter between two completely unrelated objects.

From that moment, I sought to find out whether objects beside the cage could also disclose – by bringing to light an element characteristic of them and absolutely predestined for them – the same unmistakable poetry the union of the egg and cage had managed to produce. In the course of my experiments, I came to the conviction that I always knew beforehand that element to be discovered, that certain thing above all the others, attached obscurely to each object; but this knowledge had lain as if lost in the depths of my thought.

It was the deliberateness of his method that distinguished Magritte from the more orthodox Surrealists. Although preceded by a 'frenzied contemplation' that viewed a given problem from all conceivable angles in countless sketches and variations on a theme, Magritte's paintings do not show any trace of this in their final state. In *La Philosophie dans le Boudoir*, 1947 (Fig. 1), the title of which derives from the 1795 work by the Marquis de Sade, both the dress hanging from a clothes hanger and the pair of high-heeled shoes with human toes are related to images in earlier paintings. The dress had appeared in *En Hommage à Mack Sennett*, 1934 (Collection de la Ville de La Louvière), although it was long sleeved and white and hung in a wardrobe. A pair of boot-feet with pronounced veins had appeared in *Le Modèle rouge*, 1935 (Musée National d'Art Moderne, Centre Georges Pompidou). In connection with this latter painting, Magritte was investigating 'the problem of the shoe' and 'how the most frightening things can, through inattention, become completely conscious. Thanks to *Le Modèle rouge*, we realise that the union of a human foot and a shoe is actually a monstrous custom.' Spatially, the painting is more ambiguous than *En Hommage à Mack Sennett*. The gown with its glowing breasts seems to be hanging inside a closet, yet the shoes, seemingly ready for a walk, rest on a tabletop in the immediate foreground. The hybrid forms confront the spectator directly and menacingly.

Magritte's fascination with death and the trappings of death has frequently been noted. He had personal experience with it at the age of twelve when his mother committed suicide by drowning herself. The childhood games in the graveyard at Soignies and the occasional morbid prank in later years attest to death's continuing

Fig. 3
René Magritte
L'IDOLE
Signed; also signed, titled, inscribed *15F.* and dated *1965* on the reverse, $21\frac{1}{4}$in by $25\frac{5}{8}$in (54cm by 65cm)
New York $1,210,000 (£617,347). 13.XI.90
From the estate of Catherine Schlumberger Jones

power to enthral or intrigue him. Three works painted in 1950 – *Perspective: Madame Récamier de Gérard*, *Perspective I: Madame Récamier de David* and *Perspective II: le Balcon de Manet* and a second version of *Perspective I: Madame Récamier de David* painted in 1951 (Fig. 2) – encase celebrated women of beauty and intellect (Madame Récamier and Berthe Morisot) in coffins specifically crafted to accommodate their seated or reclining forms.

It was shortly after the brief *période vache* of 1948, an interlude of deliberate levity that proved to be wildly unpopular with the general public, that Magritte began to depict a world in which everything had metamorphosed into stone. In paintings such as *Souvenir de Voyage*, 1951 (Menil Foundation, Houston), and *Le Chant de la Violette*, 1951, Magritte created an airless world in which all forms, both animate and inanimate, have been petrified. Time has stopped, just as it has in the *Perspective* series in which the coffins encase the human forms in the architectural environments created by Gérard, David and Manet. The analogy between the funereal calm of Magritte's version of the celebrated painting by David who spent the latter part of his life in Brussels, and the marmoreal splendour of much Empire art is not lost, but more is at stake than the parody of an artistic style. Magritte's ability to evoke 'astonishing poetic secrets' gives a particular resonance to his Davidian paraphrase.

L'Idole, 1965 (Fig. 3), the latest painting in the group of Magritte's from the Schlumberger Jones Collection, is as enigmatic as its title leads one to expect. The image of the bird appeared with considerable frequency in the 1960s, sometimes feathered as in *L'Homme au Chapeau Melon*, 1964, sometimes suffused with leaves, *Le Printemps*, 1965, or with a night sky, *L'Oiseau Bleu*, from around 1962. In *L'Idole* the centrally-placed bird has been petrified and seems to be of the same substance as the rocks in the foreground of the picture. If its size is to be judged by the scale of the rocks it is a very large bird indeed, flying dangerously low like a Boeing 747. The question then arises as to whether it is flying at all since in the beautifully painted, pearly light of the seascape there is no trace of movement. As in the best of Magritte's paintings, an image is presented that continues to reverberate in the mind, provoking thought and reverie, but never leading to a solution.

Henri Matisse 40

Egon Schiele
NUDE WITH GREEN STOCKINGS
Gouache, watercolour and pencil on paper, signed and dated *1912*, 19in by 12½in (48.2cm by 31.8cm)
New York $412,500 (£210,459). 14.XI.90

Opposite
Henri Matisse
LA ROBE PERSANE
Signed and dated *'40*, 31½in by 25½in (80cm by 64.7cm)
New York $4,510,000 (£2,606,936). 7.V.91
From the estate of Irene Mayer Selznick

Emil Nolde
POPPIES AND BLUE LUPINS
Signed, 1950, $26\frac{3}{4}$in by $34\frac{5}{8}$in (68cm by 88cm)
Berlin DM1,443,000 (£490,816:$839,296).
30.V.91

Oskar Schlemmer
TWO HEADS AND TWO NUDES, SILVER FRIEZE IV
Oil and tempera on canvas, 1931, 13in by $21\frac{1}{2}$in (33cm by 54.5cm)
Berlin DM521,700 (£177,449:$303,438).
30.V.91

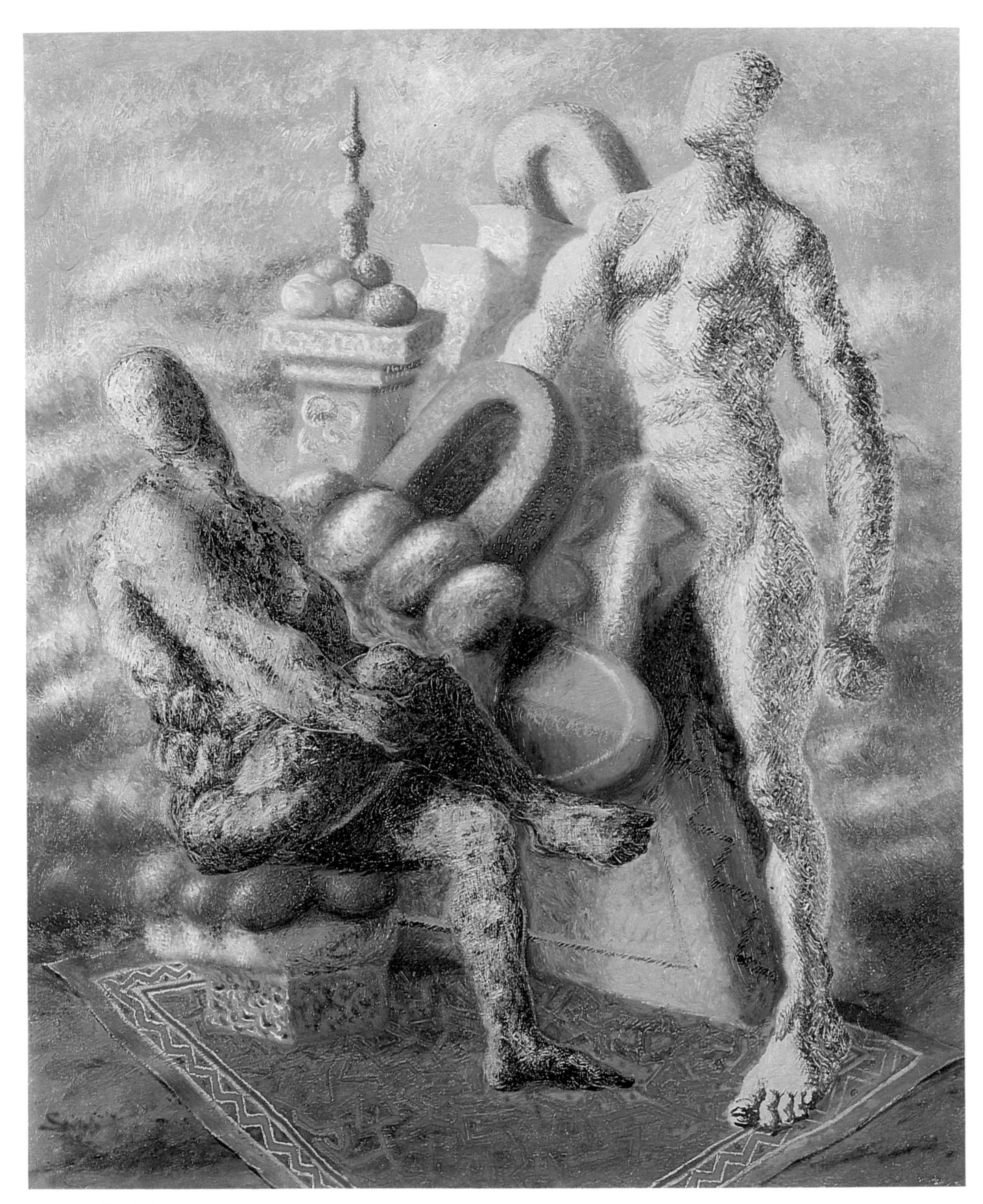

Alberto Savinio
GARDIENS D'OBJETS
Signed and dated *'929*, 28¾in by 23⅝in (73cm by 60cm)
Milan L655,400,000 (£297,368:$515,657). 28.V.91

Contemporary art

Nicolas de Staël
LE BOCAL
Signed, 1955, 28¾in by 39⅜in (73cm by 100cm)
London £572,000 ($932,360). 27.VI.91
From the Chester Beatty Collection

Opposite
Jean Dubuffet
MAISON FONDEE
Signed and dated *61*, 45¾in by 35in (116.2cm by 89cm)
New York $2,640,000 (£1,340,102). 6.XI.90

DENTISTE
PHARMA
CIE
MAISON
FONDEE
SOLDES

Robert Rauschenberg
REBUS
Oil, pencil, fabric and paper collage on canvas, 1955, 96in by 131in (243.8cm by 332.7cm)
New York $7,260,000 (£4,196,532). 30.IV.91

Opposite
Robert Rauschenberg
THIRD TIME PAINTING
Oil, paper, fabric, wood, metal, glass, chain and clock on canvas, 1961, 84in by 60in (213.3cm by 152.3cm)
New York $3,080,000 (£1,563,452). 6.XI.90
From the collection of Robert E. Abrams

ELECTRICALLY
CONTROLLED TIME
BULOVA

Opposite
Mark Rothko
SAFFRON
Signed and dated *1957* on the reverse, 69¾in by 54in (177cm by 137cm)
London £770,000 ($1,255,100). 27.VI.91

Right
Jean Fautrier
GRANDES ETENDUES
Oil and pigment on paper mounted on hessian, signed and dated *'57*, 28¾in by 36¼in (73cm by 92cm)
London £407,000 ($663,410). 27.VI.91
From the collection of Carl-Eric Björkegren

Below
Cy Twombly
UNTITLED
Oil, crayon and graphite on canvas, signed on the reverse, 1959, 57⅝in by 79in (146.5cm by 200.7cm)
New York $2,200,000 (£1,271,676). 30.IV.91

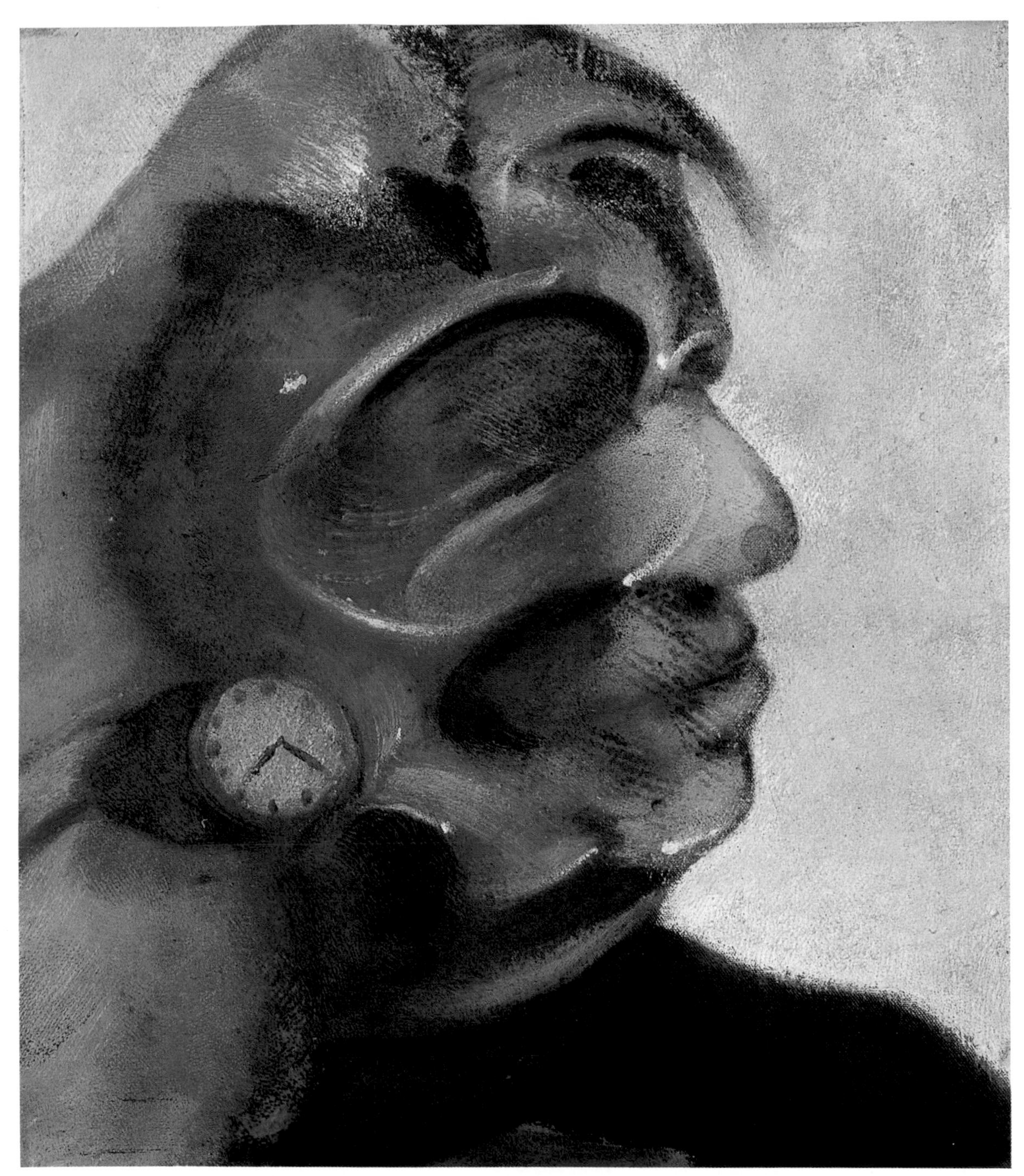

Francis Bacon
STUDY FOR SELF PORTRAIT
1973, 14in by 12in (35.5cm by 30.5cm)
London £363,000 ($591,690). 27.VI.91
From the estate of Alfred Hecht

Opposite
Karel Appel
FEMME ET CHIEN DANS LA RUE
Signed and dated '*53*, 56½in by 43⅜in (143.5cm by 110.2cm)
London £154,000 ($312,620). 6.XII.90

K. appel '53

Gerhard Richter
TOURIST (MIT 2 LÖWEN)
Signed, numbered *369* and dated *1975* on the reverse, 74⅞in by 90½in (190cm by 230cm)
London £203,500 ($413,105). 6.XII.90

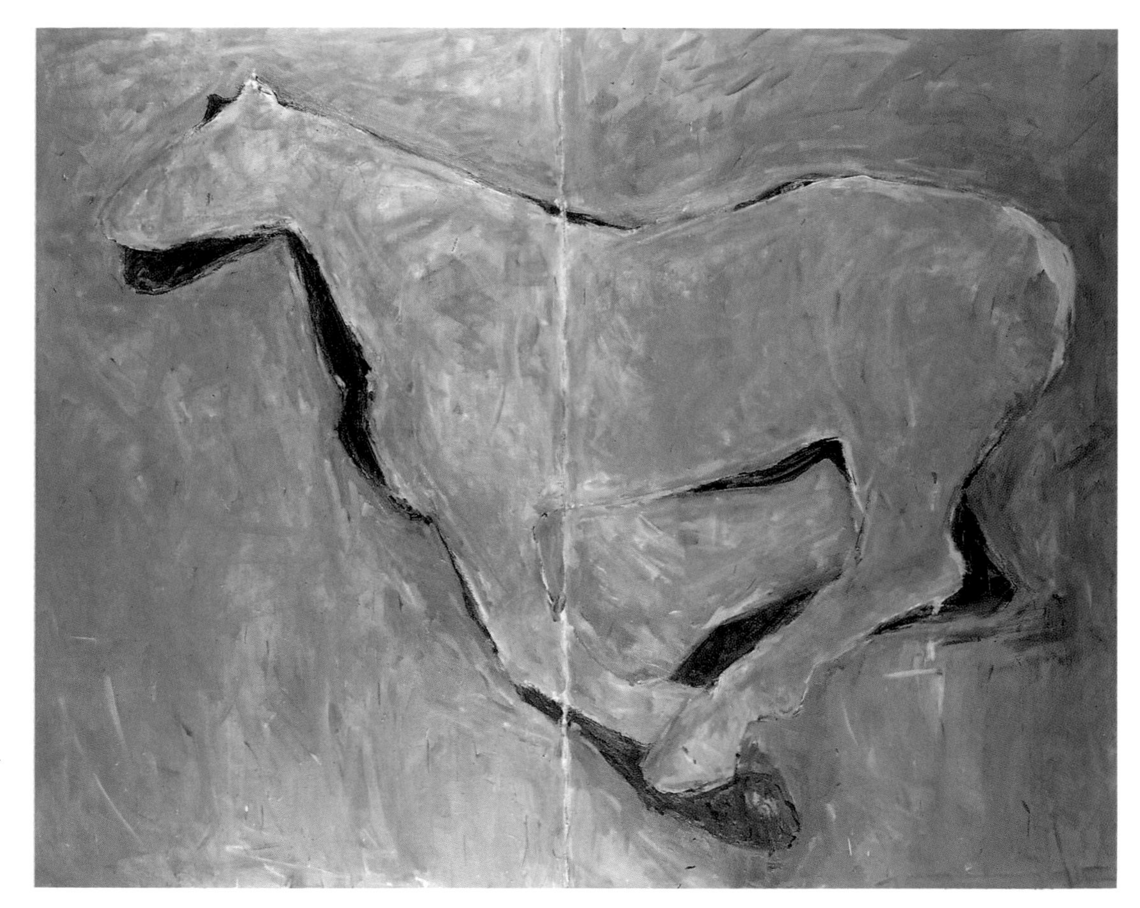

Susan Rothenberg
CABIN FEVER
Acrylic and tempera on canvas, 1976, 67in by 84in (170.2cm by 213.3cm)
New York $506,000 (£292,486). 30.IV.91

Eva Hesse
SANS II (ONE UNIT)
Fibreglass and polyester resin, 1968, 38in by 86in by 6⅛in (96.5cm by 218.5cm by 15.5cm)
New York $330,000 (£190,751). 30.IV.91

American art

Edward Hicks
PENN'S TREATY
Inscribed *Wm PENN'S TREATY with the INDIAN'S 1681*, 1847, 25in by 30in (63.5cm by 76.2cm)
New York $990,000 (£510,309). 29.XI.90
From the collection of Robert Carlen

Thomas Moran
THE GRAND CANYON
Signed and dated *1904*, 30in by 60in (76.2cm by 152.4cm)
New York $1,045,000 (£538,660). 29.XI.90

Edward Hopper
SOUTH TRURO CHURCH
Signed, 1930, 29in by 43in (73.7cm by 109.2cm)
New York $2,420,000 (£1,247,423). 29.XI.90

Opposite, above
Severin Roesen
FRUIT STILL LIFE WITH WINE GLASS IN A LANDSCAPE
Signed, 36in by 50½in (91.4cm by 128.3cm)
New York $253,000 (£130,412). 29.XI.90

Below
George Bellows
THREE CHILDREN
1919, 30in by 44in (76.2cm by 111.8cm)
New York $187,000 (£107,471). 23.V.91
From the estate of Irene Mayer Selznick

Frederick C. Frieseke
THE MIRROR
Signed and dated *1912*, 32in by 32in (81.3cm by 81.3cm)
New York $181,500 (£104,310). 23.V.91
From the collection of Wendy Willis

Harry Roseland
TO THE HIGHEST BIDDER
Signed, 1906, 60in by 32in
(152.4cm by 81.3cm)
New York $253,000
(£130,412). 29.XI.90

Prendergast

HOMER 1887

Charles Demuth
SAIL: IN TWO MOVEMENTS
Tempera on board, signed and dated *Gloucester, 1919*, 16in by 20in (40.6cm by 50.8cm)
New York $473,000 (£243,814). 29.XI.90
From the collection of Ned L. Pines

Opposite, above
Maurice B. Prendergast
GLOUCESTER
Signed, *circa* 1910–13, 20in by 28½in (50.8cm by 72.4cm)
New York $1,320,000 (£758,621). 23.V.91

Below
Winslow Homer
FODDER
Watercolour on paper, signed and dated *1887*, 13in by 19½in (33cm by 49.5cm)
New York $220,000 (£126,437). 23.V.91

Latin American, Canadian and Australian art

Fernando Botero
THREE MUSICIANS
Signed and dated *83*, 64½in by 48½in (163.8cm by 123.2cm)
New York $572,000 (£290,355). 19.XI.90
From the collection of the Minneapolis College of Art and Design

Opposite
Paul Peel
LA CAPRICIEUSE
Signed and dated *1889*, 39in by 27in (99.1cm by 68.6cm)
Toronto CAN$143,000 (£72,040: $124,294). 6.V.91

Sir Arthur Ernest Streeton
BATHERS – KILLARNEY
Oil on canvas on board, signed, 18in by 7in (46cm by 18cm)
Melbourne AUS$220,000 (£99,615:$169,491). 22.IV.91

Sir William Dobell
THE SMOKO
Oil on board, signed and dated *'50*, 30in by 27⅛in (76cm by 69cm)
Melbourne AUS$132,000 (£59,769:$101,695). 22.IV.91

Prints

William Blake
THE CHAINING OF ORC
Relief print, 1812/13, 4$\frac{1}{4}$in by 3$\frac{1}{8}$in (10.7cm by 8cm)
New York $101,750 (£59,157). 9.V.91

After Hieronymous Bosch
THE LARGE ELEPHANT WITH A FANTASTIC CASTLE ON ITS BACK
Engraving, first state of two, 15$\frac{1}{2}$in by 21$\frac{1}{4}$in (39.4cm by 53.8cm)
London £79,200 ($160,776). 6.XII.90

Paul Gauguin

NOA NOA

Woodcut, third and final state, hand printed by the artist, 1893–94, $13\frac{3}{4}$in by 8in (34.9cm by 20.2cm)
Tokyo Y26,400,000 (£95,185:$216,000).
15.X.90

Wassily Kandinsky
ORANGE
Lithograph, signed and numbered *13/50*, 1923, 18⅞in by 17¼in (47.9cm by 43.9cm)
London £82,500 ($134,475). 26.VI.91

Opposite
Pablo Picasso
BENJAMIN PERET. DE DERRIERE LES FAGOTS
The complete book, including the drypoint *La Mort du Marat*, signed and numbered *5*, Paris, 1934,
each sheet 10¼in by 5¾in (26cm by 14.6cm)
London £28,600 ($46,618). 26.VI.91

Opposite
Jasper Johns
THE SEASONS: SPRING, SUMMER, FALL and WINTER
The complete suite, comprising four etchings with aquatint, each signed, numbered *49/73* and dated *1987*
New York $187,000 (£108,721). 11.V.91

Marc Chagall
FOUR TALES FROM THE ARABIAN NIGHTS
The complete portfolio, comprising twelve lithographs, each signed and numbered *52/90*, 1948, each sheet 17in by 13in (43.2cm by 33cm)
New York $687,500 (£399,709). 9.V.91

CHUTE DE GLACE

Photographs

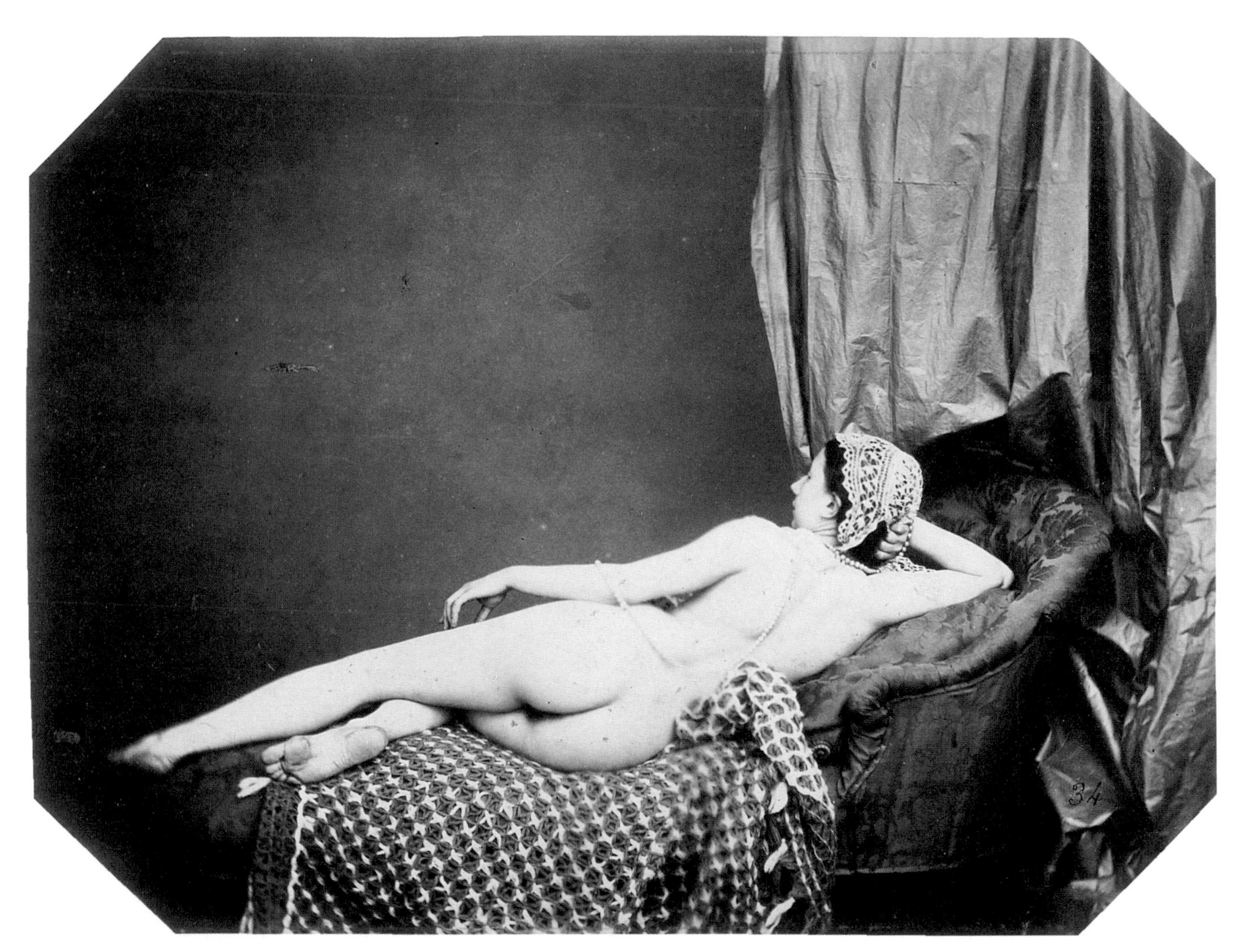

Auguste Belloc
NUDE ON DAYBED 'DE DOS'
Albumen print, *circa* 1854, 6in by 7⅞in (15cm by 19.9cm)
London £3,300 ($5,643). 9.V.91

Robert Frank
'RODEO, NEW YORK CITY, (COWBOY LEANING AGAINST TRASH CAN)'
Silver print, signed, *circa* 1955, $13\frac{1}{4}$in by $8\frac{3}{8}$in (33.8cm by 21.2cm)
London £9,900 ($16,929). 9.V.91

Tina Modotti
'ROSES, MEXICO'
Platinum print, signed on the reverse of the mount, 1924, $7\frac{3}{8}$in by $8\frac{3}{8}$in (18.7cm by 21.3cm)
New York $165,000 (£87,302). 17.IV.91

Roses, Mexico

Denise Bethel

Roses, Mexico was taken in 1924 by Tina Modotti, an Italian-born photographer and political activist who was once the lover of Edward Weston. A native of Udine, in Northern Italy, Tina Modotti emigrated to San Francisco when she was seventeen, and earned her living as a dressmaker. Around 1917, she met and married Roubaix de l'Abrie Richey, an artist and poet, and moved with him to Los Angeles. There she eventually found work as a bit player in early Hollywood films.

Sometime during the early 1920s, Modotti met the photographer Edward Weston, and their love affair, chronicled in Weston's remarkable series of portraits of her, began. In 1922 Roubaix Richey died and the following year Modotti moved to Mexico City with Weston and his young son Chandler. They spent the next three years together in Mexico, a period of intense creativity for both of them. In Mexico, Weston abandoned the pictorial mannerisms of his early career in favour of the stark realism that would characterise his mature style. And in Mexico, Modotti learned to photograph, assisting Weston in his studio and darkroom while steadily making negatives of her own. Modotti's natural talent and lyrical vision are evident in even her earliest work with a camera, as exemplified by her passionate *Roses*. In 1924, the year Modotti's *Roses* was taken, Weston wrote to a friend: 'Tina has one picture I wish I could sign with my name – that does not happen often in my life!'

The sepia-toned platinum print of crushed roses belongs to a group of early Modotti photographs in which rhythmic patterns of forms, sometimes natural sometimes man-made, fill the frame. Other works pulsate with the rounded tops of water glasses, abstract layers of stadium seats, wide-brimmed hats of a crowd of workers, or punctuated notches of sugar cane. These and a series of studies of individual plants and flowers – a calla lily, the Manito cactus – are perhaps Modotti's strongest work. In a letter of 1925, Modotti described 'the eroticism felt by different persons in some of my photographs like the calla lily – the roses, and Tepotzotlan.' When Diego Rivera reviewed a joint exhibition of Weston and Modotti's prints in 1926, he wrote, 'Tina Modotti has done marvels in sensibility on a plane, perhaps more abstract, more aerial, even more intellectual, as is natural for an Italian temperament. Her work flowers perfectly in Mexico and harmonises with our passion.'

When Weston left Mexico at the end of 1926, Modotti stayed on, supporting herself by photographing murals and other works of art. In 1927 she became a member of the Communist Party, and from that point on political activism dominated her life. Deported from Mexico in 1930, she travelled through Europe and Russia before returning to Mexico in 1939. She died in 1942, ostensibly from a heart attack, but rumours circulated that she was poisoned by political enemies. Her photographic oeuvre, though small, contains many works of great sensitivity and beauty and has ensured her position in the history of photography of the twentieth century.

Alfred Stieglitz
GEORGIA O'KEEFFE
Backed with card, matted, 1922, 7½in by 9½in (19cm by 24.1cm)
New York $99,000 (£50,510). 16.X.90

Georgia O'Keeffe met Alfred Stieglitz in 1916 and the two were married in 1924. The relationship between this master photographer and the dynamic artist has been aptly described by Estelle Jussim as a 'most intriguing collision of giant personalities'. Stieglitz took many photographs of O'Keeffe from 1917 to 1937, conceiving them as a 'composite portrait' which would record not only the physical but also the psychological changes in his sitter over time.

Opposite
Edward Weston
PALM TRUNK, CUERNAVACA
Platinum or palladium print, signed, titled and dated *1925*, 9½in by 6¼in (24.1cm by 15.9cm)
New York $154,000 (£81,481). 17.IV.91

Weston began work on this photograph on 25 November 1925 in the Cuernavaca garden of Frederick Davis, an art collector and proprietor of the Sonora News Company. Weston wrote of this study 'Why should a few yards of a white tree trunk, exactly centred, cutting across an empty sky, cause such real response? And why did I spend my hours doing it? One question simply answered – I had to!'

Printed books, autograph letters and music manuscripts

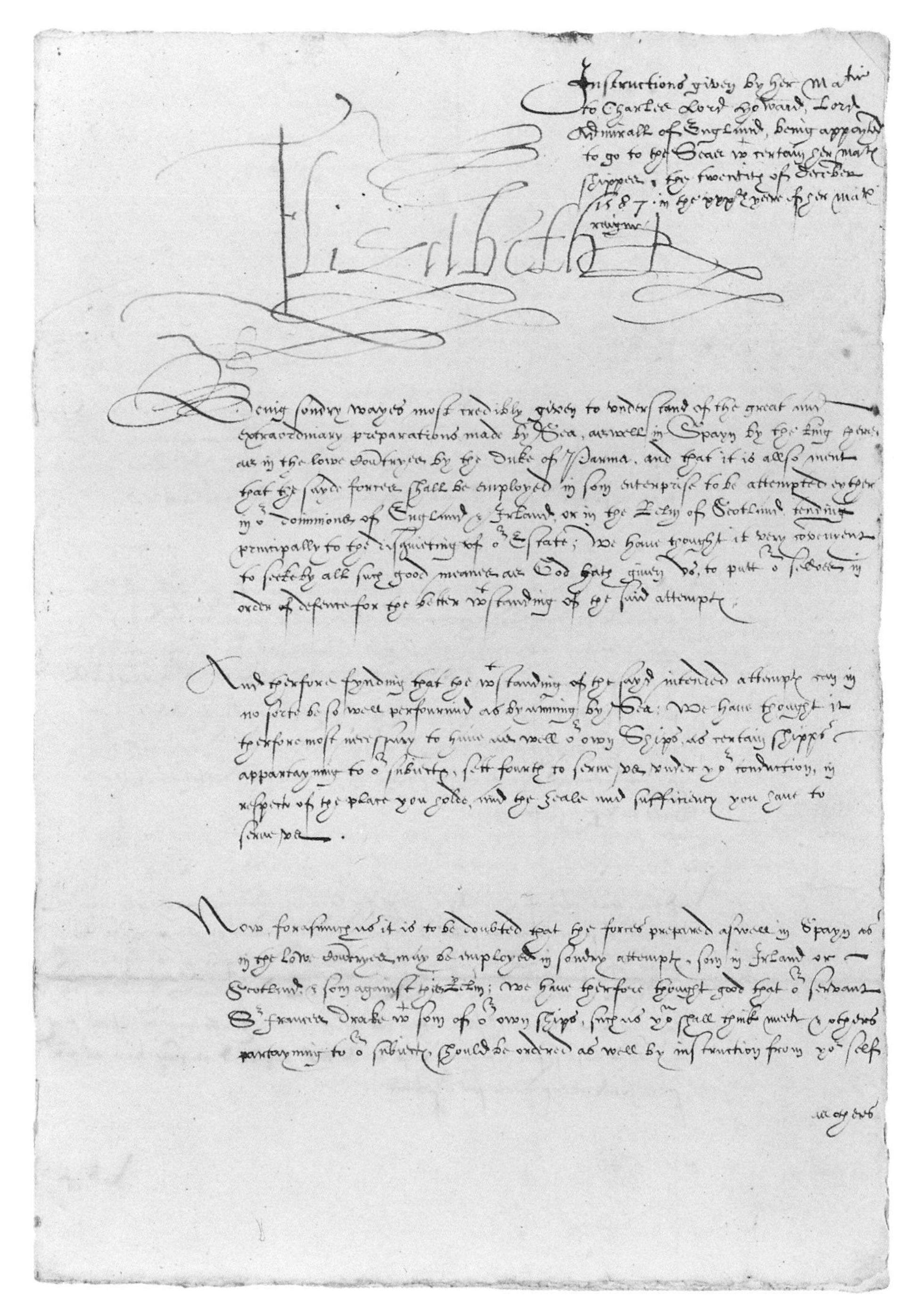

Elizabeth I
Document marking the beginning of the Armada Campaign in England, 4 pages, signed *Elizabeth R*, dated the *twentieth of december 1587*
London £49,500 ($101,475). 13.XII.90
From the collection of the 10th Duke of Northumberland

Opposite
Desiderius Erasmus
Erasmus's annotated and revised copy of *Adagia*, Johann Froben, Basle, January 1523
London £495,000 ($1,034,550). 20.XI.90

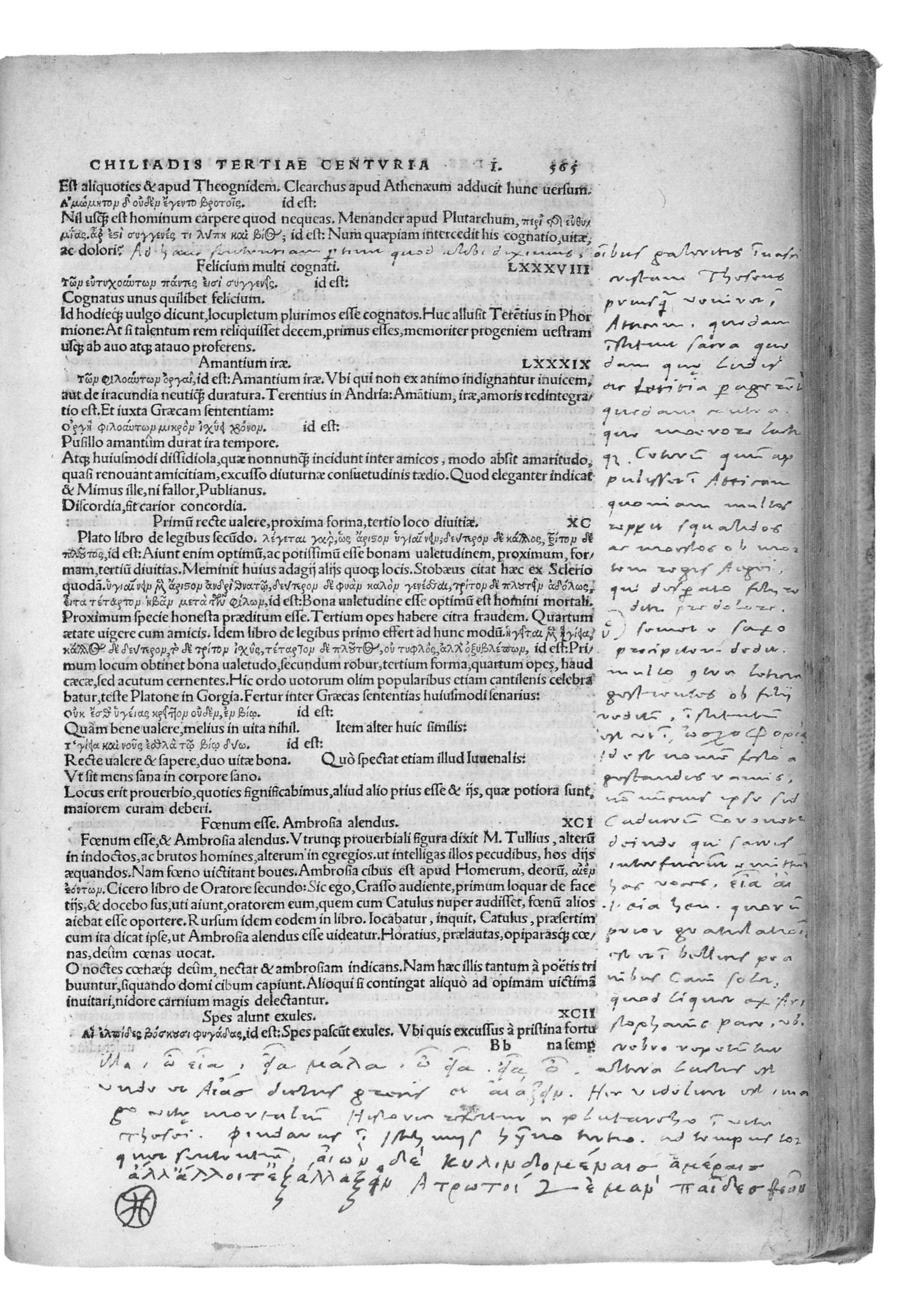

CHILIADIS TERTIAE CENTVRIA I. 565

Est aliquoties & apud Theognidem. Clearchus apud Athenæum adducit hunc uersum.
ἀμώμητον δ᾽ οὐδὲν ἔγεντο βροτοῖς. id est:
Nil usque est hominum carpere quod nequeas. Menander apud Plutarchum, περὶ τῆς εὐθυμίας. ἆρ᾽ ἐστὶ συγγενές τι λύπη καὶ βίος; id est: Num quæpiam intercedit his cognatio, uitæ, ac dolori?

Felicium multi cognati. LXXXVIII

τῶν εὐτυχούντων πάντες εἰσὶ συγγενεῖς. id est:
Cognatus unus quilibet felicium.
Id hodieque uulgo dicunt, locupletum plurimos esse cognatos. Huc allusit Terētius in Phormione: At si talentum rem reliquisset decem, primus esses, memoriter progeniem uestram usque ab auo atque atauo proferens.

Amantium iræ. LXXXIX

τῶν φιλούντων ὀργαί, id est: Amantium iræ. Vbi qui non ex animo indignantur inuicem, aut de iracundia neutique duratura. Terentius in Andria: Amātium, iræ, amoris redintegratio est. Et iuxta Græcam sententiam:
ὀργὴ φιλούντων μικρὸν ἰσχύει χρόνον. id est:
Pusillo amantûm durat ira tempore.
Atque huiusmodi dissidiola, quæ nonnunquam incidunt inter amicos, modo absit amaritudo, quasi renouant amicitiam, excusso diuturnæ consuetudinis tædio. Quod eleganter indicat & Mimus ille, ni fallor, Publianus.
Discordia, fit carior concordia.

Primū recte ualere, proxima forma, tertio loco diuitiæ. XC

Plato libro de legibus secūdo. λέγεται γὰρ, ὡς ἄριστον ὑγιαίνειν, δεύτερον δὲ κάλλος, τρίτον δὲ πλοῦτος, id est: Aiunt enim optimū, ac potissimū esse bonam ualetudinem, proximum, formam, tertiū diuitias. Meminit huius adagij alijs quoque locis. Stobæus citat hæc ex Sclerio quodā. ὑγιαίνειν μὲν ἄριστον ἀνδρὶ θνατῷ, δεύτερον δὲ φυὰν καλὸν γενέσθαι, τρίτον δὲ πλουτεῖν ἀδόλως, εἶτα τέταρτον ἡβᾶν μετὰ τῶν φίλων, id est: Bona ualetudine esse optimū est homini mortali. Proximum specie honesta præditum esse. Tertium opes habere citra fraudem. Quartum ætate uigere cum amicis. Idem libro de legibus primo effert ad hunc modū. ἡγεῖται μὲν ὑγίεια, κάλλος δὲ δεύτερον, τὸ δὲ τρίτον ἰσχύς, τέταρτον δὲ πλοῦτος, οὐ τυφλὸς, ἀλλ᾽ ὀξὺ βλέπων, id est: Primum locum obtinet bona ualetudo, secundum robur, tertium forma, quartum opes, haud cæcæ, sed acutum cernentes. Hic ordo uotorum olim popularibus etiam cantilenis celebrabatur, teste Platone in Gorgia. Fertur inter Græcas sententias huiusmodi senarius:
οὐκ ἔστιν ὑγιείας κρεῖττον οὐδὲν, ἐν βίῳ. id est:
Quàm bene ualere, melius in uita nihil. Item alter huic similis:
ὑγίεια καὶ νοῦς ἐσθλὰ τῷ βίῳ δύω. id est:
Recte ualere & sapere, duo uitæ bona. Quò spectat etiam illud Iuuenalis:
Vt sit mens sana in corpore sano.
Locus erit prouerbio, quoties significabimus, aliud alio prius esse & ijs, quæ potiora sunt, maiorem curam deberi.

Fœnum esse. Ambrosia alendus. XCI

Fœnum esse, & Ambrosia alendus. Vtrunque prouerbiali figura dixit M. Tullius, alterū in indoctos, ac brutos homines, alterum in egregios. ut intelligas illos pecudibus, hos dijs æquandos. Nam fœno uictitant boues. Ambrosia cibus est apud Homerum, deorū, αἰὲν ἐόντων. Cicero libro de Oratore secundo: *Sic ego, Crasso audiente, primum loquar de facetijs, & docebo sus, uti aiunt, oratorem eum, quem cum Catulus nuper audisset, fœnū alios aiebat esse oportere.* Rursum idem eodem in libro. Iocabatur, inquit, Catulus, præsertim cum ita dicat ipse, ut Ambrosia alendus esse uideatur. Horatius, prælautas, opiparasque cœnas, deûm cœnas uocat.
O noctes cœnæque deûm, nectar & ambrosiam indicans. Nam hæc illis tantum à poëtis tribuuntur, siquando domi cibum capiunt. Alioqui si contingat aliquò ad opimam uictimā inuitari, nidore carnium magis delectantur.

Spes alunt exules. XCII

Αἱ ἐλπίδες βόσκουσι φυγάδας, id est: Spes pascūt exules. Vbi quis excussus à pristina fortu

Bb na semp

rit opus. tñ vero aromatum·bombicis·masticis:q̄ apud Chium
duntaxat inuenitur· tantūq; ligni aloes· tantum seruoꝝ hydo/
latrarum :quantum eorum maiestas voluerit exigere· item reu/
barbarum ⁊ alia aromatum genera que ii quos in dicta arce reli
qui iam inuenisse atq; inuenturos existimo· qn̄quidem ego nul
libi magis sum moratus nisi quantum me coegerunt venti:pre/
terq̄; in villa Natiuitatis:dum arcē condere ⁊ tuta oīa esse pro
uidi. Que ⁊ si maxima ⁊ inaudita sunt:multo tñ maiora forent
si naues mihi vt ratio exigit subuenissent· Uerꝝ multum ac mira
bile hoc:nec nostris meritis correspondens:sed sancte Christia/
ne fidei:nostrorumq; Regum pietati ac religioni: quia quod hu
manus consequi nō poterat intellectus:id humanis cōcessit di
uinus· Solet enim deus seruus suos:quiq; sua precepta diligūt
⁊ in impossibilibus exaudire:vt nobis in presentia contigit:qui
ea consecuti sumus que hactenus mortalium vires minime atti
gerant:nam si harū insulaꝝ quipiam aliquid scripserunt aut lo
cuti sunt:omnes per ambages ⁊ cōiecturas·nemo se eas vidisse
asserit·vnde prope videbatur fabula· Igitur Rex ⁊ Regina prin
cepsq; ac eoꝝ regna felicissima cuncteq; alie Christianoꝝ prouin
cie Saluatori dn̄o nostro Jesu Christo agamꝰ gratias: qui tan
ta nos victoria munereq; donauit:celebrentur processiones·per
agantur solennia sacra:festaq; fronde velentur delubra· exultet
Christus in terris quemadmodum in celis exultat:quom tot po
pulorum perditas ante hac animas saluatum iri preuidet· Lete
mur ⁊ nos:cum propter exaltationem nostre fidei· tum propter
rerum temporalium incrementa:quoꝝ non solum Hispania sed
vniuersa Christianitas est futura particeps· Hec vt gesta sunt
sic breuiter enarrata. Uale· Ulis bone pridie Idus Martii·

Christoforus Colom Oceane classis Prefectus·

Christopher Columbus
Epistola . . . de Insulis Indie supra Gangem nuper inuentis, the European discovery of America, Stephan Plannck's corrected edition, Rome, 1493
New York $440,000 (£269,939). 13.VI.91

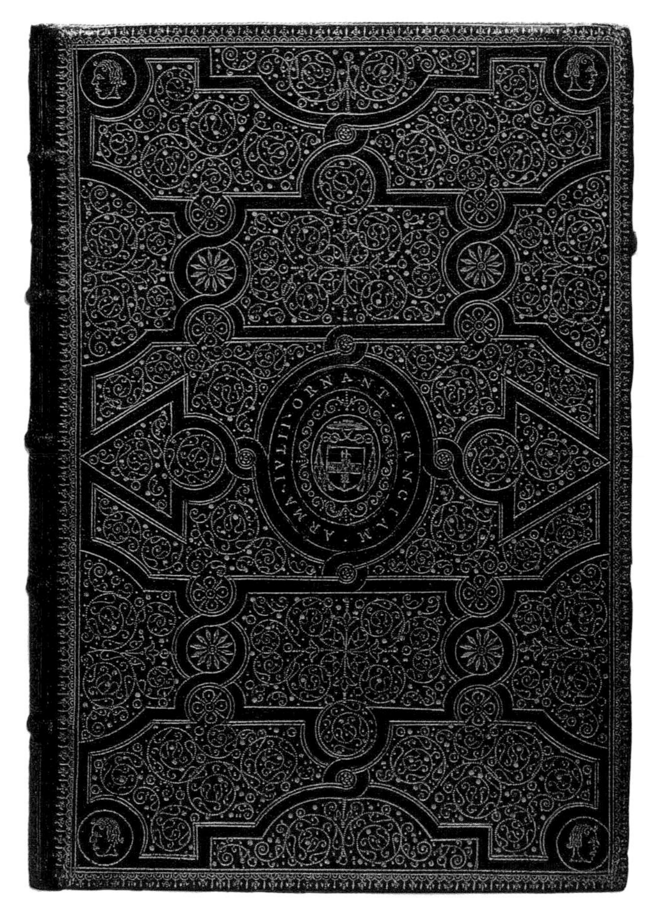

Hans Holbein the Younger
Icones historiarum, a biblical iconology illustrated with 94 Old Testament scenes, Lyons, 1547, the French red morocco binding for Cardinal Jules Mazarin bearing his arms by Florimond Badier, Paris, *circa* 1660,
$7\frac{1}{2}$in by 5in (19cm by 12.7cm)
New York $132,000 (£68,041). 11.XII.90
From the library of John M. Schiff

Long Division

Abraham Lincoln is my nam
And with my pen I wrote the same
I wrote in both hast and speed
and left it here for fools
to read 1824

Abraham Lincoln
A leaf from Lincoln's self-made schoolboy sum book, signed *Abraham Lincoln's Book* and dated *1824*,
$12\frac{1}{4}$in by $7\frac{1}{2}$in (31cm by 19.1cm)
New York $143,000 (£87,730). 13.VI.91

This leaf forms part of the earliest surviving dated writing by Abraham Lincoln, an arithmetic notebook that the future president worked on in his early teens.

IN CONGRESS, JULY 4, 1776.

A DECLARATION

BY THE REPRESENTATIVES OF THE

UNITED STATES OF AMERICA,

IN GENERAL CONGRESS ASSEMBLED.

WHEN in the Course of human Events, it becomes necessary for one People to dissolve the Political Bands which have connected them with another, and to assume among the Powers of the Earth, the separate and equal Station to which the Laws of Nature and of Nature's God entitle them, a decent Respect to the Opinions of Mankind requires that they should declare the causes which impel them to the Separation.

WE hold these Truths to be self-evident, that all Men are created equal, that they are endowed by their Creator with certain unalienable Rights, that among these are Life, Liberty, and the Pursuit of Happiness—That to secure these Rights, Governments are instituted among Men, deriving their just Powers from the Consent of the Governed, that whenever any Form of Government becomes destructive of these Ends, it is the Right of the People to alter or to abolish it, and to institute new Government, laying its Foundation on such Principles, and organizing its Powers in such Form, as to them shall seem most likely to effect their Safety and Happiness. Prudence, indeed, will dictate that Governments long established should not be changed for light and transient Causes; and accordingly all Experience hath shewn, that Mankind are more disposed to suffer, while Evils are sufferable, than to right themselves by abolishing the Forms to which they are accustomed. But when a long Train of Abuses and Usurpations, pursuing invariably the same Object, evinces a Design to reduce them under absolute Despotism, it is their Right, it is their Duty, to throw off such Government, and to provide new Guards for their future Security. Such has been the patient Sufferance of these Colonies; and such is now the Necessity which constrains them to alter their former Systems of Government. The History of the present King of Great-Britain is a History of repeated Injuries and Usurpations, all having in direct Object the Establishment of an absolute Tyranny over these States. To prove this, let Facts be submitted to a candid World.

HE has refused his Assent to Laws, the most wholesome and necessary for the public Good.

HE has forbidden his Governors to pass Laws of immediate and pressing Importance, unless suspended in their Operation till his Assent should be obtained; and when so suspended, he has utterly neglected to attend to them.

HE has refused to pass other Laws for the Accommodation of large Districts of People, unless those People would relinquish the Right of Representation in the Legislature, a Right inestimable to them, and formidable to Tyrants only.

HE has called together Legislative Bodies at Places unusual, uncomfortable, and distant from the Depository of their public Records, for the sole Purpose of fatiguing them into Compliance with his Measures.

HE has dissolved Representative Houses repeatedly, for opposing with manly Firmness his Invasions on the Rights of the People.

HE has refused for a long Time, after such Dissolutions, to cause others to be elected; whereby the Legislative Powers, incapable of Annihilation, have returned to the People at large for their exercise; the State remaining in the mean time exposed to all the Dangers of Invasion from without, and Convulsions within.

HE has endeavoured to prevent the Population of these States; for that Purpose obstructing the Laws for Naturalization of Foreigners; refusing to pass others to encourage their Migrations hither, and raising the Conditions of new Appropriations of Lands.

HE has obstructed the Administration of Justice, by refusing his Assent to Laws for establishing Judiciary Powers.

HE has made Judges dependent on his Will alone, for the Tenure of their Offices, and the Amount and Payment of their Salaries.

HE has erected a Multitude of new Offices, and sent hither Swarms of Officers to harrass our People, and eat out their Substance.

HE has kept among us, in Times of Peace, Standing Armies, without the consent of our Legislatures.

HE has affected to render the Military independent of and superior to the Civil Power.

HE has combined with others to subject us to a Jurisdiction foreign to our Constitution, and unacknowledged by our Laws; giving his Assent to their Acts of pretended Legislation:

FOR quartering large Bodies of Armed Troops among us:

FOR protecting them, by a mock Trial, from Punishment for any Murders which they should commit on the Inhabitants of these States:

FOR cutting off our Trade with all Parts of the World:

FOR imposing Taxes on us without our Consent:

FOR depriving us, in many Cases, of the Benefits of Trial by Jury:

FOR transporting us beyond Seas to be tried for pretended Offences:

FOR abolishing the free System of English Laws in a neighbouring Province, establishing therein an arbitrary Government, and enlarging its Boundaries, so as to render it at once an Example and fit Instrument for introducing the same absolute Rule into these Colonies:

FOR taking away our Charters, abolishing our most valuable Laws, and altering fundamentally the Forms of our Governments:

FOR suspending our own Legislatures, and declaring themselves invested with Power to legislate for us in all Cases whatsoever.

HE has abdicated Government here, by declaring us out of his Protection and waging War against us.

HE has plundered our Seas, ravaged our Coasts, burnt our Towns, and destroyed the Lives of our People.

HE is, at this Time, transporting large Armies of foreign Mercenaries to compleat the Works of Death, Desolation, and Tyranny, already begun with circumstances of Cruelty and Perfidy, scarcely paralleled in the most barbarous Ages, and totally unworthy the Head of a civilized Nation.

HE has constrained our fellow Citizens taken Captive on the high Seas to bear Arms against their Country, to become the Executioners of their Friends and Brethren, or to fall themselves by their Hands.

HE has excited domestic Insurrections amongst us, and has endeavoured to bring on the Inhabitants of our Frontiers, the merciless Indian Savages, whose known Rule of Warfare, is an undistinguished Destruction, of all Ages, Sexes and Conditions.

IN every stage of these Oppressions we have Petitioned for Redress in the most humble Terms: Our repeated Petitions have been answered only by repeated Injury. A Prince, whose Character is thus marked by every act which may define a Tyrant, is unfit to be the Ruler of a free People.

NOR have we been wanting in Attentions to our British Brethren. We have warned them from Time to Time of Attempts by their Legislature to extend an unwarrantable Jurisdiction over us. We have reminded them of the Circumstances of our Emigration and Settlement here. We have appealed to their native Justice and Magnanimity, and we have conjured them by the Ties of our common Kindred to disavow these Usurpations, which, would inevitably interrupt our Connections and Correspondence. They too have been deaf to the Voice of Justice and of Consanguinity. We must, therefore, acquiesce in the Necessity, which denounces our Separation, and hold them, as we hold the rest of Mankind, Enemies in War, in Peace, Friends.

WE, therefore, the Representatives of the UNITED STATES OF AMERICA, in GENERAL CONGRESS, Assembled, appealing to the Supreme Judge of the World for the Rectitude of our Intentions, do, in the Name, and by Authority of the good People of these Colonies, solemnly Publish and Declare, That these United Colonies are, and of Right ought to be, FREE AND INDEPENDENT STATES; that they are absolved from all Allegiance to the British Crown, and that all political Connection between them and the State of Great-Britain, is and ought to be totally dissolved; and that as FREE AND INDEPENDENT STATES, they have full Power to levy War, conclude Peace, contract Alliances, establish Commerce, and to do all other Acts and Things which INDEPENDENT STATES may of right do. And for the support of this Declaration, with a firm Reliance on the Protection of divine Providence, we mutually pledge to each other our Lives, our Fortunes, and our sacred Honor.

Signed by ORDER *and in* BEHALF *of the* CONGRESS,

JOHN HANCOCK, PRESIDENT.

ATTEST.
CHARLES THOMSON, SECRETARY.

PHILADELPHIA: PRINTED BY JOHN DUNLAP.

An important discovery at the flea market

Selby Kiffer

In 1989 a financial analyst from Pennsylvania who collects antique stocks and bonds bought an old and torn painting at a flea market in the Philadelphia area for $4. He thought he might use the frame to display something from his collection. After he returned home and discarded the damaged painting, he was forced to conclude that the frame was unsalvageable. In the backing of the frame, however, he found concealed a large sheet of folded paper, which he immediately recognised as an old printing of the Declaration of Independence. In early 1991 the collector showed it to Sotheby's, who confirmed that the document was a previously unrecorded copy of the first printing of the Declaration of Independence.

The newly authenticated copy brought the total of known copies of the Declaration to twenty-four, with only two others in private hands. Its condition is as remarkable as the circumstances of its discovery. Exceptionally crisp and completely unrestored, this copy is as close as possible to the condition in which it would have been taken off the press 215 years ago. Only seven of the other recorded copies are not rebacked, silked or damaged with significant loss of text.

Principally the work of Thomas Jefferson, a Virginia delegate to the Continental Congress meeting at Philadelphia, the Declaration of Independence was read and slightly modified by John Adams of Massachusetts and Benjamin Franklin of Pennsylvania. The full Congress adopted the revised Declaration on 4 July 1776 and authorised its printing by John Dunlap. Working through the night of 4 July, Dunlap set the copy in type, printed and corrected a proof, and pulled an unknown number of copies (probably between 400 and 500) which were delivered to Congress on the morning of 5 July.

Known as 'The Dunlap Broadside', this first printed version of the Declaration of Independence was the instrument by which the news of America's independence was disseminated. Copies were sent throughout the thirteen colonies, informing the colonists that 'they [were] absolved from all Allegiance to the British Crown, and that all political connection between them and the State of Great-Britain [was] to be totally dissolved.'

The Declaration of Independence, one of twenty-five surviving copies, printed by John Dunlap, Philadelphia, 4 or 5 July 1776
New York $2,420,000 (£1,484,663). 13.VI.91

Sotheby's announcement of the newly discovered copy of the Declaration commanded unprecedented media attention and sparked a nationwide search for other surviving copies. Surprisingly, a twenty-fifth Dunlap Broadside has now been discovered, or rather rediscovered. This copy had been bequeathed to the Maine Historical Society by John S. H. Fogg in 1893 but had since fallen into obscurity.

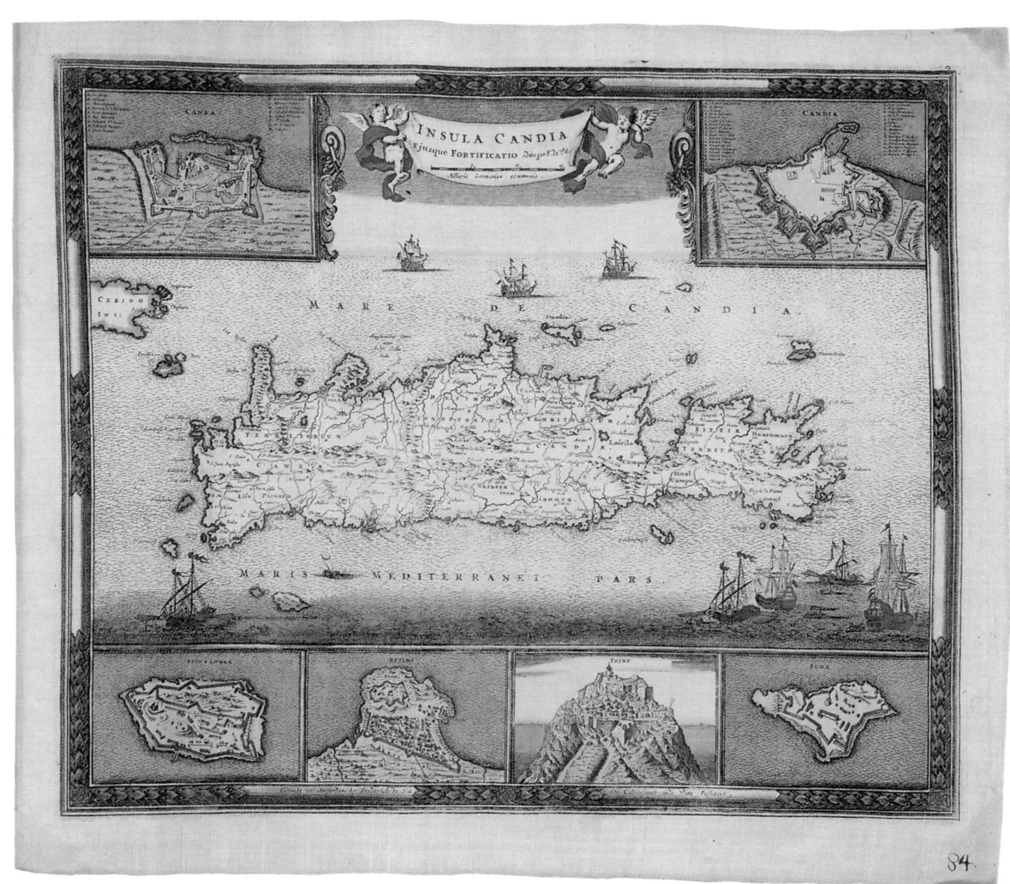

Frederick de Wit
An untitled atlas comprising 150 engraved maps and charts, printed on silk and hand coloured, Amsterdam, *circa* 1700,
21⅝in by 25½in
(55cm by 65cm)
London £63,800
($132,704). 29.XI.90

Below
An untitled manuscript map of the Guianas region, printed on vellum, with contemporary black morocco and gilt binding, England, *circa* 1596,
13⅛in by 18½in
(33.5cm by 47.2cm)
London £38,500
($80,080). 29.XI.90
From the collection of the 9th Duke of Northumberland

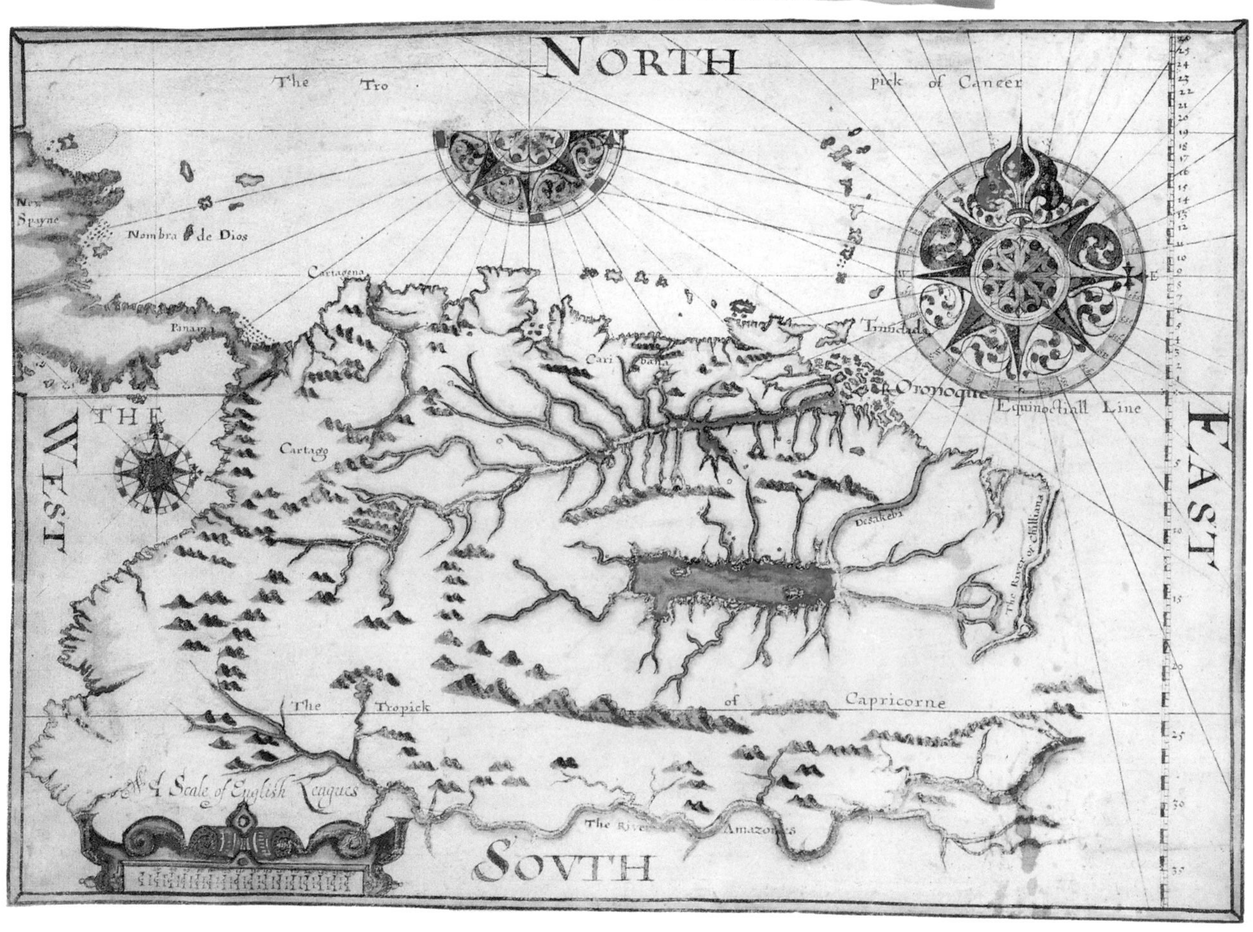

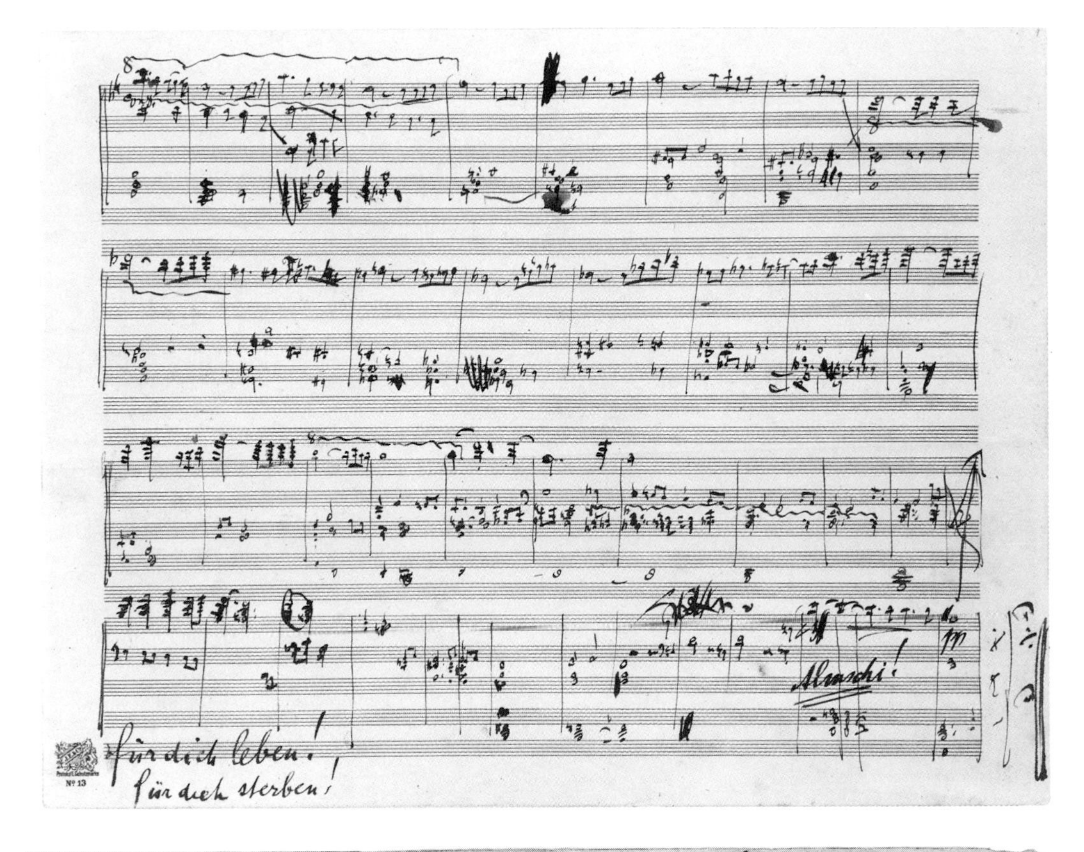

Gustav Mahler
An autograph manuscript draft of the tenth symphony, including drafts of three entire movements and a practically complete sketch of a fourth, annotated in black ink, 108 pages, mostly oblong folio, Toblach, New York and Vienna, 1910 and 1911
London £385,000 ($658,350). 17.V.91

Wolfgang Amadeus Mozart
An autograph manuscript of the fugues in F major, K.375h, C minor and E minor, K.417B^{6}, comprising three fugal expositions, possibly being drafts for the mass in C minor, K. 427, annotated in brown ink, 2 pages, probably Vienna, *circa* 1782, $8\frac{5}{8}$in by $11\frac{7}{8}$in (22cm by 30cm)
London £44,000 ($75,240). 17.V.91

Wolfgang Amadeus Mozart
The opening page from the autograph manuscripts of the Fantasia for piano in C minor, K. 475 and the Sonata for piano in C minor, K. 457, differing considerably from the published version, annotated in brown ink, the Fantasia with the autograph title *Phantasia*, unsigned, 14 pages, Vienna, 1784 or 1785
London £880,000 ($1,839,200). 21.XI.90
From the collection of the Eastern Baptist Theological Seminary

Mozart's Fantasia and Sonata in C minor

Simon Maguire

On 31 July 1990, the long-lost autograph manuscript of Mozart's Fantasia and Sonata in C minor (K. 475 and K. 457), arguably the composer's greatest works for solo piano, was discovered in a large metal safe at the Eastern Baptist Theological Seminary, Philadelphia. Composed in 1784 and 1785, the Fantasia and Sonata are regarded as prime examples of the turbulent and Romantic sides of Mozart's musical personality, in some places anticipating Beethoven's sonatas. The brooding chromaticism and dramatic contrasts of the opening of the Fantasia are particularly striking, employing the rich emotional language heard in *Don Giovanni* and the great piano concertos in D minor and C minor. The two pieces, generally performed together, have been recorded by most of the world's leading pianists; yet quite what the original text contained had been unknown for over a hundred years.

During much of the last century the manuscript belonged to the British collector Julian Marshall, but it did not appear at either of Sotheby's sales of his manuscripts. Instead, Marshall sold it to the Cincinnati industrialist William Howard Doane, for £55. All trace of the manuscript was lost when Doane took it back to America in 1889. The current edition of Köchel's catalogue of Mozart's works describes it as 'unauffindbar . . . unbekannt' ('untraceable . . . unknown').

This is the original composing manuscript in which Mozart worked out many fundamental aspects of the piece. Working manuscripts by Mozart are very much rarer than finished ones; such was his skill that he usually seems to have composed as a single creative act. Here, however, Mozart begins movements and interrupts them with others; he presents decorated passages in different versions, and revises and extends the final cadences. For example, at the very begining, Mozart scratched out his original key signature and then inserted flats and naturals within the musical text when and where required, some being squeezed between notes already written down. The very end of the work also revealed surprises, including a different, more abrupt conclusion that Mozart later extended. Perhaps the most important part of the whole manuscript is that for the slow movement of the Sonata, where some new and unrecorded music was discovered. Mozart wrote the decorated repeats of the main melody on two separate pages, one containing some passages already known, and one containing different versions that were quite unknown and unpublished.

There are many other signs of radical revisions to the manuscript, yet the fluency with which it is written down bears out Mozart's reputation for being able to compose rapidly straight onto paper. The first movement of the Sonata, in particular, appears to be composed in a single burst of creative energy, the white heat of Mozart's inspiration vividly displayed in the vigorous penmanship throughout. The manuscript was bought for the Mozarteum at Salzburg for £880,000.

(1)

Lieber Herr Freud!

Ich bin glücklich darüber, dass ich durch eine Anregung des Völkerbundes eine einzigartige Gelegenheit erhalte, mich mit Ihnen über diejenige Frage zu unterhalten, die mir beim gegenwärtigen Stande der Dinge als die wichtigste der Zivilisation erscheint: Gibt es einen Weg, die Menschen von dem Verhängnis des Krieges zu befreien? Die Einsicht, dass diese Frage durch die Fortschritte der Technik zu einer Existenz-Frage für die zivilisierte Menschheit geworden ist, ist ziemlich allgemein durchgedrungen, und trotzdem sind die heissen Bemühungen um ihre Lösung bisher in erschreckendem Masse gescheitert.

Ist es nicht erfreulich, dass ~~viele~~ unter den mit diesem Problem praktisch und beruflich beschäftigten Menschen aus einem gewissen Gefühl der Ohnmacht heraus der Wunsch lebendig geworden ist, ~~solche~~ Personen um ihre Auffassung des Problems zu befragen, die durch ihre gewohnte wissenschaftliche Thätigkeit zu allen Fragen des Lebens eine weitgehende Distanz gewonnen haben? Was mich selber betrifft, so liefert mir die gewohnte Richtung meines Denkens keine Einblicke in die Tiefen des menschlichen Wollens und Fühlens, sodass ich bei dem hier versuchten Meinungsaustausch nicht viel mehr thun kann, als versuchen, die Fragestellung herauszuarbeiten und durch Vorwegnahme der mehr äusserlichen Lösungsversuche Ihnen Gelegenheit zu geben, die Frage vom Standpunkte Ihrer vertieften Kenntnis des menschlichen Trieblebens zu beleuchten. Ich vertraue darauf, dass Sie auf Wege der Erziehung ~~und auf die Möglichkeiten hinzuweisen~~ werden hinweisen können, die auf einem gewissermassen unpolitischen Wege psychologische Hindernisse beseitigen können, welche ~~die~~ der psychologisch

Sigm. Freud

'Why War?'

Marsha Malinowski

In 1931, the League of Nations asked its International Committee on Intellectual Cooperation to 'encourage an exchange of letters between leaders of thought on the lines of those which have always taken place at the great epochs of European history; to select subjects best calculated to serve the common interest of the League of Nations and of the intellectual life of mankind, and to publish this correspondence from time to time'. Leon Steinig, a League of Nations official, travelled to Berlin in the hope of enlisting Albert Einstein's services for the project. Elaborating on his interest in the effects that education might have in removing the misunderstandings and hatred which encourage war, Einstein embraced the project. He agreed to write to Sigmund Freud on the subject of ensuring peace. Freud, however, expressed profound pessimism for the project but promised to do his best at answering Einstein's letter, thus beginning an extraordinary exchange of letters by two of the most gifted and influential minds of the twentieth century.

Einstein's letter of 28 July 1932 poses a straightforward question to Freud: 'Is there a way to liberate man from the doom of war?' Einstein proceeds to give his own answer, noting 'my customary way of thinking does not give me an insight into the depth of human wishes and feelings . . . I cannot do much more than to try to define the question and . . . enable you to discuss the problem from the vantage point of your profound knowledge of human instincts'. Einstein then focuses on the structural part of the problem, which to him seems simple, 'the creation by the various countries of a legislative and judicial authority to settle all conflicts that arise among them'. He states that each country would be obliged to respect the laws developed by this authority, to use its court in controversial cases, and to enforce its decisions. Yet Einstein concedes that there are 'powerful psychological forces' prohibiting man from reaching the goal of an international authority: 'The desire for power makes the ruling party of a nation resist any limitation of its rights to sovereignty; the leaders feel their position of power threatened.' Finally, Einstein believes war only exists because 'man has in him the need to hate and destroy'.

In his lengthy response, Freud grapples with Einstein's question in all its complexity. He agrees with Einstein on the concept of an international court of authority. On Einstein's observation of man's need to hate and destroy, Freud replies 'I can only agree with you unreservedly'. After a discourse on the link between man's aggressive and destructive instincts, Freud concludes with only a narrow ray of hope – man could end war by means of two factors – man's changing cultural disposition, and the threat of terror: 'any future war would, because of highly developed weapons of destruction, probably mean the eradication of one or perhaps both adversaries'.

This concept of peace by the threat of terror was not one which Einstein could accept. Yet seven years later he set aside these pacifistic sentiments, when he wrote to President Roosevelt to prod along research on the ultimate weapon – the atom bomb.

Albert Einstein and Sigmund Freud
An autograph letter signed by Einstein, with numerous corrections, deletions and additions, four leaves, in German, Caputh, near Berlin, 28 July 1932, 11in by 8¾in (27.9cm by 22.2cm) together with Freud's autograph reply, signed, 14 leaves, in German, Vienna, September 1932, 15½in by 9¾in (39.3cm by 24.8cm)
New York $165,000 (£85,052). 11.XII.90

Above
Guillaume Apollinaire
Le Poète Assassiné, illustrated with thirty-six original lithographs by Raoul Dufy, the contemporary blue morocco binding by Paul Bonet, Au Sans Pareil, Paris, 1926
Monte Carlo FF333,000 (£33,636:$65,294). 9.XII.90

Opposite, top left
Alan Paton
Cry, the Beloved Country, the autograph manuscript, 335 leaves, 25 September to 29 December, 1946
New York $132,000 (£80,982). 13.VI.91
From the collection of Mrs Anne Paton

Top right
Siegfried Sassoon
One of a series of 118 caricatures of Sir Osbert, Edith and Sacheverell Sitwell in pencil, pencil and watercolour and ink, *circa* 1925
London £8,800 ($14,432). 18.VII.91
From the library of Siegfried Sassoon

T. Sturge Moore
The Little School, A Posy of Rhymes, from a limited edition of 185 copies, this is one of ten copies printed on vellum, with a pictorial device by Lucien Pissarro, signed by Sybil Pye, with contemporary green morocco, vellum and gilt binding, 1906
London £8,800 ($14,872). 6.VI.91

This binding was probably designed especially for T. Sturge Moore who dedicated this book 'To Sybil Pye, the mistress of the little school, who wished these poems made for, and brought them home to children'.

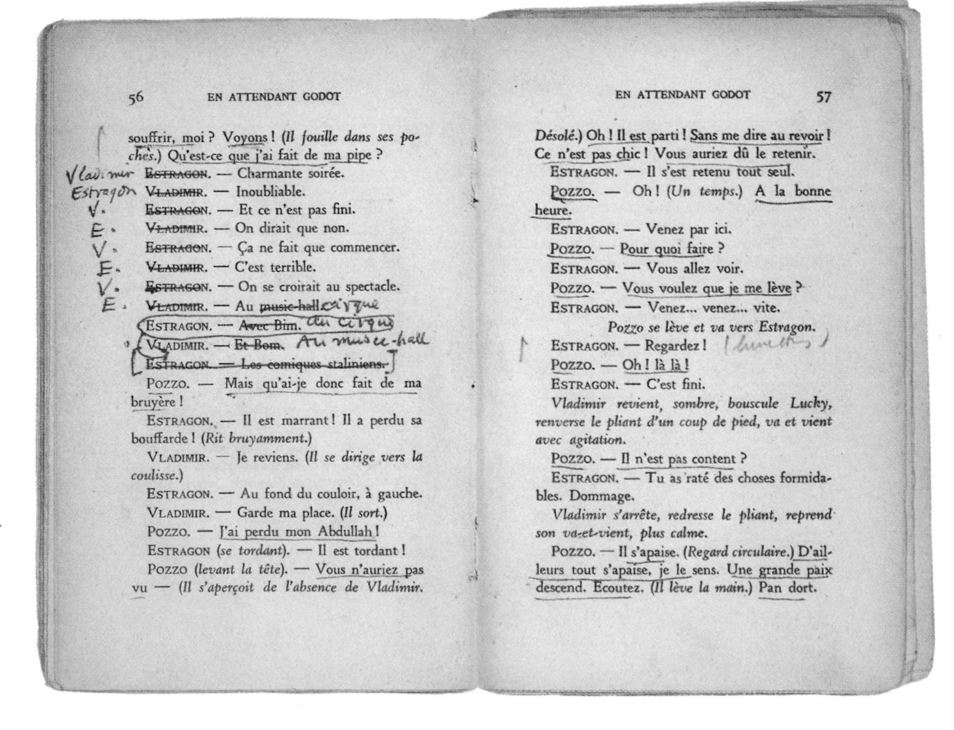

56 EN ATTENDANT GODOT

souffrir, moi? Voyons! (*Il fouille dans ses poches.*) Qu'est-ce que j'ai fait de ma pipe?
~~ESTRAGON~~. — Charmante soirée.
~~VLADIMIR~~. — Inoubliable.
~~ESTRAGON~~. — Et ce n'est pas fini.
~~VLADIMIR~~. — On dirait que non.
~~ESTRAGON~~. — Ça ne fait que commencer.
~~VLADIMIR~~. — C'est terrible.
~~ESTRAGON~~. — On se croirait au spectacle.
~~VLADIMIR~~. — Au ~~music-hall~~.
ESTRAGON. — ~~Avec Bim.~~
VLADIMIR. — ~~Et Bom.~~
~~ESTRAGON. — Les comiques staliniens.~~
POZZO. — Mais qu'ai-je donc fait de ma bruyère!
ESTRAGON. — Il est marrant! Il a perdu sa bouffarde! (*Rit bruyamment.*)
VLADIMIR. — Je reviens. (*Il se dirige vers la coulisse.*)
ESTRAGON. — Au fond du couloir, à gauche.
VLADIMIR. — Garde ma place. (*Il sort.*)
POZZO. — J'ai perdu mon Abdullah!
ESTRAGON (*se tordant*). — Il est tordant!
POZZO (*levant la tête*). — Vous n'auriez pas vu — (*Il s'aperçoit de l'absence de Vladimir.*

EN ATTENDANT GODOT 57

Désolé.) Oh! Il est parti! Sans me dire au revoir! Ce n'est pas chic! Vous auriez dû le retenir.
ESTRAGON. — Il s'est retenu tout seul.
POZZO. — Oh! (*Un temps.*) A la bonne heure.
ESTRAGON. — Venez par ici.
POZZO. — Pour quoi faire?
ESTRAGON. — Vous allez voir.
POZZO. — Vous voulez que je me lève?
ESTRAGON. — Venez... venez... vite.
Pozzo se lève et va vers Estragon.
ESTRAGON. — Regardez!
POZZO. — Oh! là là!
ESTRAGON. — C'est fini.
Vladimir revient, sombre, bouscule Lucky, renverse le pliant d'un coup de pied, va et vient avec agitation.
POZZO. — Il n'est pas content?
ESTRAGON. — Tu as raté des choses formidables. Dommage.
Vladimir s'arrête, redresse le pliant, reprend son va-et-vient, plus calme.
POZZO. — Il s'apaise. (*Regard circulaire.*) D'ailleurs tout s'apaise, je le sens. Une grande paix descend. Ecoutez. (*Il lève la main.*) Pan dort.

Samuel Beckett
Beckett's working rehearsal copy used for the original production of *Waiting for Godot* with autograph annotations, later inscribed for *John & Bettina with much love & gratitude from Sam London 31.12.64*, Les Editions de Minuit, Paris, 1952
London £33,000 ($67,650). 13.XII.90
From the collection of John Calder

LIBERTY

Virgil's elegy

John Russell

Virgil Thomson with his fellow musicians, Aaron Copland, Gian Carlo Menotti, Samuel Barber and William Schuman, one of a group of eleven photographs, 1940s–80s
New York $770 (£389). 11.X.90
From the estate of Virgil Thomson

Opposite
One of fifteen portraits of Virgil Thomson by various photographers, 1930s–80s
New York $1,980 (£1,000). 11.X.90
From the estate of Virgil Thomson

Whether we like it or not, where we live is what we are. Our surroundings cannot lie. This was conspicuously the case with Virgil Thomson, the composer, critic, autobiographer, and black-belt conversationalist who died in September 1989, not far short of his 93rd birthday, at the Chelsea Hotel in New York.

He had lived there since 1940 and was in all things neat, sharp, exact, and unforgetful. Not the man to leave his front door simply ajar, he propped it open an inch or two with a brick covered with carpet for that express pupose. But then everything in Thomson's apartment was there for a purpose. The word 'slovenly'

Florine Stettheimer
PORTRAIT OF MARCEL DUCHAMP
Signed and dated 1923, 30in by 26in (76.2cm by 66cm)
New York $110,000 (£56,701). 29.XI.90
From the estate of Virgil Thomson

Above, right
A silk brocade vest made for Gertrude Stein, by Alice B. Toklas, *circa* 1920–30
New York $19,800 (£10,000). 11.X.90
From the estate of Virgil Thomson

might never have been coined . . . In a little drawer near Thomson's bed, his pocket datebooks for the past sixty and more years – all identical in size – were filed in chronological order . . . From the 1920s and 30s – the heyday of good and cheap living in France – there were the books that every intelligent expatriate brought back with him. But there were also books that harked back to the American country music of long long ago. As for the fruit and vegetables in the kitchen, they rhymed with the still lifes that his friend Maurice Grosser had painted in 1932. Even as Thomson lay dying, nine pairs of shoes, polished as well as ever, lay waiting at the foot of his bed in case he wanted to get up and go out.

His apartment was not in the least 'done up'. No canon of orthodox taste could be applied to it. But wherever visitors looked, and all the more so if they were encouraged to open a drawer, a box file, a cupboard, or a bookcase, they knew that only one man could have lived in these rooms. And they also knew that that man was the composer of *Four Saints in Three Acts, The Mother of Us All*, and *Lord Byron*; the collaborator of Gertrude Stein; and the equal of Schumann, Berlioz, and Debussy as a commentator on other men's music.

In conversation, as in his surroundings, Virgil Thomson had perfect pitch. The right word came out at the right time, with the right weight and at the right speed. The sound was flat, abrupt, laconic. If he ever hesitated, it was for effect and not because he did not know what to say . . . He had split second timing. If he sometimes seemed combative in his conversational style, it was because he liked to go straight to the point.

He favoured large, commodious, unflimsy pieces of furniture, and he was very good at getting them from people who were anxious to be rid of them. When the American Academy of Arts and Letters no longer knew what to do with an enormous bookcase of burled walnut and ebony, Thomson took over and had it shipped down to the Chelsea.

When his old friend the architectural historian Henry-Russell Hitchcock was encumbered with a three-piece bedroom set that had been given to his grandparents on their marriage, Virgil Thomson knew just where to put the walnut bed with a Gothic headboard, the washstand, and the marble-topped bureau. (The bureau was to do double duty as a sideboard or buffet when there were a lot of people for dinner.)

When anyone admired his dining table, with its black enamelled top and delicately curved chromium legs, he paid tribute to Minna Lederman, the editor of *Modern Music*, who had passed it on to him. He loved it partly for the date of its making, 1932, which was also the year in which he began to enjoy, at the Liberal Club at Harvard, the talk that he later described as 'the finest anywhere'.

Things pleased him for private reasons and not because they would impress others. He could have collected art, but he only had paintings and sculpture and drawings by people he knew and liked – Grosser, Florine Stettheimer, Leonid Berman. He had some photographs by Man Ray, but he never showed them. He had works by Jean Arp and Yves Tanguy, bright stars in the modernist heavens, but they didn't get star billing.

What he really liked did not have to be (and rarely was) what others thought of as fancy. He had a kidney-shaped table that had belonged to Gertrude Stein and was left to him by Alice B. Toklas. The red velvet S-shaped chair on which two people can talk sitting face to face, and almost nose to nose, was a present from Lincoln Kirstein's sister, Mina Curtiss, who was no mean judge of the high comforts of Paris in the nineteenth century . . .

Looking round the Chelsea apartment one last time, this visitor remembered what Virgil Thomson had said of his concierge in Paris when she died at the age of 84: 'A life so long, a person so fulfilled, gives little wish to alter history.' And it was as true of him as it was of her.

Illuminated manuscripts

The prayerbook of the Anti-Pope Clement VII, in Latin, illuminated manuscript on vellum, 75 leaves, with 15 large miniatures, Avignon, *circa* 1378–83, $5\frac{3}{4}$in by $4\frac{3}{8}$in (14.6cm by 11cm)
London £220,000 ($354,200). 18.VI.91
Now in the Bibliothèque Municipale, Avignon

Clement VII was the first anti-pope of the Western Schism. He was elected pope in opposition to Urban VI on 20 September 1378, and took up residence in the papal palace in Avignon. He died in 1394 without ever successfully proving his sole claim to the papal throne. This prayerbook was his most intimate manuscript, compiled for his private use. It is probably the manuscript described as being kept in the chamber of the *Cerf Volant*, *circa* 1383. It includes his arms and devices on almost every page, and is the finest of about a dozen surviving manuscripts illuminated in Avignon in the late fourteenth century. The miniature illustrated here shows the anti-pope being presented to the Virgin and Child by his patron saint St Clement.

Opposite
The Annunciation, the Visitation, the Nativity of Christ and the Annunciation to the Shepherds, miniature on a single leaf from an illuminated manuscript Psalter on vellum, diocese of Hildesheim, probably Braunschweig, *circa* 1239, $8\frac{7}{8}$in by $6\frac{1}{8}$in (22.4cm by 15.5cm)
London £264,000 ($549,120). 29.XI.90

Aue maria
annūcio uobis gaudiū magnū

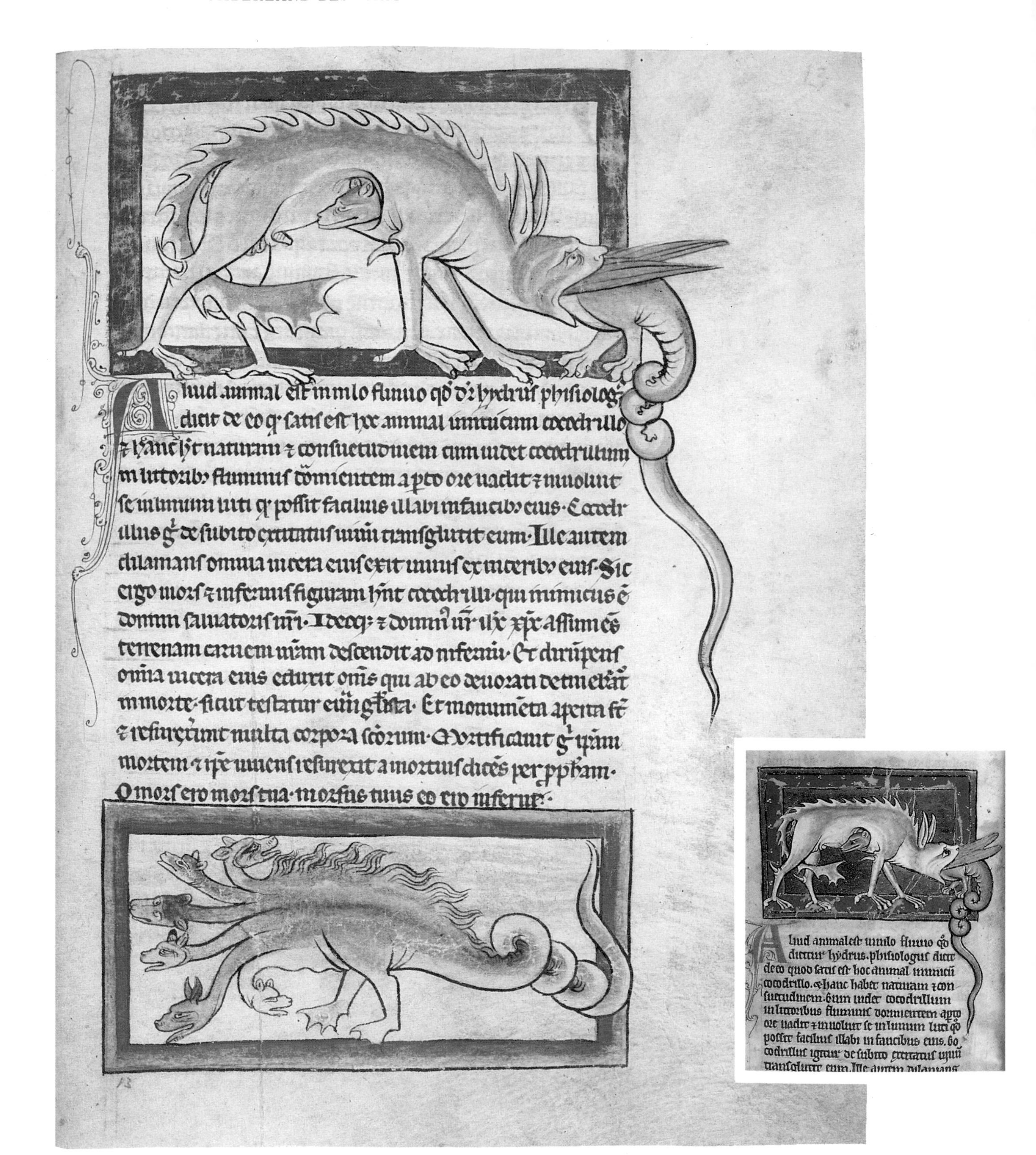

Aliud animal est in nilo flumio qd' d'r hydrus phisiolog'
dicit de eo q' satis est hoc animal inimicum cocodrillo
et hanc h't naturam et consuetudinem cum uidet cocodrillum
in litorib' fluminis dormientem a p'to ore iacit et inuoluit
se in limum luti q' possit facilius illabi in faucib' eius. Cocodr
illus g' de subito excitatus uiuu' transglutit eum. Ille autem
dilamans omnia uiscera eius exit uiuus ex uisceribus eius. Sic
ergo mors et infernus figuram h'nt cocodrilli. qui inimicus e'
domini saluatoris n'ri. Ideoq; et domin' n'r ih'c xp'c assumens
terrenam carnem n'ram descendit ad infernu'. Et dirumpens
o'nia uiscera eius eduxit o'ms qui ab eo deuorati detinebant'
in morte. sicut testatur eu'ngelista. Et monumenta aperta s't
et resurrexerunt multa corpora s'corum. Mortificauit g' ip'am
mortem et ip'e uiuens resurrexit a mortuis dicens per p'ph'am.
O mors ero mors tua. morsus tuus ero tibi inferne.

Aliud animal est in nilo flumio qd
dicitur hydrus. phisiologus dicit
de eo quod satis est hoc animal inimicu'
cocodrillo. et hanc habet naturam et con
suetudinem. cum uidet cocodrillum
in litoribus fluminis dormientem apto
ore iacit et inuoluit se in limum luti qd
possit facilius illabi in faucibus eius. Co
codrillus igitur de subito excitatus uiuu'
transglutit eum. Ille autem dilamans

The Northumberland bestiary and its group

Ann Payne

Fig. 1
The Northumberland bestiary, in Latin, illuminated manuscript on vellum, 74 leaves, with 112 miniatures, England, perhaps Northern England, *circa* 1250–60, 8¼in by 6¼in (21cm by 15.8cm)
London £2,970,000 ($6,177,600). 29.XI.90
From the collection of the 9th Duke of Northumberland

Folio 13*v*, *The hydrus*, is an aquatic snake which hates crocodiles. When it sees one asleep with its mouth open, it will rush off and roll in the mud so that it can slip down the crocodile's throat. The crocodile then wakes up and gulps it down and the hydrus bursts its way out of the crocodile's belly, as in the miniature here.

Fig. 2 (Inset, detail)
The hydrus, folio 12*v*, from a bestiary in the Royal Collection (Royal MS 12 C xix)
(Reproduced by courtesy of the British Library).

In September 1187 Philip, Canon of Lincoln, gave to the Augustinian Priory of Worksop (also called Radford), some fifteen miles distant, a collection of six manuscripts which included the Meditations of St Anselm, a Mappa Mundi and a bestiary 'ad edificationem fratrum'. It was a generous gift. The bestiary volume, for instance, which carried an inscription recording the event, was a handsome, finely illuminated example of a class of manuscript that was becoming increasingly popular in England – an illustrated compendium describing the supposed nature and habits of over a hundred beasts and birds flavoured with stories pointing a Christian moral.

Written about 1185, probably at Lincoln, the Worksop Priory bestiary (now New York, Pierpont Morgan Library, M. 81) is thought to be the earliest example extant of a small group of bestiaries closely related in both text and illumination. Other manuscripts in this group are a late twelfth-century bestiary now in Leningrad (State Public Library, MS Lat. Q.v.V.I), a bestiary in the Royal Collection at the British Library (Royal MS 12 C xix) dating from around 1200 (see Fig. 2), and our present manuscript, the Northumberland bestiary of the mid thirteenth century, from Alnwick Castle (see Fig. 1). The recent sale at Sotheby's of the Northumberland bestiary presents an opportunity to reconsider the group.

The main sources used by compilers of medieval Latin bestiaries were a translation of a Greek book of anonymous authorship known as the *Physiologus* ('Natural Historian'), and the more down-to-earth but inventive *Etymologies* of St Isidore of Seville of the seventh century. Early Christian writers looked for the message of God in all natural phenomena. The fervently ideological *Physiologus* could find in ancient reports of a bird called the 'phoenix' which sacrificed itself in fire and then came back to life a manifestation in the natural world of the truth about Christ's Passion and Resurrection. St Isidore, a less spiritual interpreter of nature, was impressed by a possible derivation of the name 'phoenix' from a colour known as 'phoeniceus' or from an Arabic word for 'unique'. With additional material provided by such writers as Solinus, St Ambrose, Hugh of St Victor and others, the expanded Latin bestiary supplied a wide readership with entertaining folklore, the thrill of the monstrous and exotic, and sober Christian teaching, often liberally illustrated with appealing pictures.

The Cambridge scholar M. R. James, in the introduction to his facsimile edition of a twelfth-century bestiary (CUL MS Ii.4.26) for the Roxburghe Club (1928), divided Latin bestiaries produced in England into four basic families. Our quartet of manuscripts is very close in range and content to James's second family, but owes a little more to the *Physiologus* in the manner of the first. The *Physiologus* dealt randomly with a limited number of beasts whose supposed habits lent themselves to allegorical interpretation. Isidore's zoological range was wider, and he classified his creatures into domestic animals, wild beasts, serpents and so on. Like the second family bestiary our group has a range of animals to rival Isidore's and a similar classification, while retaining most of the parables and allegories of the *Physiologus*. It differs from the second family in preferring in some cases the text of the *Physiologus* to that of Isidore (the siren, the doves), and in staying more faithful to the Latin versions of the *Physiologus* in its order of dealing with many of the subjects.

Because of such differences the Worksop group of bestiaries has sometimes been labelled 'transitional'. However, in its scope, its content and the fineness of its illustrations the group can be regarded as in no way inferior to the second family model, even if, judging by a count of surviving manuscripts, the second family version seems to have become generally the most popular.

Iconographically it is clear that the four manuscripts of the Worksop group follow a single cycle. The miniatures, though striking – often beautiful – in design, are largely conventional: confronted rams butting heads, inter-spiralling serpents, the elephant with a turret on its back, two turtledoves with beaks crossed as if in Continental greeting. It is not surprising therefore that some of the pictures from our group, as if from standard model books, have close parallels in other groups of bestiaries; the Leningrad bestiary illustration of a ship stranded on the back of a whale, its terrified crew struggling to raise the mast while one of their number crawls naked up the backstay reappears, for example, in very similar guise in a British Library second family bestiary (Harley MS 4751) and elsewhere. Within the group the pictures are close and without doubt related (although certainly not in every respect). The degree of actual copying is difficult to assess since medieval artists seldom felt constrained to absolute fidelity to their models. One suspects a number of intermediate stages between, for instance, the Worksop bestiary and the Royal manuscript. At least one of these may have involved copying by pricking and pouncing, since the direction in which some of the animals are facing has become reversed in a way that might be caused by pouncing from the *verso* of the transfer sheet.

From the Royal bestiary several important folios with miniatures are missing. Comparison with the other members of the group gives an indication as to their number and nature. We have here no fox, ape, griffin, bear, siren or bonnacon; some half a dozen more beasts have gone, a similar number of birds and all the fish. Illustrations to the prefatory material, showing scenes of the Creation and of Adam naming the animals, have also been removed. Textually the Worksop and Royal bestiaries would appear to have been very close. Indeed the layout of the texts runs in some passages so parallel as to produce identical word-breaks at the ends of lines and pages. The Royal bestiary is thought to have been made, not in the Midlands, but in the North of England, perhaps at Durham, about the year 1200. Though within the same illustrative tradition, one was not copied directly from the other, but rather each shares common models. Dissimilarities in the detail of the pictures confirm this – the beaver of the Royal bestiary is saving itself from its pursuer in the prescribed manner by detaching its own testes (the hunter's prize) with a bite; the Worksop beaver, on the other hand, having baulked at this sacrifice, has been fatally lanced by the hunter's spear.

Above
Fig. 3 (Detail)
The Northumberland bestiary, folio 8, *The lions*, mightiest of beasts. When lion cubs are first born, they lie dead for three days, until on the third day their father comes and breathes life into them, as in the miniature here.

Below
Fig. 4 (Detail)
The lions, folio 6, from a bestiary in the Royal Collection (Royal MS 12 C xix)
(Reproduced by courtesy of the British Library).

Above, left
Fig. 5 (Detail)
The parrot, folio 40*v*, from a bestiary in the Royal Collection (Royal MS 12 C xix)
(Reproduced by courtesy of the British Library).

Right
Fig. 6 (Detail)
The Northumberland bestiary, folio 34*v*, *The parrot*, which greets people of its own accord. It can learn very many human words, especially in the first two years of its life. Its beak is so thick that it can land on it with safety from a great height. The parrot in the present miniature looks very sad.

Much closer to the Royal than the Worksop manuscript is the Northumberland bestiary, made also perhaps in Northern England, but some fifty years later. The text is very similar, and most of the illustrations throughout are as close to the Royal pictures as freehand copying might be expected to produce. However, there are differences of style. The mid thirteenth-century Northumberland artist simplified. He made no attempt to reproduce the thick ornate borders of the Royal manuscript or its coloured grounds. He used no gold, no body colour, but worked more informally in a tinted wash drawing. (Such tinted drawing was at this time common to both bestiary and apocalypse, the best known exponent being Matthew Paris of St Albans who used it to great effect in his narrative works.) The precise relationship between the two manuscripts will probably never be conclusively determined, but there seems nothing to preclude the possibility that the Northumberland bestiary was copied straight from the Royal. In producing the text the Northumberland scribe thoughtlessly bequeathed to his artist rectangular blanks whose proportions differed from those of the Royal model, and so time and again the Northumberland artist has been forced into rather awkward modifications in order to get the subject in. Where the panel devoted to lions in the Royal manuscript is compositionally considered and orderly (Fig. 4), the equivalent panel in the Northumberland bestiary (Fig. 3), done to the very same design, is cramped for room on the right; the artist has allowed the correct space to the standing lion's front but has had to compress and rearrange the lion's hindquarters. In the case of the dogs he is given a square space to be filled with a long, horizontal panel. The oversight of one complete picture-space by the scribe obliged the artist to squeeze both the saura and the stellio serpents into the same panel.

It is not only for this reason that the Northumberland copy gives an impression of haste. Its scribe made a number of careless omissions, to be corrected – most calligraphically – in the margins; and the 'dorchon' (goat) might have had some currency as the 'drachon' but for a timely amendment by a contemporary hand. On the other hand the Northumberland bestiary contains an element of interesting novelty in a field where there was little innovation. The compilers were working almost wholly to reinforce traditional understanding and beliefs and not with any desire for a fresh interpretation. Their purpose was a didactic one, to convey a theological message, not to attempt an accurate description of wildlife, even when an artist might be portraying creatures that must have been familiar, like the owl or the hedgehog. In the Northumberland bestiary the artist shows a new readiness to substitute the realistic for the conventional. The parrot of the Royal manuscript is the usual undistinguished bird, more akin to a sea bird than a parrot (Fig. 5). The Northumberland artist has seen a real parrot, or a picture that knowledge told him was a better likeness, because his parrot is in colour and form a respectable portrait – and with a doleful enough aspect fairly to reflect admonitions in the text that a parrot is best taught to speak with blows from an iron bar (Fig. 6). Elsewhere, the artist 'corrects' the limb positions of a running horse and remedies the proportions of the hedgehog.

The pictures of the fourth member of the group, now in Leningrad, have much in common with those of the Worksop bestiary. They are thought of as sister manuscripts and indeed are roughly similar in date. Because of their closeness, a North Midlands origin for the Leningrad version has also been suggested. There are, however, interesting diffferences between the text of the Leningrad bestiary and that of the other three manuscripts. For example, following the tradition of the *Physiologus* and the bestiaries of the first family, the Leningrad bestiary still deals with the weasel and the asp in a single chapter: the former creature, whose sex-act was thought to involve the penetration of the ear, being likened to people who listen to the word of God; the latter, able to plug its ear with the tip of its own tail, being likened to those who stop up their ears against heavenly voices. The Worksop bestiary, applying a little more strictly its animal classification, has restricted its asp to a proper place among the serpents. It seems odd that the bestiary that is thought to be the later of the two should be continuing with a version of the text already rendered somewhat outmoded by the more orderly arrangement of its sister manuscript. It is tempting to conclude from this that either the Leningrad bestiary is itself in fact the earlier work, or it is copied from an early version without knowledge of the 'corrected' Worksop form. Taking the place of the asp beside the weasel in the Worksop, Royal and Northumberland bestiaries is a verse from *De Mundi Universale* of Bernardus Silvestris of Tours, describing in entertaining couplets characteristics associated with a number of animals, including – in a very rare appearance in a bestiary – the hare whose ears spring up when it is running away. Another verse by Bernardus Silvestris occurs in all the manuscripts of the group except the Leningrad between the dogs and the sheep.

One other manuscript, even later than the Northumberland, may be said to have some connections with the group. The Isabella Psalter (Munich, Staatsbibl. MS gall.16), made for the wedding in 1308 of Isabella of France to Edward II of England, contains in some of its lower margins a sequence of bestiary pictures in the same distinctive order as our manuscripts. This postscript to the group takes us back to Worksop Priory. The Isabella Psalter's place of origin is not known for certain, but it has been linked (so closely as to suggest that its decoration, in part at least, came from the same workshop) with the Tickhill Psalter known to be from Worksop. John Tickhill, scribe of the Psalter which bears his name, served, until his removal for 'maladministration and incontinence', as Prior of Worksop. Canon Philip's largesse to Worksop in 1187 was accompanied by a fierce injunction that the manuscripts were at no time to be removed from the priory on pain of excommunication under the wrath of God. In the face of such anathema it is at least possible that his bestiary gift remained at Worksop to provide, a century later, a guide – if not for the content of the pictures, at least for their order – to the makers of the Isabella Psalter.

Johannes Birk
The Chronicle of Kempten Abbey and the Life of its founder St Hildegard, in German, manuscript on paper, 147 leaves, with 59 coloured drawings, Swabia, dated *1499*, 12in by 8in (30.3cm by 20.2cm)
London £209,000 ($336,490). 18.VI.91

Opposite
Jean Froissart
The Chronicles of the Hundred Years' War, in French, illuminated manuscript on vellum, 263 leaves, with 198 miniatures by the so-called Master of Petrarch's Triumphs, Rouen, *circa* 1505–10, 19⅝in by 13⅜in (50cm by 34cm)
London £1,375,000 ($2,213,750). 18.VI.91
From the libraries of Cardinal d'Amboise and Baron Horace de Landau

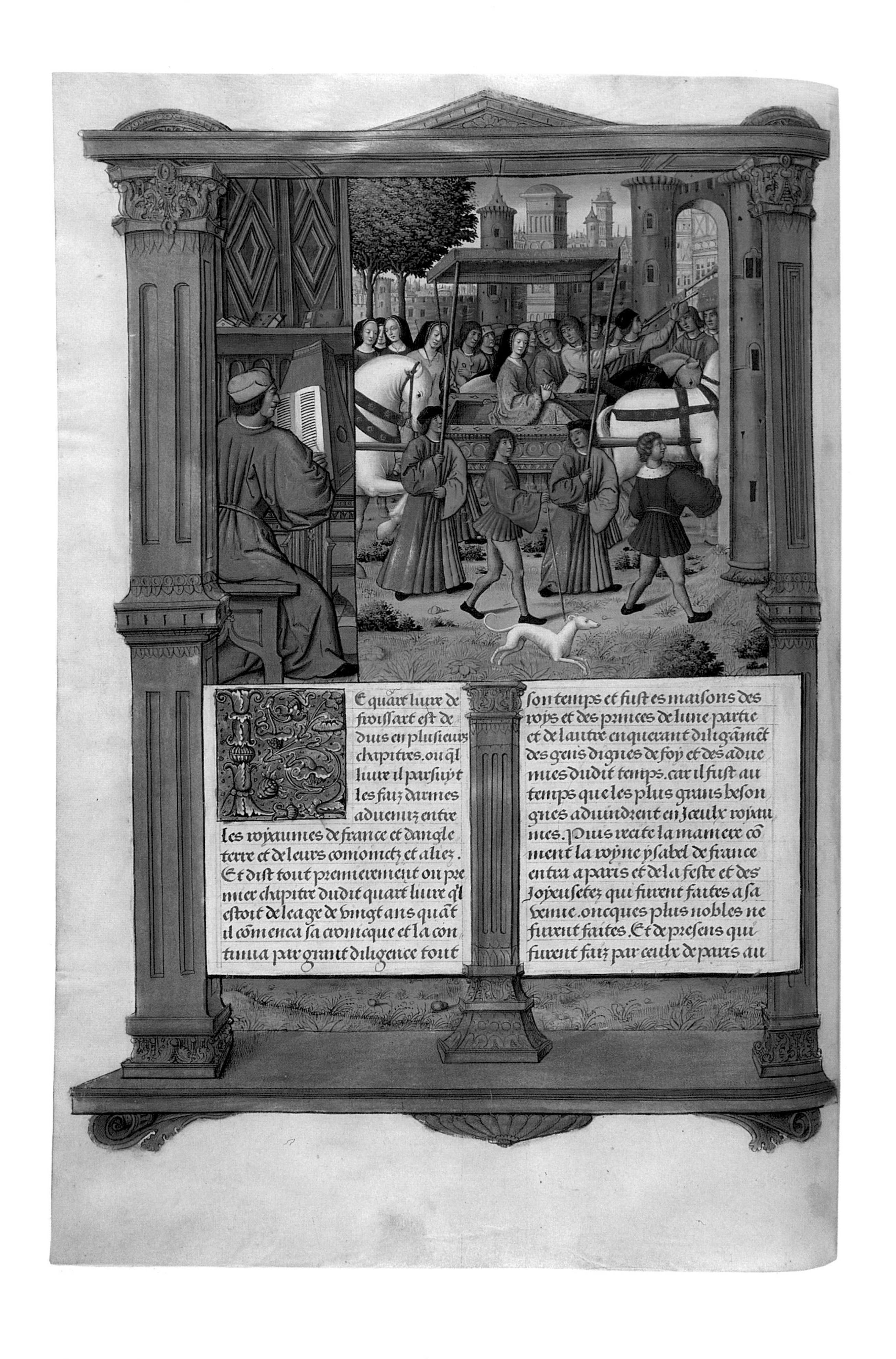

E quart liure de
froissart est de
duis en plusieurs
chapitres. ou q̄l
liure il parsuyt
les faiz darmes
aduenuz entre
les royaumes de france et dangle
terre et de leurs conioinctz et aliez.
Et dist tout premierement ou pre
mier chapitre dudit quart liure q̄l
estoit de leage de vingt ans quāt
il cōmenca sa cronicque et la con
tinua par grant diligence tout
son temps et fust es maisons des
roys et des princes de lune partie
et de lautre enquerant diligāmēt
des gens dignes de foy et des adue
nues dudit temps. car il fust au
temps que les plus grans beson
gnes aduindrent en iceulx royau
mes. Puis recite la maniere cō
ment la royne ysabel de france
entra a paris et de la feste et des
ioyeusetez qui furent faites a sa
venue. oncques plus nobles ne
furent faites. Et de presens qui
furent faiz par ceulx de paris au

Apostol, with commentaries, in Church Slavonic, illuminated manuscript on paper, 393 leaves, Russia, late fifteenth – early sixteenth century, $11\frac{1}{4}$in by 8in (28.5cm by 20.5cm)
London £57,200 ($118,976). 29.XI.90
From the library of Paul M. Fekula

Opposite
Persian poetry and prose manuscript on paper, by Sa'di, copied by Imad al-Husaini, Aleppo, dated *1595*, with gold and silver decorated borders, Tabriz, second quarter sixteenth century and Esfahan, $11\frac{1}{2}$in by $7\frac{1}{4}$in (29.1cm by 18.4cm)
London £39,600 ($81,972). 12.X.90

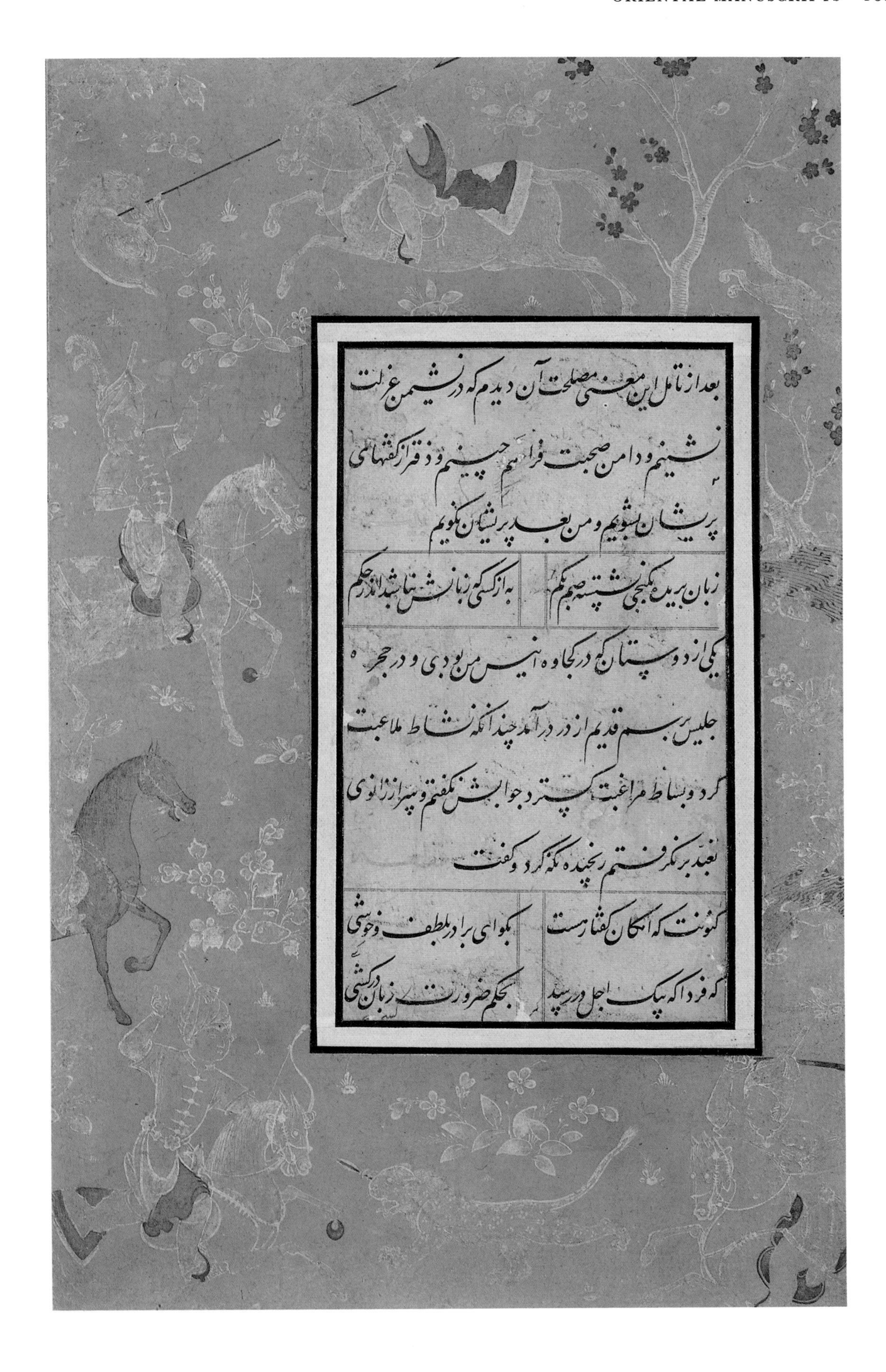
بعد از تامل این معنی مصلحت آن دیدم که در نشیمن عزلت
نشینم و دامن صحبت فراهم چینم و دفتر از گفتهای
پریشان بشویم و من بعد پریشان نگویم
زبان بریده بکنجی نشسته صم بکم
به از کسی که زبانش نباشد اندر حکم
یکی از دوستان که در کجاوه انیس من بودی و در حجره
جلیس برسم قدیم از در درآمد چندانکه نشاط ملاعبت
کرد و بساط مداعبت گسترد جوابش نگفتم و سر از زانوی
تعبد بر نگرفتم رنجیده نگه کرد و گفت
کنونت که امکان گفتار هست
بگو ای برادر بلطف و خوشی
که فردا که پیک اجل در رسید
بحکم ضرورت زبان درکشی

The Mughal emperor Humayun receiving dignitaries, gouache with gold, with three lines of Persian text in a panel, attributed to the artist Bahman, Mughal, *circa* 1590, $12\frac{3}{4}$in by $7\frac{5}{8}$in (32.5cm by 19.5cm)
London £66,000 ($111,540). 26.IV.91

From a dispersed royal Mughal historical manuscript of large dimensions. The subject, showing Humayun in Qandahar, presumably after his return to India in 1555, indicates that the manuscript covered specifically Mughal history. It could well have been a copy of the *Akbarnama* or possibly a history of Humayun himself.

A lord seated on a throne listening to musicians, a page from the 'Chawand' *Ragamala, Sri Raga*, attributed to Nasiruddin, Chawand (Mewar), 1605, $6\frac{1}{4}$in by $6\frac{1}{4}$in (16cm by 16cm)
New York $52,250 (£30,029). 27.III.91
From the Carter Burden Collection

The Fath 'Ali Shah portrait

Diana Scarisbrick

Fig. 1
Portrait of Fath 'Ali Shah Qajar, with titles of Fath 'Ali Shah and a poem within gold cartouches, also with use of gold for the jewels and their settings, by Mihr 'Ali, Qajar, probably Tehran, signed and dated *AH 1225*, 1810, 7ft 9¼in by 3ft 11¼in (237cm by 120cm)
London £126,500 ($213,785). 26.IV.91

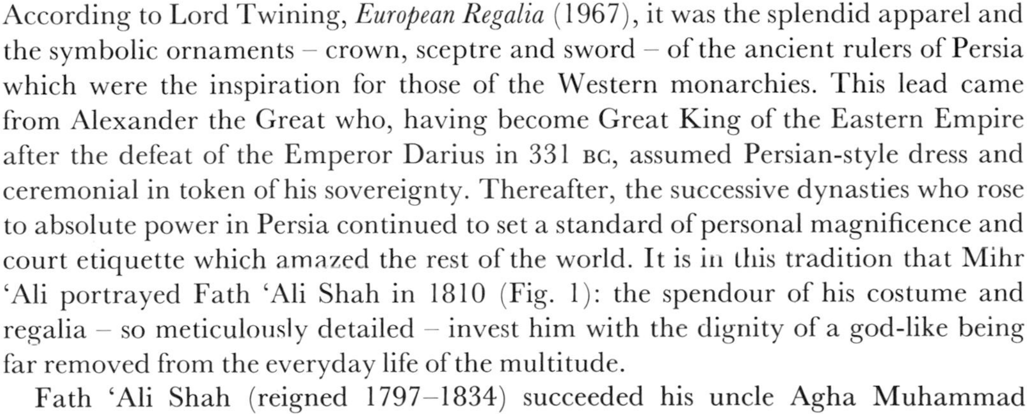

According to Lord Twining, *European Regalia* (1967), it was the splendid apparel and the symbolic ornaments – crown, sceptre and sword – of the ancient rulers of Persia which were the inspiration for those of the Western monarchies. This lead came from Alexander the Great who, having become Great King of the Eastern Empire after the defeat of the Emperor Darius in 331 BC, assumed Persian-style dress and ceremonial in token of his sovereignty. Thereafter, the successive dynasties who rose to absolute power in Persia continued to set a standard of personal magnificence and court etiquette which amazed the rest of the world. It is in this tradition that Mihr 'Ali portrayed Fath 'Ali Shah in 1810 (Fig. 1): the spendour of his costume and regalia – so meticulously detailed – invest him with the dignity of a god-like being far removed from the everyday life of the multitude.

Fath 'Ali Shah (reigned 1797–1834) succeeded his uncle Agha Muhammad Khan, founder of the Qajar dynasty which reigned until Reza Shah Pahlavi took over in 1925. Whereas his uncle was a warrior and cunning politician, Fath 'Ali Shah was a poet and a connoisseur. He did however do everything possible to maintain the absolute authority inherited from his uncle, who for his sake had 'raised a royal palace and cemented it with blood'. A priority was the establishment of the collection of state jewels which consisted principally of the vast quantity of gold, silver, jade, diamonds, pearls and coloured stones removed from the treasury of the Mughal emperors by the Persian ruler Nadir Shah during the invasion of India in 1739. Once Fath 'Ali Shah had appropriated this fabulous collection from Nadir Shah's heirs he began to commission regalia thickly encrusted with gems, enhanced by brilliant red, green, and royal blue enamels for the glorification of the Qajar dynasty. Some of the ornaments depicted in the portrait survived until modern times when they were displayed in the Bank Melli of Tehran by order of the late Muhammad Reza Shah.

Fig. 2
The Kiani crown, from the Persian crown jewels, height without *jiqas* 12⅝in (32cm)
(Reproduced by courtesy of the Royal Ontario Museum, Toronto).

In the portrait Fath 'Ali Shah is shown, as at a court levée, kneeling beside a cushion on a rug – both richly embroidered with pearls and precious stones. The wide cuffs, shoulders, the hem and open seams of his traditional grey tunic are similarly stiff with jewelled embroidery, and hanging from his sleeves and across his chest are quantities of deep red spinels or rubies, some of them doubtless inscribed with the names and dates of Mughal emperors.

Instead of a turban he wears the most picturesque of all the Persian crown jewels, the Kiani crown, of tall cylindrical design encrusted with numerous diamonds, 1,800 pearls, 300 emeralds, 1,500 rubies and spinels, many of them uncut, mounted over foil in yellow gold (Fig. 2).

Above the circlet of ruby and diamond triangles and medallions there is a deep pearl pavement interspersed with yet more diamonds framed in rubies, and huge emeralds meeting at a cluster in the centre. The mitred top is outlined with pearls enclosing gem-studded triangular motifs. Inside there is a domed red velvet cap crossed by jewelled arches intersecting at a 120 carat red spinel, said to have come from the throne of the Mughal Emperor, Aurangzib (1658–1707). The Shah did of course own several other crowns, and one of them bore an inscription translating 'Help from God and Speedy Recovery'.

Three heron plumes – each pinned with three large white pearls – give further emphasis to royal dignity. These black tufts, which the Mughal emperors first wore in their turbans, and the *jiqa* or jewelled aigrette attached to the front of the crown derived from Mughal India.

Fig. 3
The Fath 'Ali Shah *jiqa*, from the Persian crown jewels, overall height 8in (20.5cm)
(Reproduced by courtesy of the Royal Ontario Museum, Toronto).

Although the *jiqa* in the portrait – a rich diamond, emerald and ruby cluster weighed down by heavy diamond drops – is not in the collection today there are several others similar including one with plumes emerging from a sunburst, which are recorded as belonging to Fath 'Ali Shah (Fig. 3). Despite their distinctive Mughal character, there is a theory, put forward by Sue Stronge of the Victoria and Albert Museum, that these aigrettes might have originated in Europe. Several versions are illustrated in the museum's design album of Arnold Lulls, court jeweller to James I, which could have been sent to India as presents.

On his sleeves are the bazù bands, or ornaments for the bazù – that part of the arm above the elbow – which like the three tufts of heron plumes were reserved for the king and his sons. As befitted insignia of such importance they are centred on the two most celebrated Golconda diamonds in the Persian crown jewels. That worn on the left arm is the Great Table Diamond which the French gem merchant, Jean-Baptiste Tavernier saw in India in 1642 and longed to buy for himself. It is a light pink diamond of exceptional size and limpidity called the *Darya-i Nur* (Sea of Light; Fig. 4). It now bears the name of Fath 'Ali Shah and the date of his death, 1834, but is smaller than it was in his lifetime, for part was removed and recut as a brilliant, now known as the *Nur ul-Ain* (Light of the Eye). This beautiful pink drop-shaped stone was set by Harry Winston in the centre of a tiara of coloured diamonds for the Empress Farah in 1959. The other huge diamond set in the middle of the right bazù band known as the *Taj-i-Mah* or 'Crown of the Moon' is also still in the collection, though no longer mounted.

Fig. 4
The Darya-i Nur (Sea of Light) pink diamond, from the Persian crown jewels, overall height $2\frac{7}{8}$in (7.2cm)
(Reproduced by courtesy of the Royal Ontario Museum, Toronto).

Hidden beneath the Shah's long glossy black beard is a rope of pearls – each as big as a hazelnut – crossed over at the breast. More beautiful pearls hang from the tassel capped with a great emerald which falls from the jewelled belt encircling the elegant wasp waist. This magnificent mosaic of gems, which is clasped with a round diamond and ruby buckle, terminates in a long tag encrusted with pearls interspersed with hexagonal emerald cameos and intaglios engraved by Mughal court artists. Although the belt was broken up and the gems and pearls reset into other ornaments both the dagger and sword worn on it survive. They are also richly encrusted with gemstones, with a large ruby red spinel set in the tip of the guard. The sword was the Shah's particular favourite, made by a swordsmith who inscribed the watered steel blade 'Work of Kalb 'Ali Son of Asadullah Isfahani' and 'The Sultan Fath 'Ali Shah Qajar Father of the Sword'. The scabbard is paved with pearls between medallions of diamonds and coloured stones, and there is another large spinel in the centre of the gem-studded hilt (Fig. 5).

While the sword and dagger are emblematic of military glory, the mace, which lies on the rug, is the sign of judicial authority (Fig. 6). Here the mosaic of diamonds and red spinels stands out against a translucent green emerald ground. Similarly luxurious is the bottle – perhaps for fruit juice – which is close by.

This gorgeous display of the riches of Persia was intended to convey the dazzling splendour of the autocrat whose titles were 'Centre of the Universe, Object of the World's Regard, Cousin of the Sun and Moon, Point of Adoration of the World'. Not only were his subjects expected to prostrate themselves before him at court, but even his portrait commanded the same respect. When Mirza Abdul Hassan, ambassador to the court of George III, saw a similar portrait in the offices of the East India Company when he visited in 1811, he was so 'overwhelmed by the beauty of the Qibleh of the Universe' that he bowed low until his head was on the level of his feet. Even more astonishing to English travellers was the honour paid to such portraits hidden in wooden boxes. Sir John Malcolm, who was at the port of Abushehr at the same time as some Indian envoys were bringing home to their ruler a portrait from the Shah, said in his *Sketches of Persia* (1827) that the governor and people processed outside the gates to make their obeisance to the enclosed image and that a salute was fired as it entered the city. The ceremonies were repeated on embarkation and the English resident much criticised for refusing to join in 'the mummery'.

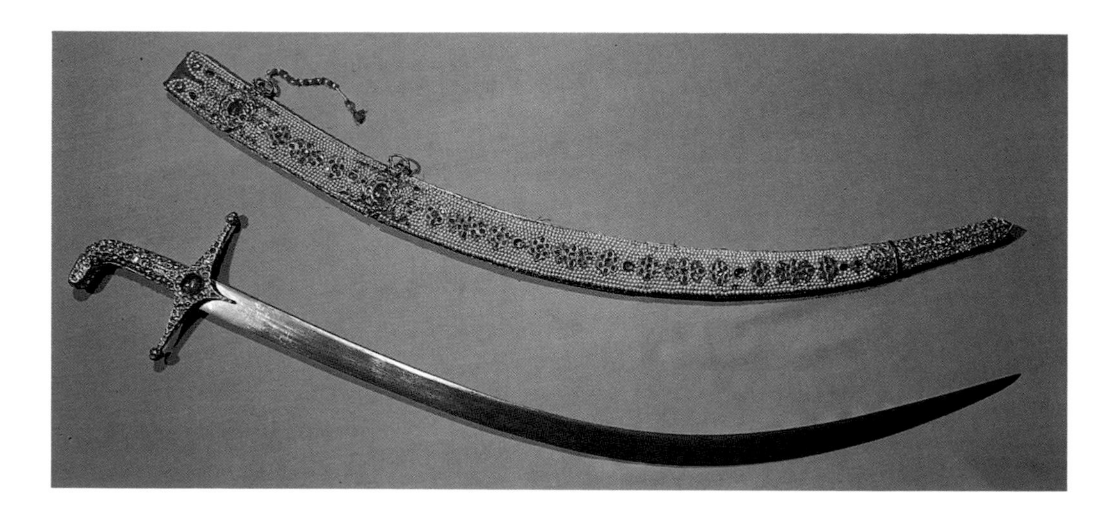

Fig. 5
The favourite sword of Fath 'Ali Shah, from the Persian crown jewels, overall length $40\frac{1}{8}$in (102cm)
(Reproduced by courtesy of the Royal Ontario Museum, Toronto).

Fig. 6
The mace, from the Persian crown jewels, length $28\frac{3}{4}$in (73cm)
(Reproduced by courtesy of the Royal Ontario Museum, Toronto).

Fig. 1
One of two Qajar tents, Central Persia, second quarter nineteenth century, rectangular tent approximately 13ft 9in by 10ft 6in (420cm by 320cm); circular tent, diameter approximately 17ft 9in (540cm)
London £66,000 ($110,220). 24.IV.91

Qajar tents of Muhammad Shah

Figs 2 and 3
Two *mihrab* from one of the tent panels, enclosing two silk and metal thread embroidered men in Qajar costume.

When one of the two Qajar tents to be sold on 24 April 1991 was erected in Sotheby's London salerooms, it gave rise to many murmurs of recognition (Fig. 1). For although such almost complete examples are now extremely rare, references to royal tents frequently occur in Persian literature and manuscript art. This is hardly surprising when one considers the peripatetic world of the Islamic courts. With much of the royal schedule taking place out of doors, or away from permanent residences, tents developed a traditional and central role as travelling audience chambers, temporary garden rooms, and accommodation for hunting expeditions.

The figures and decorative elements depicted on the two tents sold in April bear out such uses: the larger of the two – a rectangular tent – sported fine naturalistic details of courtiers, one carrying a gun, and another a falcon (Figs 2 and 3). The smaller, circular, tent showed a profusion of flowering branches supporting birds. It also carried an inscription in Persian *nasta'liq*: 'As-Sultan Muhammad Shah Ghazi' and 'Kamtarin banda dar-gah Fath 'Ali'. This translated reads: 'For the sultan Muhammad Shah, the conqueror' and 'the court's most humble servant Fath 'Ali'.

Muhammad Shah was the third ruler of the Qajar dynasty and reigned from 1834 to 1848. His predecessor and grandfather Fath 'Ali Shah had made extraordinary efforts to add to the prestige and authority of the crown, and established a remarkable collection of jewels and regalia (see the article on pages 172–75). Muhammad Shah attempted to maintain this policy of strength through display, but in the process brought Persia close to financial ruin.

The two tents belong to this period of flamboyant expenditure, and represent the very finest quality of workmanship. Unusually, dye has been floated on some areas to achieve a more naturalistic effect: clouded sky appears behind the figures of the courtiers, and three-dimensional modelling can be seen on some of the animals depicted on the roof panels. The number of colours used (eleven) also indicates a surprising level of quality. From all this it seems likely that the tents were made in a court workshop, probably in Tehran (though it is worth mentioning that the pieced wool flannel technique used is more usually associated with later work from Rascht on the Caspian Sea).

Muhammad Shah's reign saw his country move much closer to European ways – he himself eventually discarded traditional dress in favour of the frock-coat and epaulettes of a European monarch – and many of the traditions of Persian royal life were never to see the light of day again.

These two splendid Qajar tents can therefore be seen as some of the very last embodiments of a magnificent culture as it turned to face the modern world – elegant testimonies to a life well lived.

Oriental rugs and the collection of the J. Paul Getty Museum

Ian Bennett

Fig. 1
A silk and metal thread 'Polonaise' rug, Esfahan, Central Persia, first half seventeenth century, approximately 6ft 11in by 4ft 11in (211cm by 150cm)
New York $231,000 (£117,857). 8.XII.90
From the J. Paul Getty Museum

Opposite
Fig. 2
A silk and metal thread 'Polonaise' rug, Esfahan, Central Persia, first half seventeenth century, approximately 6ft 8in by 4ft 8in (203cm by 142cm)
New York $440,000 (£224,490). 8.XII.90
From the J. Paul Getty Museum

While the late J. Paul Getty did not consider Oriental rugs as one of his major collecting interests, it is clear from the quality of his acquisitions and the very high prices he was willing to pay, that he took them seriously, as did many other great American collectors during the first decades of this century. It is arguable that Getty himself was the last of this famous pre-War generation. He made two of his most significant acquisitions in the 1930s, the white ground Getty 'Coronation' carpet and the Robinson-Yerkes 'Ardebil' carpet (both now in the Los Angeles County Museum). No sixteenth-century Safavid carpets of the art historical importance and condition of these two examples have been seen on the open market since World War II, although a very small number have changed hands privately.

The catalogue for the recent sale of carpets from the J. Paul Getty Museum reads like a mini *Who's Who* of early twentieth-century art dealing and collecting. Apart from Getty, one could read among the provenances the names of Kevorkian, Salomon, Duveen, Rothschild, Yerkes, Kelekian, Mortimer Schiff, Pierpont Morgan, Elbert Gary, Martha Baird (Mrs John D. Rockefeller) and Lionel Harris: a veritable galaxy of art market history.

The Getty sale included two examples of the perennially popular group of Safavid weavings, the so-called 'Polonaise' type with silk pile. These can be attributed to the looms established by Shah Abbas in Esfahan in around 1601–1602. Documented examples show that they continued to be made throughout most of the seventeenth century and were extremely popular among European royalty and nobility. The least expensive of the two Getty examples is in many ways the most interesting (Fig. 1). The rug had been illustrated in the second of the three splendid volumes published by the K. K. Österreichisches Handels-Museum in Vienna between 1892 and 1896 (Vol. II, pl. XCIX). The plates in these volumes were themselves selected from the huge exhibition of Oriental carpets held at the museum in 1891, the first and probably the greatest ever to have been assembled. Sir C. Purdon Clark, who wrote the entry for this rug in the 'Vienna Books', as they are generally called and

Fig. 3
A Mughal carpet, possibly shaped to accommodate a dais, Lahore, North-West India, mid seventeenth century, approximately 14ft 8in by 8ft 11in (447cm by 272cm)
New York $297,000 (£151,531). 8.XII.90
From the J. Paul Getty Museum

John Kimberly Mumford, who wrote the text for the 1910 auction catalogue of the Yerkes Collection, both considered this as one of the most beautiful and richly colourful examples of its kind to have survived. Despite the flattering nature of the watercolour reproductions used in the Yerkes catalogue, it does seem to have been in excellent condition in 1910 and, indeed, an outstanding example. Its quality is further shown by the fact that the prices in 1910 for the four other Yerkes 'Polonaise' rugs ranged between $3,500 and $7,700, but the Getty example made a resounding $12,300, a price which, in real terms, would equal $1.5 million today.

The prices fetched over the last 70 years by another closely related group of Safavid weavings included in the Getty sale illustrate how the 1929 Crash depreciated the value of carpets of this type by an astonishing factor of at least ten. The red-ground Esfahan rugs, extremely popular with early twentieth-century collectors, achieved prices of between $75,000 and $78,000 at the Benguiat sale in 1925 and $50,000 (i.e. the equivalent in real terms to $5 million today) at the Gary sale at the American Art Association in 1928. Ten years later, these rugs were fetching only between 525 guineas (then equivalent to about $2,750) and 840 guineas ($4,400) at the John Schiff sale in London in 1938. The Getty 'Polonaise' rug mentioned above seems to have followed a similar pattern, dropping to $3,900 at the Schiff sale the following year in New York.

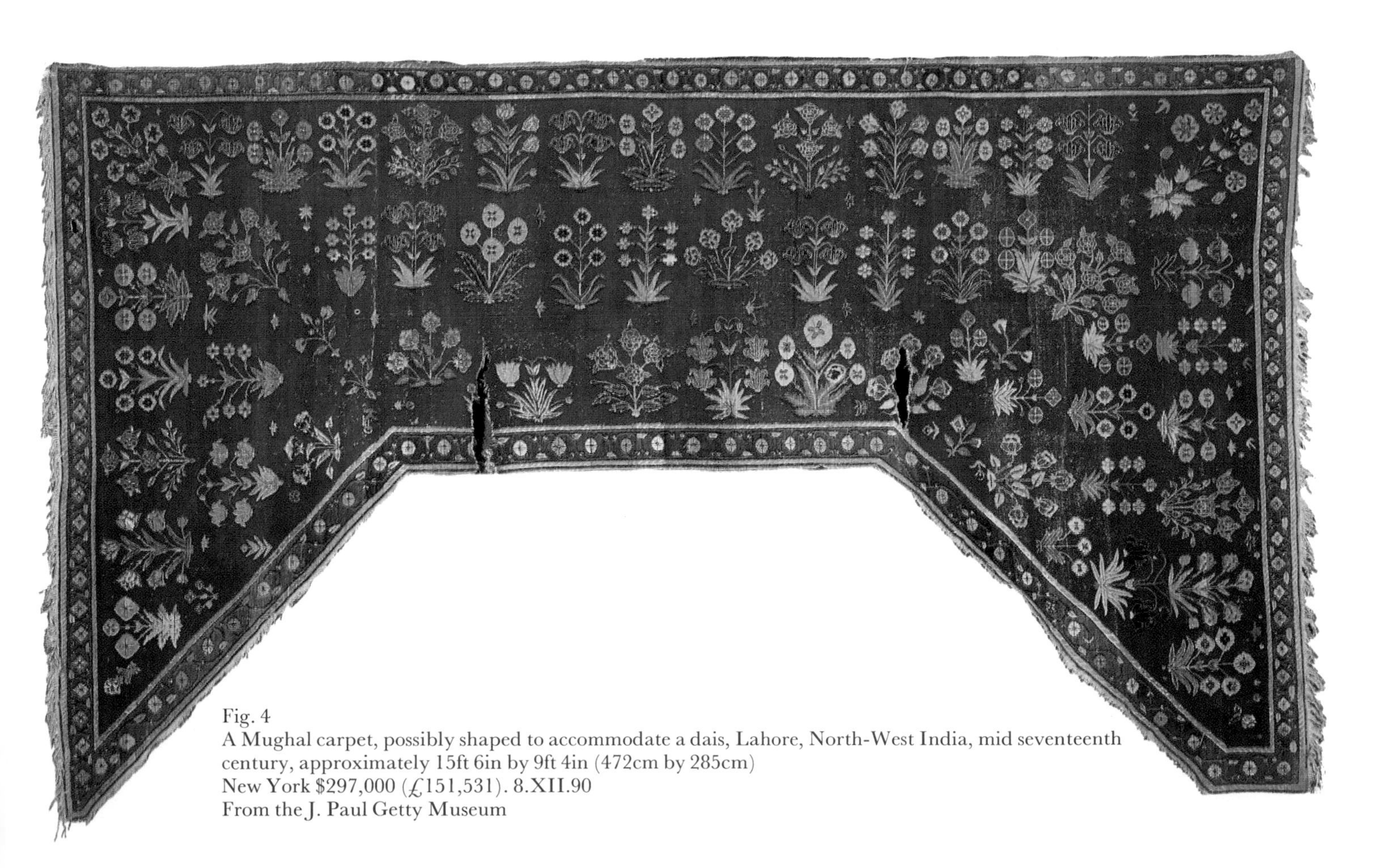

Fig. 4
A Mughal carpet, possibly shaped to accommodate a dais, Lahore, North-West India, mid seventeenth century, approximately 15ft 6in by 9ft 4in (472cm by 285cm)
New York $297,000 (£151,531). 8.XII.90
From the J. Paul Getty Museum

The more expensive of the two Getty 'Polonaise' rugs (Fig. 2) had been purchased at the first of the two Kevorkian sales in London in 1969 for only £6,600 (then $15,840), which further illustrates the stagnancy of the market in the decades after 1929. Virtually a pair to the often illustrated example in the Cleveland Museum of Art, this rug had suffered little of the wear and fading evident in many of the 300 or so 'Polonaise' rugs to have survived.

Fading could, however, be seen on the most expensive rug of all those sold in New York last December (although not in the Getty sale), the extremely rare early seventeenth-century 'Polonaise' with an all-silk foundation and no metal (Fig. 5). Most rugs of this type are woven on a predominantly cotton base with extensive silver brocading.

Further evidence of the great rise in value of major 'Classical' carpets over the last twenty years was given by the three seventeenth-century Mughal Jaipur 'shrub' carpets in the Getty sale (see Figs 3 and 4). These three made a total of $847,000, as opposed to the £12,200 (then $29,280) they had cost at the first Kevorkian sale in 1969 in London. The second Kevorkian sale the following year contained the most expensive of the Jaipur 'shrub' carpets in the collection, which was bought by the Metropolitan Museum in New York, for £14,000 (then $34,160) and only one other complete, or almost complete, example has been on the market since, the fragmented but still magnificent rectangular Michaelian carpet now in the al-Sabah Collection, which made $99,000 at auction in New York in 1980. The rectangular-shaped one of the three Getty carpets sold in 1990, it is worth noting, would seem to be the pair to the example now in the Keir Collection. All these carpets, of whatever shape, are associated with the Maharajah of Jaipur's palace at Amber, which was completed in the 1630s. They are presumed to have been woven in Lahore and a substantial number still remain at Jaipur, including rectangular, almost round and 'lintel'-shaped examples.

The Getty sale demonstrated a number of interesting things about the 'Classical' Oriental carpet market, both past and present. Values were cut dramatically by the 1929 Crash and in real terms, some might argue, have never recovered. Yet equally as dramatic is the rise which appears to have taken place during the last two decades. Compared with other works of art of such quality, great carpets are still not expensive, even at the Getty level of prices, but it is good to see them being taken seriously again.

Opposite
Fig. 5
A silk Esfahan rug, Central Persia, early seventeenth century, approximately 7ft 6in by 5ft 6in (229cm by 168cm)
New York $506,000 (£258,163). 8.XII.90

A Kazakh rug,
approximately 5ft by 4ft
(152cm by 122cm)
London £10,450
($17,452). 24.IV.91

Opposite
A Persian shrub and
arabesque carpet, probably
Kerman, late sixteenth–
early seventeenth century,
approximately 11ft 6in by
9ft 5in (351cm by 287cm)
London £236,500
($489,555). 11.X.90

This carpet exemplifies the splendour and magnificence of Safavid carpet weaving. It belongs to a group generally classified as 'vase' carpets in reference to the Chinese vase motifs which appear in several examples, and to a structural feature shared by the group. It depicts flowering plants and trees demonstrating the Safavid love of nature. Carpets such as this provided an indoor alternative to lavish gardens; a mental and visual retreat.

A Timurid jade cup

John Carswell

One of the most surprising objects to come over the counter in the past year was a jade cup, inlaid with gold. Because of its dragon handle, it was first shown to the Chinese department, who in turn suggested it might be Indian. This was not so far off the mark, as the cup had been acquired in India many years ago; and Mughal jades are famous. In fact, further research showed it to be Timurid, probably made in Central Asia, perhaps at Samarkand.

The cup is carved from semi-transluscent dark green nephrite, with an incised ring on the slightly everted rim; the dragon handle has a supporting bracket below. The body is finely engraved and inlaid with gold, with scalloped medallions linked by curving spiral stems, and the gold inlay is further enhanced with fine engraving, the cartouches with minutely beaded frames and the leaves with tiny spiral tendrils, of such delicacy that they can hardly be appreciated by the naked eye.

The cup belongs to a group of Timurid hardstone vessels of the first half of the fifteenth century, in particular to jade cups in the British Museum, the Ardebil Shrine in Iran, the Museum of Decorative Arts in Vienna, and in Benares, the latter being inscribed to Ulugh-Beg Gurgani. The vessels served as wine-cups and the handle for suspension from a belt or saddle.

The Timurid ruler Ulugh-Beg (1394–1449) was known to have a particular taste for jade, and at the end of his campaign against the Mughals in 1424–25 ordered his troops to transport back to Samarkand two enormous blocks of nephrite. One of these was used to fashion the tomb cover of his famous grandfather, Timur-Shakespeare's Tamberlaine. This jade cover is of exactly the same colour as the jade cup, and the ornamental decoration is of similar design. The cover had a large hunk missing at one corner, and it is tantalising to speculate that the cup might have been carved from just such a fragment.

A jade cup in the Gulbenkian Museum in Lisbon also has a dragon handle, and is actually dedicated to Ulugh-Beg ibn Shahrukh. The dragon's head was a popular motif in Timurid art, and a series of double-headed dragon candlesticks have very similar heads to the jade examples. Dragons also appear on wood and ceramics, and on silk textiles. On the other hand, the elaborate gold inlay is unique on this particular type of dragon cup. Finally it is not without interest that the cup was acquired in India. The Mughals were fascinated with their Timurid ancestry and this led to an appreciation of Timurid works of art. It is not hard to imagine that this splendid example may have once graced the Mughal court.

A Timurid gold inlaid jade cup, early fifteenth century, diameter 3⅛in (8cm)
London £132,000 ($273,240). 10.X.90

A glass ewer, with *kufic* inscription, Baghdad, ninth – tenth century, height 4⅜in (11cm)
London £6,160 ($12,751). 10.X.90

A glass goblet, early sixteenth century, height 7⅜in (18.8cm)
London £8,800 ($18,216). 10.X.90

Above
An Iznik pottery dish, early sixteenth century, diameter 16in (40.6cm)
London £39,600 ($67,320). 25.IV.91

The dish is modelled on an early fifteenth-century Chinese blue-and-white dish, possibly even one of the original examples now in the Topkapi Saray Museum.

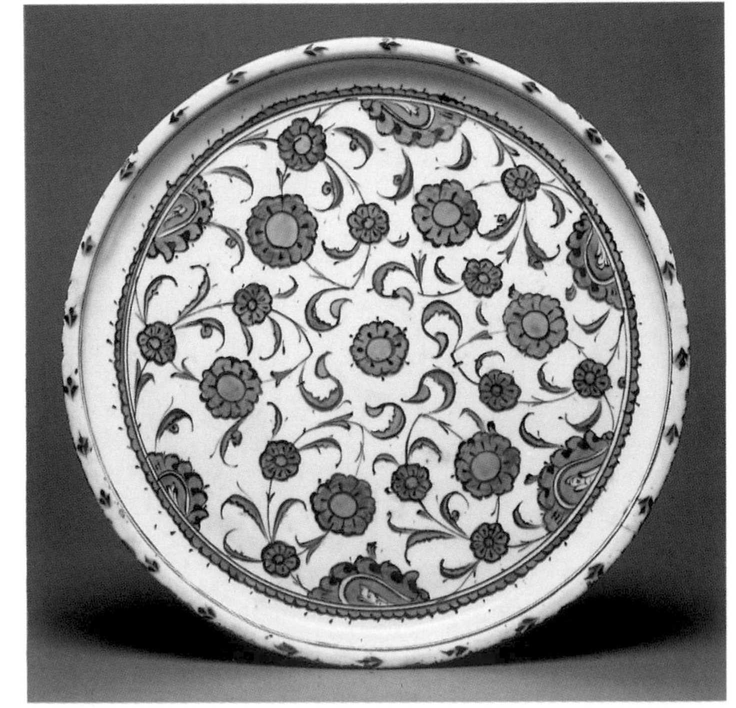

Right
An Iznik blue and turquoise pottery dish, early sixteenth century, diameter 10in (25.3cm)
London £57,200 ($118,404). 10.X.90

The six-fold design based on an implicit hexagon derives from much earlier prototypes, such as the tiles in the Murad II mosque at Edirne of the first half of the fifteenth century, themselves based on early fifteenth-century Chinese porcelain prototypes. This dish epitomises the early Iznik blue and turquoise style with the artist breaking away from the imposed designs of the *nakkashane* and adopting a more individual and painterly approach.

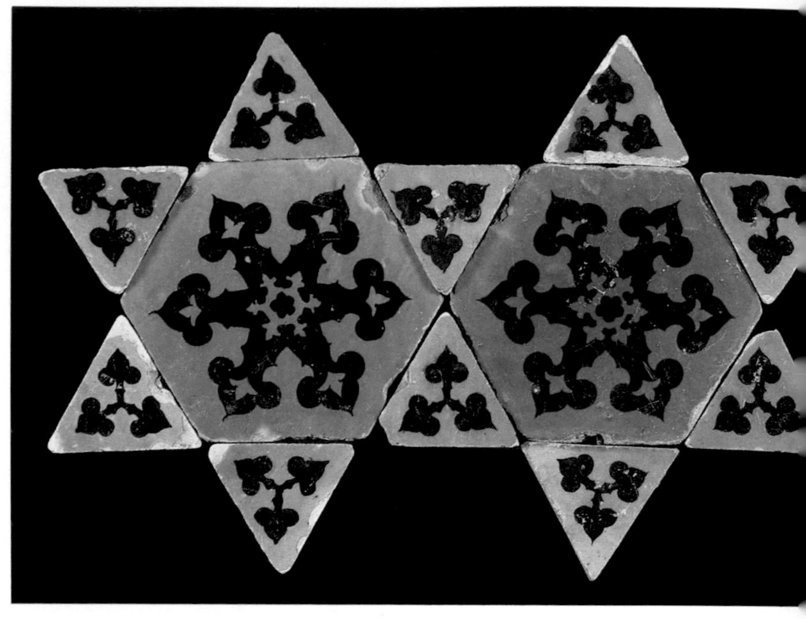

Above, left
A *cuerda seca* pottery tile from the Dome of the Rock, Jerusalem, *circa* 1550, 7½in (19cm)
London £3,520 ($5,984). 25.IV.91

Right
Two hexagonal and ten triangular pottery tiles from the Dome of the Rock, Jerusalem, *circa* 1550, hexagons 5¾in (14.5cm) across; triangles 3in (7.6cm) each side
London £8,250 ($14,025). 25.IV.91

An underglaze pottery tile from the Dome of the Rock, Jerusalem, *circa* 1550, 7½in (19cm)
London £7,700 ($13,090). 25.IV.91

A gold gem-set diadem, North-West Morocco, eighteenth–nineteenth century, the velvet backing and ties later, length approximately 21½in (54.5cm)
London £37,400 ($63,580). 25.IV.91

Diadems of this type were worn as part of the bridal finery in the Kabylie area of Morocco and this gem-set example would have been worn by an important member of the community.

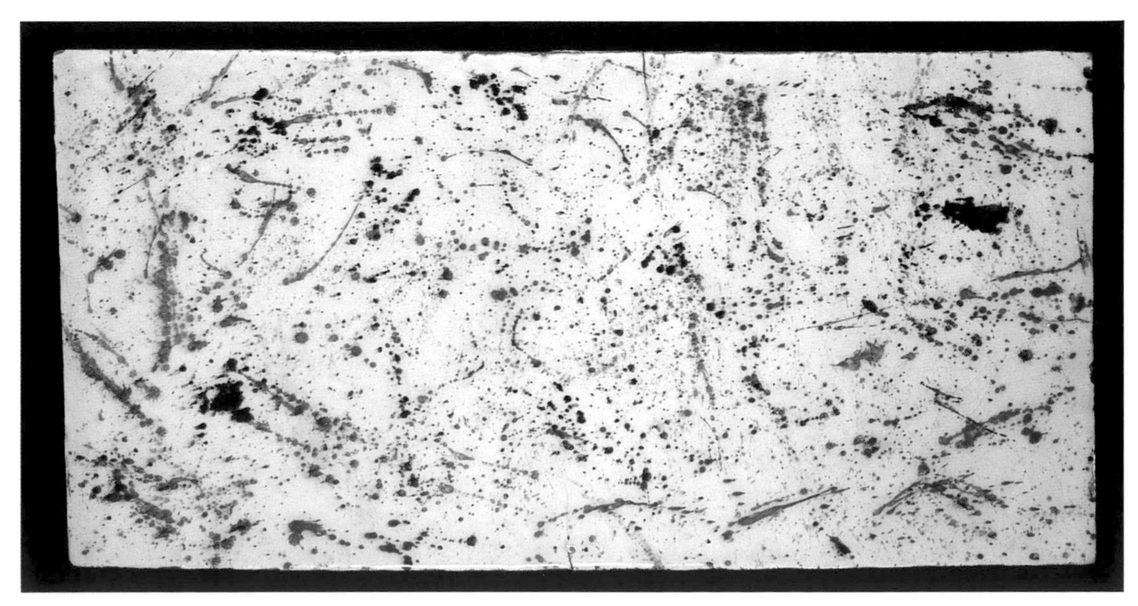

A pottery tile, seventeenth century, length 27¼in (69.2cm)
London £11,000 ($18,700). 25.IV.91

Indian art

A post-Gandhara bronze figure of the Bodhisattva Maitreya, Swat Valley, *circa* seventh century, height 5¼in (13.2cm)
London £35,200 ($58,784). 24.IV.91

Opposite
A buff sandstone stele of a Yogini, Uttah Pradesh or Madhya Pradesh, tenth century, height 34in (86.4cm)
New York $104,500 (£53,316). 5.X.90
From the Pan-Asian Collection

Japanese art

A carved wood figure of the Bodhisattva of Compassion, possibly Sho Kannon, fourteenth century, height 40½in (103cm)
New York $176,000 (£103,529).
24.IV.91

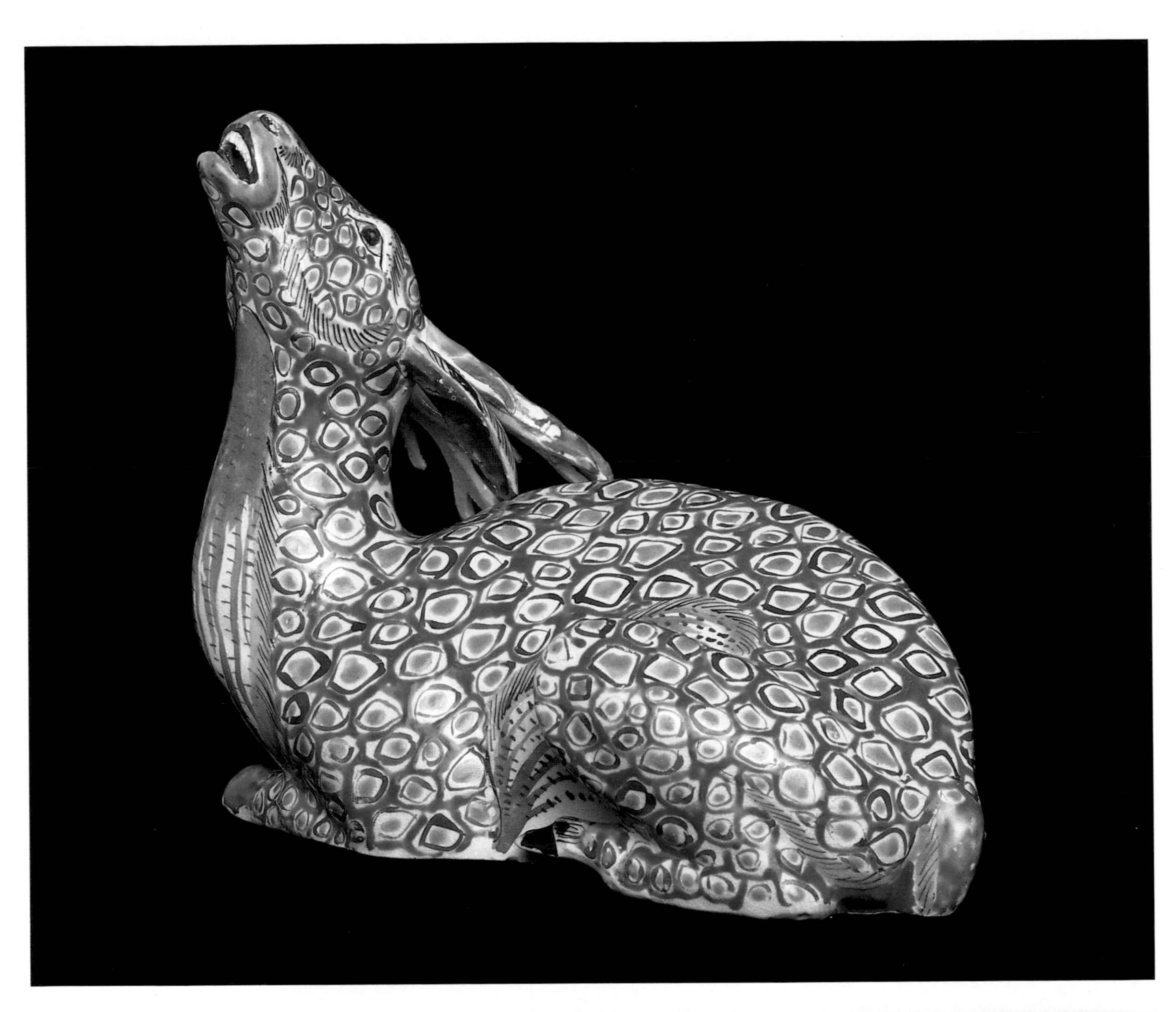

A Kakiemon-style model of a stag, *circa* 1680, length 8½in (21.8cm) London £192,500 ($398,475). 23.XI.90

A pair of Nabeshima cups, late seventeenth–early eighteenth century, diameters 3½in (8.9cm) London £41,800 ($75,240). 21.III.91

Opposite
An earthenware vase by Kinkozan and Sozan, signed, the base inscribed *James Robinson Esq with Mr G. Kobayashi's Compliments*, *circa* 1908, height 21¾in (55.3cm)
London £39,600 ($71,280). 21.III.91

Right
An ivory netsuke of a Manchurian crane by Kaigyokusai Masatsugu, signed, nineteenth century, 1¾in (4.5cm)
London £104,500 ($188,100). 21.III.91
Formerly in the collection of Imai Kenzo

In the realm of Japanese netsuke there are a large number of minor examples, a quantity of good examples and very few masterpieces. Among the latter group is the 'Imai Crane'. The Japanese have tended to regard the netsuke as a dress accessory, but Imai Kenzo was perceptive enough to respect the pieces as art forms and their makers as artists. Kaigyokusai Masatsugu was one of the last traditional netsuke artists from Osaka and his work has been a source of inspiration to twentieth-century artists.

Below, left and right
A pair of iron vases and covers by Mitsutoshi Ikkokusai, signed, Meiji period (1868 – 1912), heights 8⅝in (22cm)
London £35,200 ($63,360). 21.III.91

Below, centre
An iron koro and cover by Mitsutoshi Ikkokusai, signed, Meiji period (1868–1912), height 7¼in (18.5cm)
London £52,800 ($95,040). 21.III.91

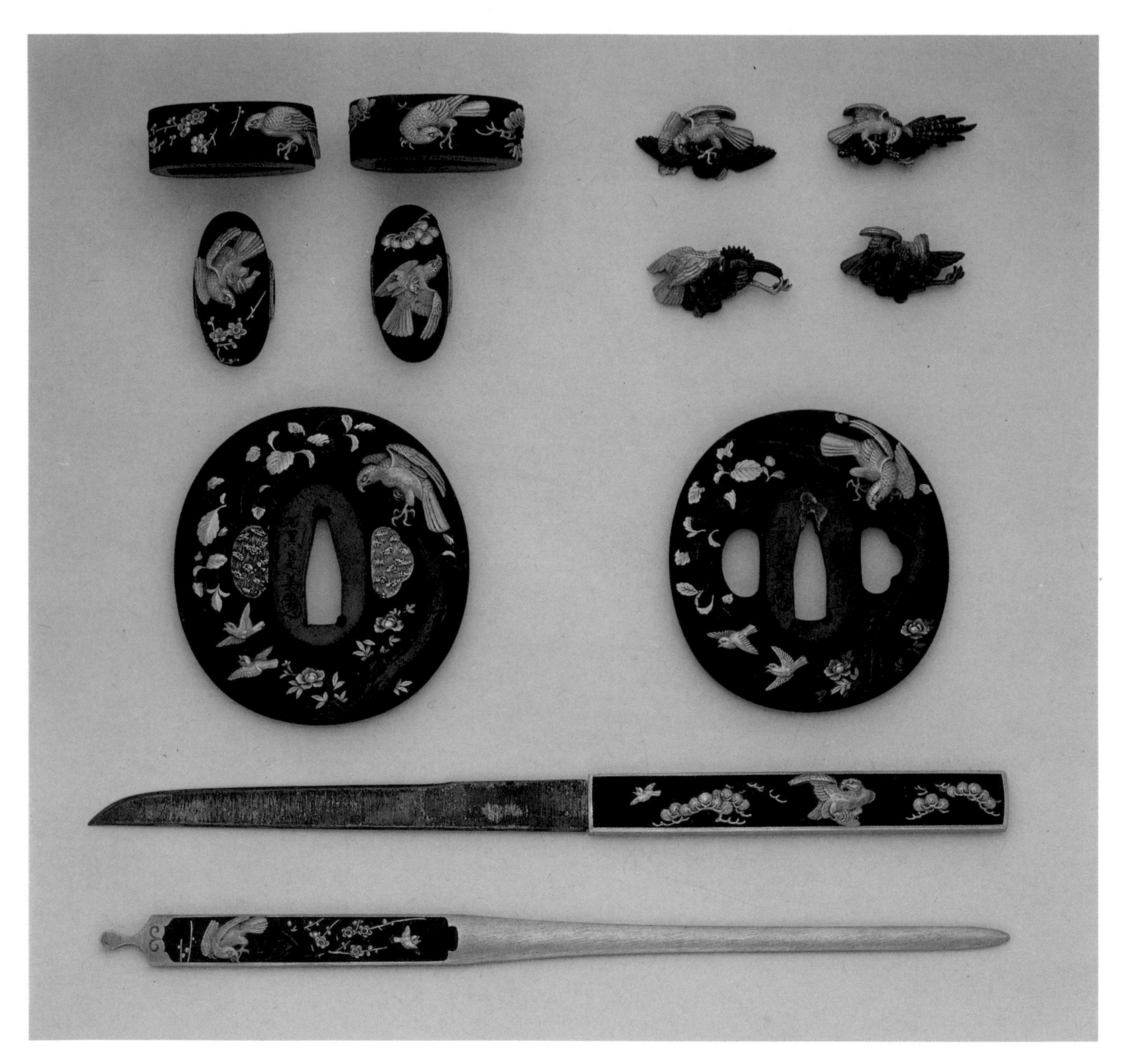

The Roy G. Cole Collections

Nyr Indictor

Last year Sotheby's New York offered two extraordinary collections belonging to Roy G. Cole, a retired Canadian businessman. The first was a large group of Japanese prints, which sold in June 1990, and the second a group of sword fittings and other works of art which was sold in December.

An accomplished sportsman, Mr Cole has maintained a lifelong interest in marksmanship and fishing. Mr Cole became enamoured of arms and armour at a very young age. 'As a boy of twelve,' he says, recalling his first purchase, 'I traded my penny bank . . . for a flintlock pistol . . . Later in the same year, I purchased at the Eastwood Estate Auction sale in Hamilton, Ontario, Canada, an oil painting of a white dove by the early Canadian artist Crostwaite for $2.50.' This seems to have been the beginning of a lifelong passion for collecting. A collection always reveals much about the collector, and it is interesting to consider the extraordinary diversity of the two Cole sales with this in mind.

Most collections of Japanese prints focus on the classical *Ukiyo-e* ('Floating World') scenes by Harunobu, Utamaro, Hokusai, Hiroshige: artists who have been studied and collected in the West since the late nineteenth century. Mr Cole chose instead to focus on contemporary print artists, working in the traditional woodblock medium but in a style that shows considerable Western influence. Many of these artists were virtually unknown to the Western world and had only a limited audience within Japan. Mr Cole's ability to detect the importance of this body of work forty years before scholars and collectors would devote serious attention to them is testimony both to his discerning taste and his business acumen. He made a point of buying different versions of prints he particularly liked, and this has helped make the catalogue of his Japanese prints collection an invaluable reference work.

Mr Cole's collection of sword fittings and other works of art revealed his fascination with the metalworker's craft and demonstrated a preference for the wide range of soft metal alloys. Japanese swords are traditionally fitted with a *tsuba* (handguard), a *fuchi* and a *kashira* (handle-end ornaments), and a pair of *menuki* (grips). While some of these fittings are very plain and functional, many are exceedingly ornate and were never intended for use in battle. Mr Cole purchased variations of similar compositions between the 1940s and 1960s, a time when interest in Japanese art was low and Japanese collectors themselves could not afford to buy extensively. He is modest about his accomplishments, often attributing successful purchases to his advisors. However, it is clear from his ability to discover masterpieces in a wide range of different areas, that Mr Cole's achievements are very much his own.

Opposite, above
A complete set of gold and *shakudo* sword fittings for a *daisho*, by Ishiguro Koreyoshi, nineteenth century
New York $187,000 (£96,392). 13.XII.90
From the Roy G. Cole Collection

Below
An iron and gold *shinshinto tachi* blade, in Komai-style mounts, attributed to Mishina Tajima (no) Kami Kanemitsu, nineteenth century, length 36¼in (92cm)
New York $60,500 (£31,186). 13.XII.90
From the Roy G. Cole Collection

Fig. 1
Toshusai Sharaku
A bust portrait of the actor Iwai Hanshiro IV as Shigenoi in the play *Koi Nyobo Somewake Tazuna*, performed at the Kawarazaki theatre in 1794, signed, with censor's seal *kiwame* and publisher's mark *Tsutaya Jusaburo*, 14⅞in by 9¾in (37.8cm by 24.7cm)
Tokyo Y59,400,000 (£241,886:$318,328). 15.IV.91
From the Walter Amstutz Collection

Sharaku is the most inexplicable phenomenon in *Ukiyo-e*, or indeed in Japanese art. Not only is he one of the most truly original of all the print designers, with a power of concentrated expressiveness in his portrait heads and disturbing contortionism in his figure compositions, but he appeared on the *Ukiyo-e* scene suddenly in 1794 as an unprecedented master, without, apparently, any apprentice work remaining to attest to a formal training, and ended his career in less than a year after designing some 150 prints, almost entirely devoted to Kabuki. The rarity of these prints, put down to their lack of popularity among the Edo Kabuki followers, coupled with his enormous present-day reputation in Japan as well as the West, makes them among the most sought-after of all Japanese prints.

The Walter Amstutz Collection of Japanese prints

Jack Hillier

The Amstutz Collection sold by Sotheby's in Tokyo in April 1991 was among the finest assemblages of Japanese prints to come on to the market in recent years.

The piecing together of the collection was one of many extraordinary achievements in a remarkable life. Born in Switzerland in 1902, Dr Amstutz first made his name as a leading figure in skiing and mountain climbing. As a ski-instructor he taught kings and princes, and even introduced his own spring heel, the 'Amstutz'. His climbing exploits were equally impressive, and he conquered some 800 peaks, including fifty of the highest Alps. In his late twenties Amstutz turned to publishing and developed a keen interest in graphics, introducing a bi-monthy journal of the graphic arts, and in 1963 founding the De Clivo Press in Dubendorf. Amstutz also gained fame for his diplomatic activities. As a keen Anglophile he contributed much to furthering relations between Switzerland and Great Britain, and in 1984 achieved the rare distinction for a foreigner of being appointed Honorary Officer of the Most Excellent Order of the British Empire.

With such a full life one wonders how Amstutz found time to pursue all his collecting activities (oriental prints represent only a part of his commitments). It seems that he is the type of connoisseur to whom an interest in any particular artistic sphere leads to a desire to possess. His collecting has therefore not been restricted to one or two exclusive areas, and the walls of his house have displayed with informed eclecticism paintings and drawings by such widely divergent artists as Constantin Guys and Henry Fuseli, alongside others by Katsushika Hokusai and Ando Hiroshige.

The leaning towards Japanese prints was initiated in part by an early admiration for Hokusai's *Great Wave* print and the endeavour to secure an impression. This led to a wider study of Japanese graphics and, by the end of the last war, systematic buying in Paris and London where prints could be acquired in galleries or at auctions, either singly or in sizeable groups.

It is difficult to identify specific provenance, but the prints allow some general conclusions to be drawn. The very strong showing of Utamaro, Harunobu and Sharaku prints points to the influence of the first band of European collectors, who in the years before the First World War were particularly devoted to these artitsts.

The Utamaro prints, with a high percentage of the 'Large Heads' (bust-portraits) and the half-lengths (with dramatic *contraposti*) were central to the collection. Some are rare, but one deserves special mention as comprising the only recorded impressions of two sheets of a triptych, of which the third is completely unknown. Prints by Toshusai Sharaku are also notoriously rare. There were six in the collection including that of Iwai Hanshiro IV as Shigenoi in the play *Koi Nyobo Somewake Tazuna* performed in 1794 (Fig. 1). A few years earlier than Sharaku, Katsukawa Shunko had experimented with the 'Large Head' portraits that may have owed something to the example of portrait bust engravings imported from Europe. His print of Segawa Kikunojo in a play of 1788 is one of the pioneer masterpieces of the type (Fig. 2). Another print presumed unique is the Sugimura Jihei, an exceptionally large size genre scene of the Kan'ei-ji Temple, with the great bronze effigy of Buddha prominent among the cherry trees.

It would be wrong, however, to give the impression that Amstutz sought out rarities: he was primarily concerned to bring together prints of artistic worth, truly representative of the Japanese print at its most archetypal. Hence the great variety of techniques exemplified: *sumi-e* (ink prints, sometimes touched up with hand-colouring); *urushi-e* (hand-coloured outlines with added lacquer); *benizuri-e* (printed with two colours, typically in green and pink, like the theatrical print by Toyonobu); blown technique with atomised colour (*fuki-e*); and the full colour-print, the so-called 'brocade print' *nishiki-e*.

The gentle Harunobu, designer of many of the earliest broadsheet colour-prints, has always elicited warm affection, especially with his enchanting *musume* peopling scenes that are nearer fantasy than everyday life. None is more delightful than the 'night-piece', *Plum Beside the Water*, from this collection.

Among the numerous great landscapes of Hokusai and Hiroshige, two underline their unique and contrasting gifts: Hokusai's *Red Fuji* (actual title *Fine Wind, Clear Morning*), sublimely simple and controlled; and Hiroshige's *Shono 'White Rain'*, utterly atmospheric, with the wind sweeping the rain in strong diagonal sheets that engulf the travellers.

Nor should it be overlooked that the collection was exceptional in having a foundation of six Chinese colour-prints of the seventeenth century. The largest repository of Chinese prints of this kind is the British Museum which, through the beneficent Hans Sloane, acquired twenty-nine specimens brought back from Japan in 1692–93 by Englebert Kaempfer, a German surgeon attached to the Dutch fleet, by whose name they have always been known. The printing technique differed from that finally evolved by the Japanese, but despite that, it has always been suggested that the introduction of colour-printing in Japan was encouraged by the Chinese success. It was typical of Dr Amstutz's appreciation of the history of the colour-woodcut that he should have wished to have examples of the earliest successful prints in the medium.

The size of the great print collections has perforce dwindled since the first were formed in the late nineteenth century when Japan disregarded its own triumphs in graphic art and allowed vast collections to be formed in the West. Nowadays, the accepted model is that of the wealthy American Louis Ledoux, who set a notional limit of approximately 200 prints, each of outstanding merit, and liable to substitution in the event of prints adjudged superior becoming available. Dr Amstutz pursued a similar aim, and after making notable additions in such sales as the Popper (New York, 1972) and the Vever (London, 1974–75), was quite prepared to shed items that fell below the impressively high standard of the collection in general. By the time the collection came to Sotheby's rooms in Tokyo in April 1991 it was of a size and consistency in quality that led to its being admired for its 'enviable balance'.

Fig. 2
Katsukawa Shunko
A bust portrait of the actor Segawa Kikunojo III as Yuki Onna (the Snow Woman) in the play *Genji Saiko Kogane no Tachibana*, performed at the Ichimura theatre in 1788, signed, 14$\frac{3}{4}$in by 10in (37.4cm by 25.4cm)
Tokyo Y15,400,000 (£62,711:$82,529). 15.IV.91
From the Walter Amstutz Collection

Shunko was the closest follower of his master Shunsho and from the mid 1770s onwards designed a great number of actor prints, many of them of the highest quality and often challenging comparison with Shunsho's own. In the last years of the next decade he lost the use of his right arm and continued to draw with his left hand (a number of paintings exist with the signature 'Shunko painted this with his left hand'). The 'Large Heads' (*okubi-e*) considered as his most important innovation in the *Ukiyo-e* print – he is renowned as the first to adopt this bust portrait style – were made in the late 1780s and early 1790s and are exceedingly rare.

Suzuki Kiitsu
THE THIRTY-SIX IMMORTAL POETS
Hanging scroll, ink and colour on silk, signed, with one seal *Shukurin*, 43in by 27¾in (109cm by 70.5cm)
New York $363,000 (£213,529). 24.IV.91

The Thirty-six Immortal Poets is an eleventh-century Heian-period compilation based upon poetry from the eighth-century *Manyoshu* and other works up to the late tenth century. From the time of this imperial compilation, the Thirty-six Poets became a celebrated group, frequently depicted individually in handscroll and album formats with an appropriate poem accompanying each portrait. The theme continued into the Edo period as a favourite subject particularly among Tosa and Rimpa artists. The great Rimpa master, Ogata Korin was the first to explore the decorative potential by combining all thirty-six figures in a single composition. Kiitsu clearly imitated Korin's composition and also painted the entire mount to resemble old brocade and a Rimpa-style textile of scattered fans on a stream. The meticulous attention to decorative detail continues to the roller ends which are inlaid with the identical motif in mother-of-pearl.

Opposite
A pair of six-fold Rimpa screens, ink, colour and *gofun* on gold paper, seventeenth century, 24¼in by 67⅛in (61.5cm by 170.5cm)
London £121,000 ($250,470). 22.XI.90

Following the tradition of the Sotatsu school studio screens, these screens depict favourite Japanese garden flowers, simply gathered in clusters and represented alone without additional adornments. Although the screens do not bear the usual Sotatsu studio *Inen* seal, the formal Rimpa composition and the technique of the *tarashikomi* (fusing one pigment into another) indicate that they were made in workshops run by Sotatsu's followers.

Chinese art

A sancai-glazed pottery figure of a caparisoned Fereghan horse, Tang Dynasty, height 27½in (69.8cm)
London £462,000 ($771,540). 11.VI.91
From the collection of James W. and Marilynn Alsdorf

Opposite
An Archaic bronze food vessel (*ding*), Western Zhou Dynasty, height 12¼in (31.1cm)
New York $275,000 (£138,889). 27.XI.90
From the C. C. Wang Collection

A blue-and-white dish, with Persian/Arabic inscription, Yuan Dynasty, diameter $18\frac{7}{8}$in (48cm)
Hong Kong HK$7,700,000 (£581,132:$987,179). 30.IV.91

Opposite, above
A *famille-rose* bowl, mark and period of Yongzheng, diameter $3\frac{5}{8}$in (9.2cm)
Hong Kong HK$1,980,000 (£128,739:$254,172). 13.XI.90
From the Goldschmidt Collection

Below
A *doucai* stemcup, mark and period of Yongzheng, height $3\frac{3}{8}$in (8.5cm)
New York $220,000 (£111,111). 27.XI.90
From the collection of Ira and Nancy Koger

A *Huanghuali* folding horseshoe-back armchair (*yuanhoubei jiaoyi*), sixteenth–seventeenth century, height 39½in (100.3cm)
New York $176,000 (£89,340). 19.X.90
From the collection of Mrs Rafi Y. Mottahedeh

Opposite
An imperial enamel and gilt-bronze musical automaton clock, Qianlong, height 32in (81cm)
London £220,000 ($451,000). 11.XII.90

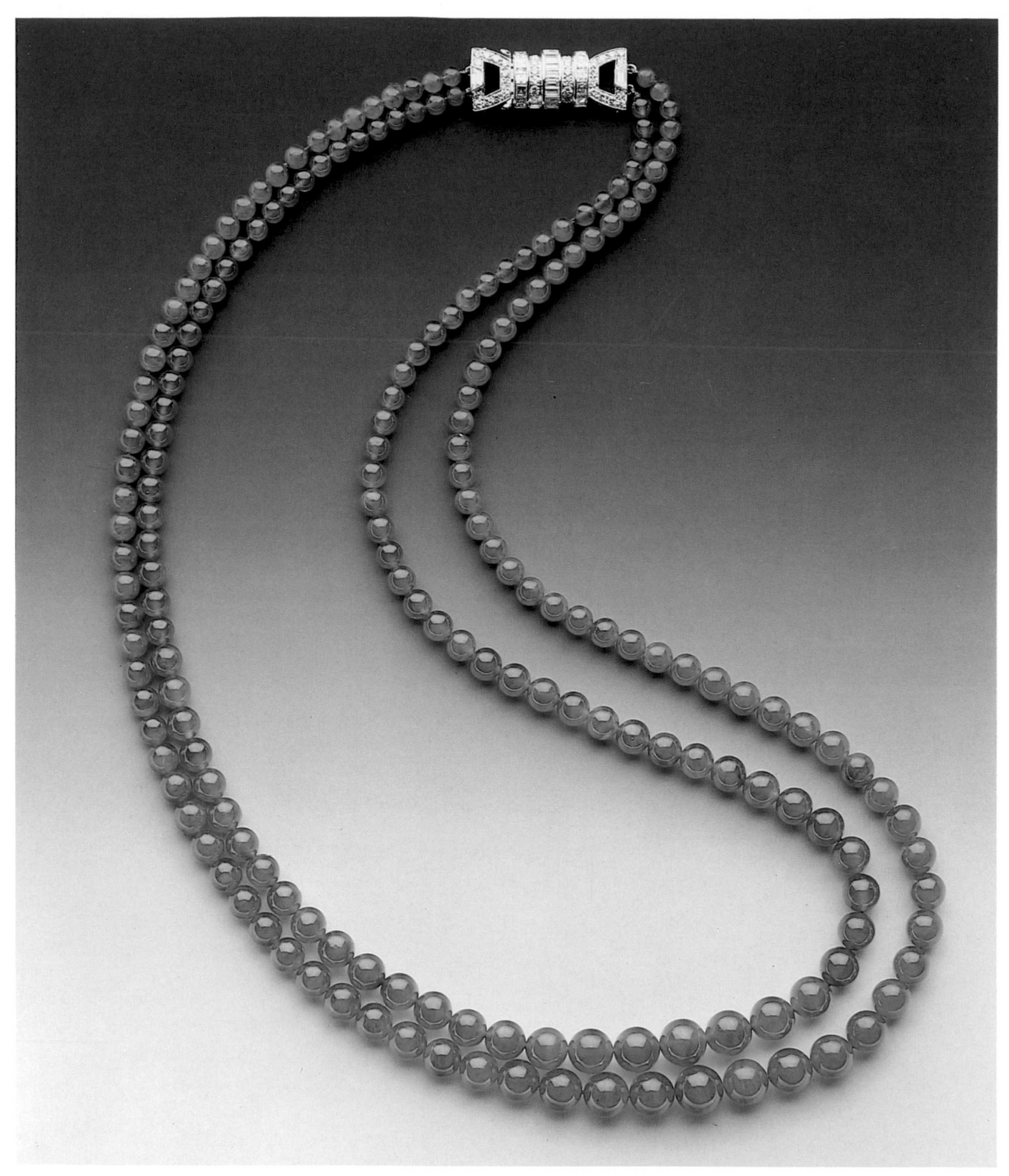

A double-strand jadeite bead necklace
Hong Kong HK$8,360,000 (£630,943:$1,071,795). 1.V.91

Above
Shitao (Yuanji)
ALBUM OF LANDSCAPES
One from an album of ten leaves, ink and colour on paper, each inscribed, with five seals of the artist and with numerous collectors' seals, seventeenth century, $9\frac{3}{8}$in by $14\frac{1}{2}$in (23.8cm by 36.8cm)
New York $308,000 (£178,035). 29.V.91

Right
Zhang Daqian
MIST AT DAWN
Ink and colour on paper, signed and dated fifty-seventh year, *wu shen*, 1968, with three seals of the artist, $39\frac{1}{2}$in by $55\frac{1}{8}$in (100.5cm by 140cm)
Hong Kong HK$2,090,000 (£157,736:$267,949). 2.V.91

Tribal art

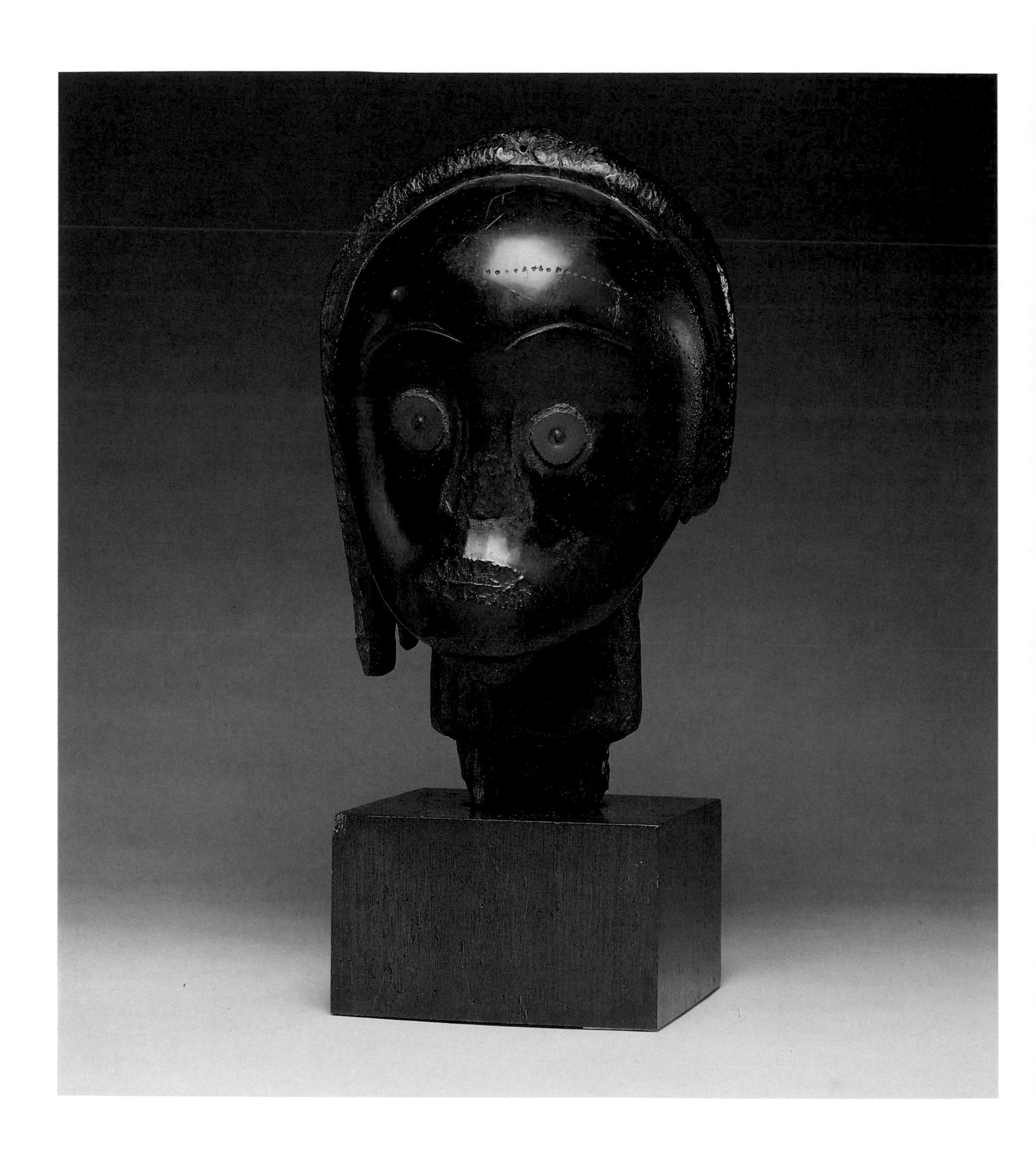

Opposite
A Fang reliquary guardian head (*nlo bieri*), height 15¾in (40cm)
New York $797,500 (£404,822).
20.XI.90

Right
A Senufo female rhythm pounder (*pombibele*), height 35¾in (90.8cm)
New York $1,017,500 (£581,429).
15.V.91

Rhythm pounders from the Senufo tribe in the North Ivory Coast are among the finest and most celebrated works of African art. They are also among the rarest objects in the corpus of African sculpture as less than six of this type and quality are known to exist. They exemplify the essence of African art by blending movement and sculpture, dance and art, fusing in their elegant shapes both time and space. This figure evokes both the intellectual control and spiritual powers of the fully initiated woman, the total self-command and authority of an important matriarch. Despite creating a portrait of someone who has attained her rank in advanced age, the Senufo artist has shunned any sign of physical age and represented only the glory of her youthful beauty. The Senufo themselves call these figures *pombibele* which means 'children of the Poro'. They are used by the men's and women's secret societies in commemorative funeral and initiation rites. They were renamed rhythm pounders in Western literature since it has been reported that young initiates would swing the statue slowly from side to side, striking the ground in a synchronised beat with the drums and horns.

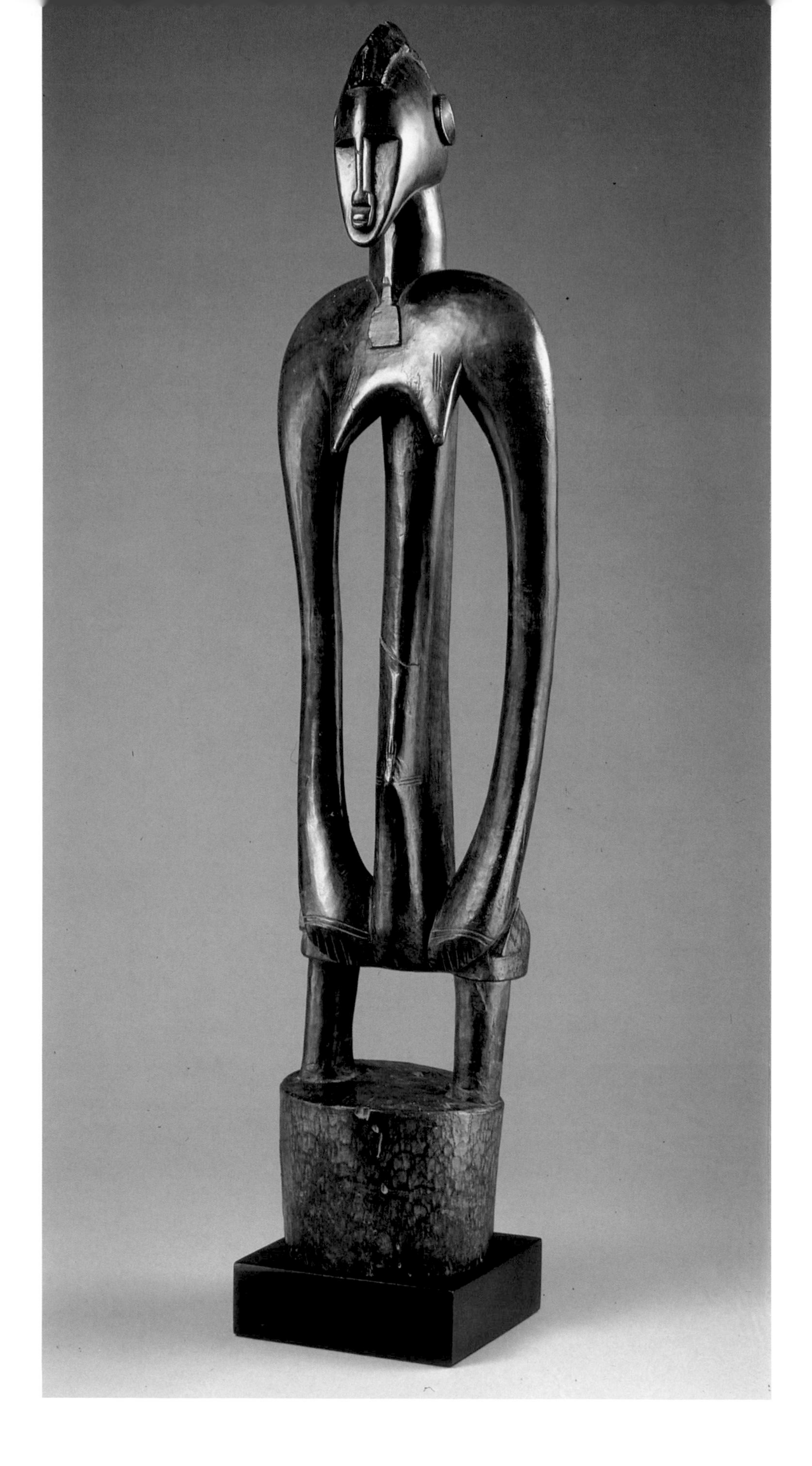

Opposite
A Benin bronze equestrian figure, height 23in (58.4cm)
London £495,000 ($801,900). 17.VI.91

This figure is certainly among the largest and most complex works of art ever cast by Benin artists. There are only twelve known examples of this type of sculpture; the closest example, which has the similar backward tilt of the horse, is in the collection of the Museum of Mankind (No. 1903.7 – 18.1). Horses were kept and used at the Benin court throughout the seventeenth and eighteenth centuries; they would have been stabled inside the palace complex and brought out for ceremonial purposes; it has been reported that the king made his annual public appearance on horseback, surrounded by footmen, cavalry, musicians, dwarfs and leopards. Equestrian bronzes would have been displayed on the ancestral altars of former kings of Benin.

A Cook Islands *tao* wood staff god, Mitiaro Island, 16⅝in (42.2cm)
London £68,200 ($110,484). 17.VI.91
From the collection of the British Rail Pension Fund

A Sioux pictorial beaded and fringed hide vest, length 23in (58.4cm)
New York $39,600 (£21,176). 25.IX.90
From the collection of the New Hampshire Historical Society

A Tlingit iron ornament, height 8in (20.3cm)
New York $50,600 (£29,080). 21.V.91

Opposite
An Olmec serpentine mask, Guerrero region, Middle Preclassic, *circa* 1150–550 BC, height 7½in (19cm)
New York $429,000 (£246,552). 14.V.91

Antiquities

A Roman bronze table, late Roman Republic – early Imperial, *circa* 50 BC – AD 50, width 32in (81.3cm)
New York $176,000 (£109,317). 18.VI.91

Opposite
A Roman cut glass beaker, inscribed *Drink may you live forever, circa* fourth century AD, height 4⅜in (11cm)
London £143,000 ($233,090). 8.VII.91

An Egyptian polychrome limestone relief fragment carved with the head of a king, probably Ptolemy I Soter, early Ptolemaic period, *circa* 305–280 BC, height 12⅜in (31.4cm)
New York $99,000 (£50,254). 28.XI.90

Opposite
An Egyptian bronze figure of a cat, Twenty-second – Twenty-sixth Dynasty, 945–525 BC, height excluding base 7⅛in (18.1cm)
New York $159,500 (£80,964). 28.XI.90
From the collection of the late Sir William van Horne

A Cycladic marble beaker with an anthropomorphic representation, Early Bronze Age I,
circa 3000–2800 BC, height $4\frac{1}{8}$in (10.4cm)
London £68,200 ($118,668). 23.V.91
From the Thétis Collection

Opposite
An Achaemenid limestone relief fragment, carved with the heads of two horses in profile, from a chariot group, Persepolis, first half fifth century BC, height $14\frac{3}{4}$in (37.5cm)
London £319,000 ($653,950). 13.XII.90

The 'Ouseley' relief, originally acquired by Sir Gore Ouseley, Ambassador Extraordinary and Plenipotentiary at the Court of Persia from 1810 to 1815, is now identified as being related to a fragment in the British Museum. Together they joined to form a section of the grand decorative scene glorifying the king which lined the East Wing North stairway leading to the audience hall of the palace at Persepolis, in what is now Iran. Ouseley visited Persepolis in 1811, and afterwards donated some of the many antiquities found there to the British Museum. This relief, however, is one of the artefacts he kept for his own collection, and it was subsequently passed through the family.

Coins

A silver decadrachm of Syracuse by Cimon, *circa* 405 BC, showing the head of Arethusa surrounded by four dolphins
New York $407,000 (£210,881). 4.XII.90

The late fifth-century Sicilian decadrachms of Syracuse are considered to have been struck to mark the defeat of the Carthaginian forces in 405 BC. This example is one of the most perfectly preserved specimens known, with the signature of the artist displayed on the hairband of the water-goddess, sacred to Syracuse.

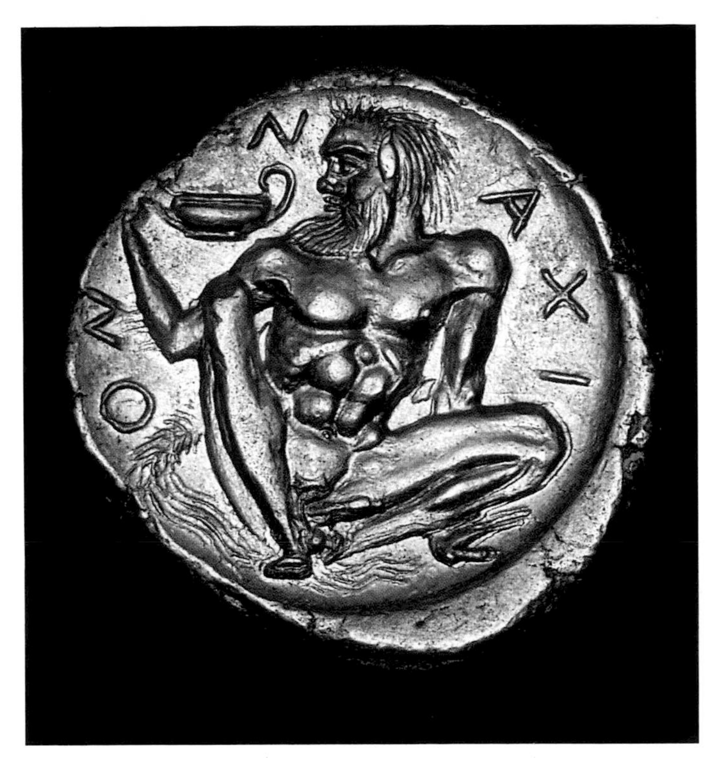

Greek, Tetradrachm of Naxos, *circa* 460 BC
New York $165,000 (£85,492). 4.XII.90
From the Nelson Bunker Hunt Collection

Roman, Aureus of Maxentius (AD 306–312), struck at Ostia
New York $170,500 (£88,500). 4.XII.90
From the Nelson Bunker Hunt Collection

Byzantine, Histamenon of Zoë and Theodora,
(April–June 1042)
New York $99,000 (£51,295). 6.XII.90
From the William Herbert Hunt Collection

Islamic, Mughal rupee of Jahangir dated *AH 1019*
(AD 1610), from the collection of 8,526 Islamic coins
London £165,000 ($295,350). 4.IV.91
From the Nelson Bunker Hunt Collection

European works of art

A North French gilt-bronze seated figure of a young friar, *circa* 1280, height 2⅝in (6.9cm)
London £104,500 ($166,155). 4.VII.91

Opposite
A North German bronze lion aquamanile, early thirteenth century, length 9½in (24cm)
London £93,500 ($148,665). 4.VII.91

Below
A North French gilt-bronze miniature figure of a sleeping youth, *circa* 1220–30, height 1⅜in (3.5cm)
London £209,000 ($332,310). 4.VII.91

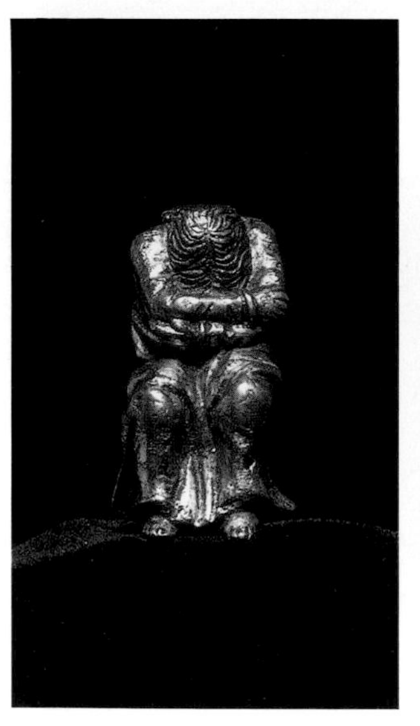

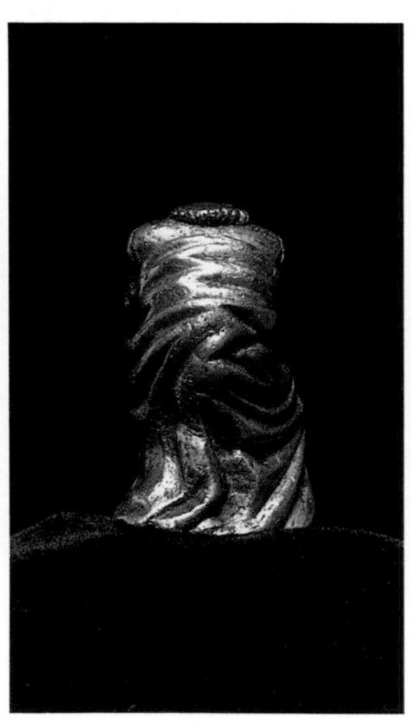

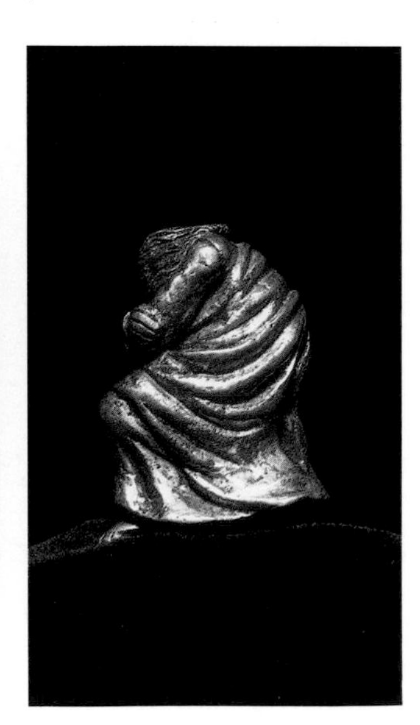

A pair of South Netherlandish or North French painted and gilt limewood groups, depicting kneeling donors, attendant friars and patron Saints Catherine and Augustine, *circa* 1510–20, heights (left) 25½in (65cm) and (right) 23¾in (60.5cm)
London £77,000 ($157,850). 13.XII.90

A bronze figure of Apollo, second half sixteenth century, height 12¾in (32.4cm)
New York $72,600 (£42,706). 1.VI.91

Nineteenth-century sculpture

Charles-Henri-Joseph Cordier
SAID ABDALLAH DE LA TRIBU DU DUFOUR
Bronze, with onyx plinth, signed, 1848, overall height 21in (53.5cm)
London £46,200 ($84,546). 15.III.91

Born in Cambrai, Charles Cordier (1827–1905) was as a boy apprenticed to a jeweller, before studying at the Ecole des Beaux-Arts in Paris and then with the sculptor François Rude. He first exhibited at the Paris salon in 1847 but soon became fascinated by the nobility and elegance of foreign races, travelling extensively in North Africa. His interest and skills combined perfectly with the French national interest in the various racial types since their conquest of Algeria and he was commissioned by Constant Dumenil, the director of the Museum of Natural History in Paris, to sculpt a series of busts for an ethnographic gallery.

A pair of allegorical ivory figures, probably Dieppe, third quarter nineteenth century, heights 31in (78.7cm)
New York $79,750 (£40,689). 21.II.91

Sir Alfred Gilbert
ICARUS
Bronze, *circa* 1884, height 19in (48.5cm)
London £35,200 ($72,864). 23.XI.90

Opposite
Edward Hodges Baily
THE TIRED HUNTER
Marble, signed and dated *1851*, height 73¼in (186cm)
London £88,000 ($182,160). 23.XI.90

This neo-classical marble figure is one of Baily's major works. Born in Bristol, the son of a ship's carver, Baily studied under John Flaxman in London for seven years before joining the gold and silversmith firm of Rundell and Bridge. He worked as chief modeller for the company for twenty-five years, where he received a number of commissions for public works including the reliefs of naval and military subjects for Marble Arch, and for the Throne Room at Buckingham Palace. His best known work is perhaps the figure of Nelson on top of the central column in Trafalgar Square, executed between 1839 and 1843. *The Tired Hunter* was one of four works executed by Baily for Joseph Neeld, the great nephew of Philip Rundell.

Russian works of art, portrait miniatures and vertu

A Cretan icon of Saint John the Evangelist, attributed to Angelos Akontantos, *circa* 1430–50,
17⅜in by 14⅛in (44cm by 36cm)
London £121,000 ($250,470). 30.XI.90

Back row, from left to right, including
A silver-gilt presentation cup and cover, maker's mark of R. & S. Garrard & Co., London, 1909, height 20$\frac{7}{8}$in (53cm), SF9,350 (£3,740:$6,448)
A portrait miniature of King Manuel II of Portugal by Arthur Vieira de Mello, signed and dated *1908*, height 4$\frac{3}{4}$in (12cm), SF3,520 (£1,408:$2,428)

Front row, from left to right, including
A gold, silver and enamel paperknife, length 9$\frac{5}{8}$in (24.5cm), SF10,450 (£4,180:$7,207)
Two diamond-set commemorative rings, late eighteenth century, SF14,300 (£5,720:$9,862)
A gold, enamel and diamond collar chain and breast star of the military Order of the Tower and Sword, by Santos Leite, Lisbon, SF55,000 (£22,000:$37,931)
A jewelled gold and enamel cigar case, *circa* 1887, width 4$\frac{3}{4}$in (12cm), SF11,000 (£4,400:$7,586)
These items from the collection of King Manuel II of Portugal were sold in Geneva on 16 May 1991.

Far left, above
A Swiss jewelled gold and enamel vinaigrette, *circa* 1810, width $1\frac{5}{8}$in (4.2cm)
Geneva SF30,800 (£12,320:$21,241). 16.V.91

Below
A Roman micromosaic panel by Antonio Aguatti, signed, *circa* 1825, width $2\frac{3}{4}$in (7cm)
Geneva SF20,900 (£8,360:$14,414). 16.V.91

Left
Pierre Adolphe Hall
A YOUNG LADY, POSSIBLY THE ARTIST'S DAUGHTER ADELAIDE VICTORINE
Circa 1785, height 3in (7.8cm)
Geneva SF44,000 (£17,886:$35,200). 15.XI.90

Far left
A Fabergé hardstone carving of a baboon, *circa* 1900, height $3\frac{1}{8}$in (8cm)
Geneva SF85,800 (£34,878: $68,640). 15.XI.90

Left
A Fabergé gold and carved chalcedony pelican, *circa* 1900, height $3\frac{1}{8}$in (8cm)
New York $35,200 (£21,463). 19.VI.91

A French pearl-set gold and enamel snuff box by Pierre-François Drais, Paris, 1778, maker's mark, width 3in (7.5cm)
Geneva SF99,000
(£39,600:$68,276).
16.V.91

A Fabergé gold, enamel, purpurine and diamond presentation snuff box, maker's mark of Henrik Wigström, 1908–17, width $3\frac{3}{4}$in (9.4cm)
Geneva SF88,000
(£35,772:$70,400).
15.XI.90

Jewellery

A pear-shaped diamond weighing 101.84 carats
Geneva SF15,950,000 (£6,483,740:$12,760,000). 14.XI.90

A fancy pink diamond weighing 28.67 carats, mounted as a ring
New York $4,620,000 (£2,357,143). 25.X.90

A marquise-shaped diamond weighing 48.28 carats, mounted as a ring
New York $3,850,000 (£1,964,286). 25.X.90

A sapphire and diamond necklace by Cartier, late nineteenth century
New York $2,475,000 (£1,447,368). 23.IV.91
From the estate of Thora Ronalds McElroy

A diamond corsage ornament by Cartier, Paris, 1906
New York $209,000 (£122,222). 23.IV.91
From the estate of Thora Ronalds McElroy

Heiress to the fabulous Scott-Strong fortunes, Thora Ronalds McElroy was born at New York's Plaza Hotel in 1907. Her father, Reginald Ronalds, was one of Teddy Roosevelt's Rough Riders, and her mother, Thora Scott Strong, inherited a fortune in coal, railroads and newspapers from her parents.

From tiaras to spectacular choker-necklaces and bodice ornaments, the McElroy jewels belong to a truly glamorous era. American business tycoons who built financial empires during the late nineteenth and early twentieth centuries considered themselves the royalty of this booming time and looked to the eighteenth century for inspiration. It was not unusual for social events, like masquerades and balls, to recreate the pomp and splendour of the court of Versailles. For their jewels, these tycoons turned to Cartier, who wedded the delicate garland style of the eighteenth century with a virtuosity and exuberance appropriate to the new era. Emulating the opulence of the Belle Epoque, corsage ornaments were worn together with choker-necklaces and tiaras. Cartier produced a number of bodice ornaments for their clients, usually favouring the traditional motifs of flowers, wreaths and bows. The McElroy Collection included a bodice ornament of two elaborate sprays of lilies designed by Cartier (see above). Her collection also featured a spectacular sapphire and diamond necklace (see opposite), once owned by Mary Scott Townsend, which was bequeathed to Thora by her cousin Mathilde Townsend Welles.

A diamond bracelet by Cartier, *circa* 1925
New York $286,000 (£167,251). 23.IV.91
From the estate of Thora Ronalds McElroy

A diamond bow brooch possibly by Bapst, mid nineteenth century
New York $77,000 (£39,896). 4.XII.90

Opposite
An aquamarine, sapphire and diamond necklace by Cartier, *circa* 1935
St Moritz SF275,000 (£110,887:$214,844). 23.II.91

Opposite
A diamond necklace by Van Cleef & Arpels
$1,045,000 (£533,163)
A pair of diamond earclips by Van Cleef & Arpels
$22,000 (£11,224)
These jewels from the estate of Mrs Jack L. Warner were sold in New York on 25 October 1990.

Right
A pair of sapphire and diamond earclips by Boucheron, the sapphires weighing 59.53 and 67.17 carats, *circa* 1935
St Moritz SF825,000 (£332,661:$644,531). 23.II.91

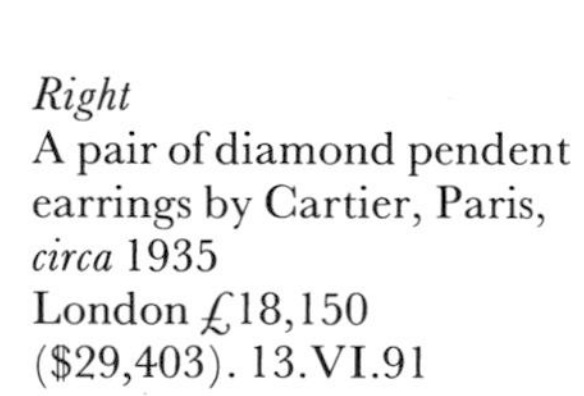

Right
A pair of diamond pendent earrings by Cartier, Paris, *circa* 1935
London £18,150 ($29,403). 13.VI.91

Far right
A sapphire and diamond pendant-brooch by Harry Winston, the sapphire weighing 151.02 carats, *circa* 1960
New York $1,100,000 (£561,224). 25.X.90
From the estate of Libbie Moody Thompson

The dazzling Daisy Fellowes

Daisy Fellowes dressed as Hippolyta for the Beistegui Ball in Venice, 1951, wearing her Cartier necklace (Photograph by Cecil Beaton).

Opposite
A coloured gemstone and diamond necklace and a pair of emerald and diamond pendent earrings by Cartier, 1936
Geneva SF3,850,000 (£1,540,000:$2,655,172). 15.V.90
Formerly in the collection of Daisy Fellowes

In May 1991 a magnificent diamond and coloured gemstone necklace was sold at Sotheby's Geneva for £1.54 million, setting a record for a suite of Art Deco jewellery (see opposite). It was bought by Cartier who had originally created the necklace and will now form part of the Cartier Collection, based in Geneva.

During the 1920s and 1930s Cartier created exceptional jewels set with carved coloured gemstones in which Eastern and Western tastes fused together. This necklace was one of the most outstanding examples of this style, and was made in 1936 for Daisy Fellowes, who brought the gemstones back from India herself.

Daisy Fellowes acquired jewellery for her collection throughout her life, adding some of the very best pieces designed during this period. She was born Daisy Decazes, daughter of the 4th Duc Decazes and granddaughter of the sewing machine industrialist Isaac Merritt Singer. After the death of her first husband the Prince de Broglie in 1918, she married the Hon. Reginald Fellowes. From the 1920s she became one of the leading figures in the social and fashion world, a darling of café society and renowned for the studied simplicity of her dress.

She became fashion editor-in-chief for *Harpers Bazaar* and was hailed by *Vogue* as the best dressed woman in the world. In around 1933 she purchased from Cartier the famous light pink diamond of 17.47 carats known as the *Tête de Bélier* (ram's head) which reputedly was given by Catherine the Great to her favourite, Potemkine. To complement the stone the famous designer Elsa Schiaparelli created the new 'shocking pink' colour. The diamond was unfortunately stolen in 1939, since when there has been no record of it.

In the late 1940s Daisy Fellowes commissioned a panther brooch in sapphires and diamonds, the first creation of Jeanne Toussaint, modelled on the emblem of the Order of the Golden Fleece, and in 1960 she purchased one of the first hardstone 'Chimera' bracelets also created by Jeanne Toussaint. Both pieces became favoured motifs of the House of Cartier.

Besides jewels, Daisy Fellowes collected works of art: English silver, extravagant chandeliers, *genre* paintings by Boldini, and curiosities such as ostrich eggs mounted by the eighteenth-century English goldsmith, James Cox. These were displayed in her magnificent house in rue de Lille, Paris which was decorated by Georges Geffroy, a prominent French interior designer, and where she lived from 1945 until her death in 1962.

Works of art from Daisy Fellowes' collection have rarely been seen at auction and never before had such a superb piece of her jewellery been offered for sale – a piece that is surely one of Cartier's most spectacular creations of the 1930s.

An emerald and diamond cluster ring by Van Cleef & Arpels, New York, 1961
London £209,000 ($428,450). 10.XII.90
From the collection of the late Ava Gardner

A ruby and diamond cluster ring
St Moritz SF2,035,000 (£820,565:$1,589,844). 23.II.91

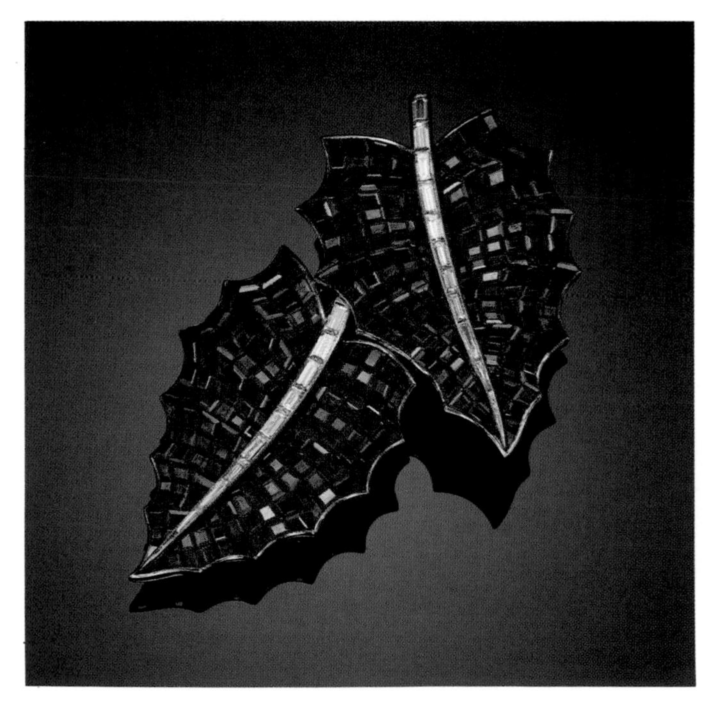

An invisibly-set ruby and diamond leaf brooch by Van Cleef & Arpels, New York
New York $159,500 (£97,256). 12.VI.91

A ruby and diamond double-clip brooch, *circa* 1940
London £13,200 ($27,060). 10.XII.90
From the collection of the late Mrs Dorothea Allen

An emerald and diamond pendant-brooch, *circa* 1820
£41,800 ($85,690)
An emerald and diamond necklace, *circa* 1830
£198,000 ($405,900)
These jewels from the collection of Viscount Windsor's Children's Settlement Trust were sold in London on 10 December 1990.

An aquamarine and amethyst orchid brooch by Cartier, *circa* 1940
St Moritz SF132,000 (£53,226:$103,125). 23.II.91

Opposite
An emerald and diamond necklace by Bulgari, *circa* 1960
Geneva SF440,000 (£178,862:$352,000). 14.XI.90

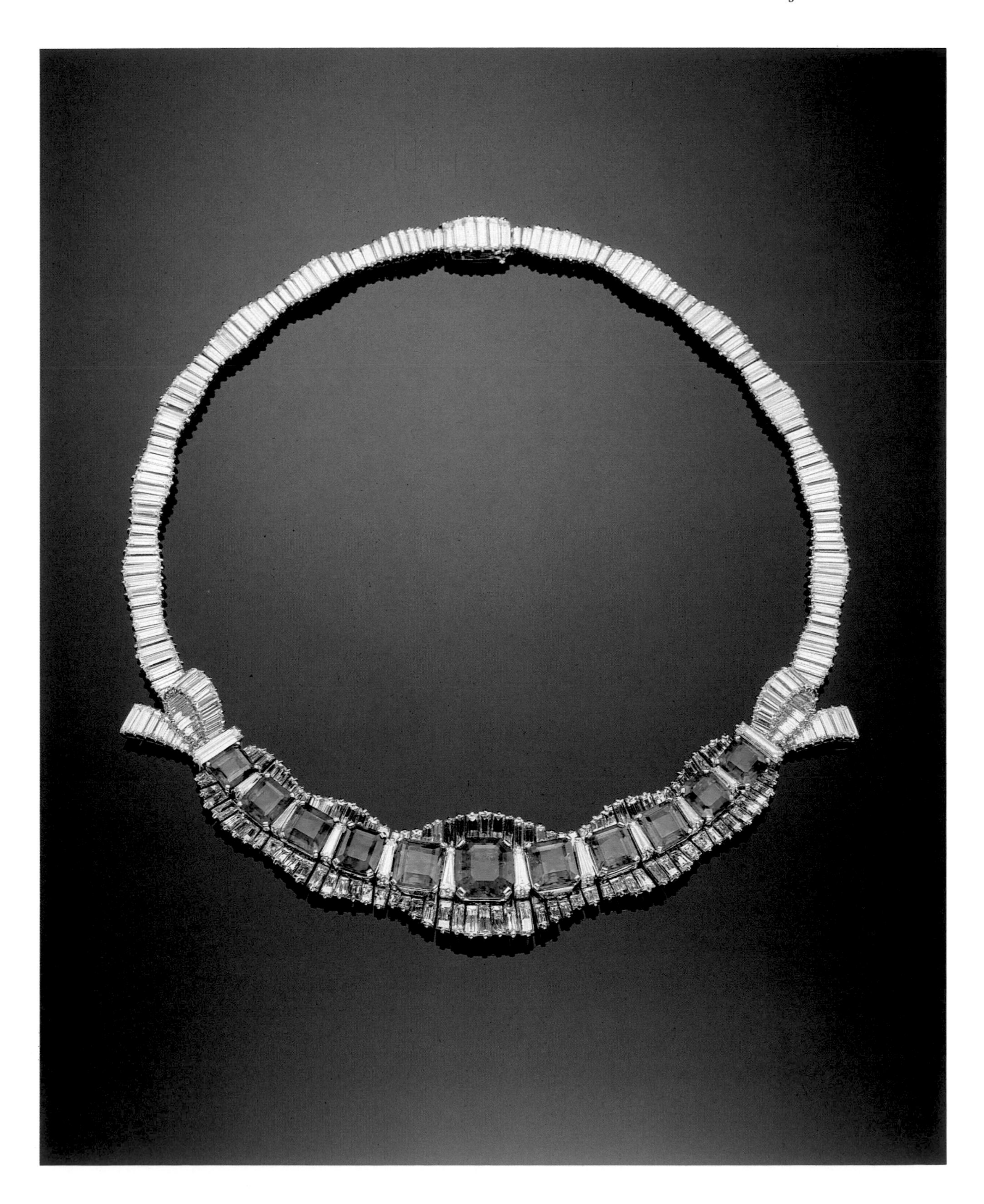

A gold and enamel bracelet by Bapst et Falize, 1890
London £17,600 ($28,512). 13.VI.91

A coloured stone and diamond articulated banner brooch commemorating victory in the Great War, by Cartier, 1919
Geneva SF165,000 (£66,000: $113,793). 15.V.91

From top to bottom
A yellow diamond and onyx bracelet by Cartier, Paris, 1962
SF253,000 (£101,200:$174,483)
A yellow diamond and onyx brooch by Cartier, Paris, 1957
SF418,000 (£167,200:$288,276)
A pair of yellow diamond and onyx pendent earrings by Cartier, Paris, 1961
SF550,000 (£220,000:$379,310)
These jewels from the collection of Barbara Hutton were sold in Geneva on 15 May 1991.

Silver

A French silver-gilt revolving inkstand, maker's mark of Martin-Guillaume Biennais, Paris, 1809–19, height 10¼in (26cm)
Geneva SF495,000 (£197,211:$339,041).
13.V.91

Opposite
A German parcel-gilt table fountain, maker's mark of Melchior Gelb I, Augsburg, *circa* 1625–30, height 25⅛in (64cm)
Geneva SF968,000 (£393,496:$774,400).
12.XI.90

A George II soup tureen and cover, maker's mark of George Wickes, London, 1735, length over handles 16½in (42cm)
New York $181,500 (£92,132). 12.X.90

The arms boldly emblazoned across the body of this tureen and the crest on the lid are those of Lord North (1704–90) to whom George Wickes delivered '2 Fine Terreens' in April 1736.

Opposite
A caster, maker's mark of Philippe-Jacques Langlois, Paris, 1710, height 9¼in (23.5cm)
Monte Carlo FF721,500 (£72,879:$141,471). 9.XII.90

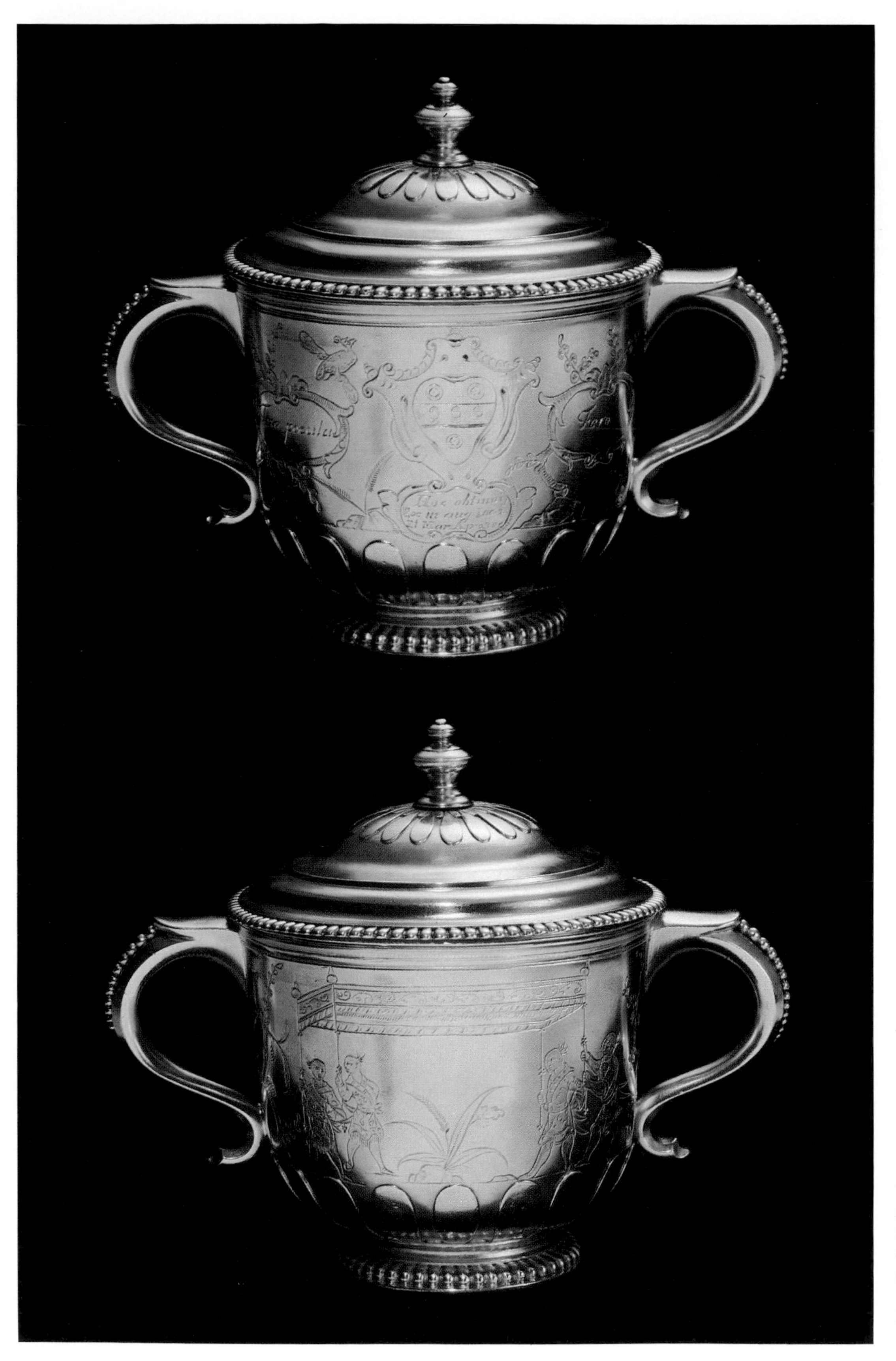

Two views of a James II silver-gilt chinoiserie cup and cover commemorating the Coronation of James II, *circa* 1685, height 5¼in (13.3cm)
New York $126,500 (£73,547). 19.IV.91

A George II silver-gilt salver, maker's mark of Lewis Pantin, London, *circa* 1735, diameter $17\frac{1}{2}$in (44.2cm)
London £82,500 ($157,575). 28.II.91

The arms are those of Frederick Lewis, Prince of Wales, eldest son of George II who appointed George Wickes as his goldsmith in the early 1730s. The salver does not bear Wickes' maker's mark but he is known to have bought items in from other silversmiths such as Lewis Pantin, the grandson of one of the first Huguenot silversmiths to take refuge in London in the late seventeenth century.

A Victorian parcel-gilt 'Gothic' ewer set with enamel and jewels, maker's mark of John Hardman & Co., Birmingham, 1855, height 14$\frac{3}{4}$in (37.5cm)
New York $66,000 (£38,372). 19.IV.91

Opposite
A set of four silver-gilt salt cellars, maker's mark of Paul Storr for Rundell, Bridge & Rundell, London, 1811–13, lengths 4$\frac{3}{4}$in (11.8cm)
London £66,000 ($126,060). 28.II.91

Lucien Falize's neo-Gothic clock

Above
On the opposite face to the main dial, three smaller cloisonné dials show the names of the days of the week (with the maker's mark of ring and pearl), the names of the months (with flowers representing the four seasons), and the thirty-one days of the month (with a winged sandglass).

'The architecture of the clock corresponds approximately to the year 1512', wrote Falize. 'It is inspired by those buildings erected by French masters under the reign of Louis XII . . . in architecture, the flowery gothic style still dominated.' Lucien Falize, the second generation of a Parisian family specialising in gold cloisonné jewellery, turned to the decorative arts of the fourteenth to sixteenth centuries for inspiration. His fascination with the period is especially evident in this clock, dating from 1881. Charles Blanc, who examined the clock while it was still incomplete, wrote in his *Grammaire des Arts Décoratifs* (1882) that Falize endeavoured to rediscover the engraving and enamelling techniques of the sixteenth century, and felt that he had not achieved this goal until the creation of this clock.

Falize designed the clock for Alfred Morrison, his greatest English patron. A well-known English collector and connoisseur, Alfred was the second son of James Morrison, himself a great collector, who had purchased Constable's *The Lock* in 1824 (see article on pages 48–55). Morrison *fils* was an eclectic collector, who filled his houses at Fonthill and 16 Carlton House Terrace with paintings, engravings, furniture, Chinese porcelain, Roman glass, textiles, autographs and letters. The *Dictionary of National Biography* (1901) wrote of him '[he] specially interested himself to seek out artistic craftsmen in all countries and employed them for years in the slow and careful production of masterpieces . . . In this manner he became the possessor, and in a way, the originator, of many remarkable specimens, which he was proud to believe equalled anything produced during the most famous periods of artistic excellence.'

Lucien Falize spoke fondly of his patron and the partnership they formed in the creation of a number of designs, including a vase exhibited at the Exposition Universelle of 1889. 'As for the Sassanian Vase, it belongs to Mr Alfred Morrison . . . I take great pleasure in acknowledging the debt owed to his impeccable taste and special trust he placed in me . . . allowing me to undertake and complete a work of art for which I am truly proud'.

After the death of Alfred Morrison in 1897, the clock remained in the family until 1938 when it was sold by his grandson, John Granville Morrison. It next appeared in 1955 at Parke-Bernet Galleries in New York and was sold for $5,000. Today the clock is housed in the Metropolitan Museum of Art in New York.

Opposite
A French silver, gold and hardstone neo-Gothic clock set with enamels, designed by Lucien Falize, the modelling by M. L. Chedeville, goldsmithery and enamelling by Bapst & Falize, the movement by Le Roy et Fils, signed, Paris, 1881, height 17¾in (45cm)
New York $330,000 (£191,860). 19.IV.91

Clocks and watches

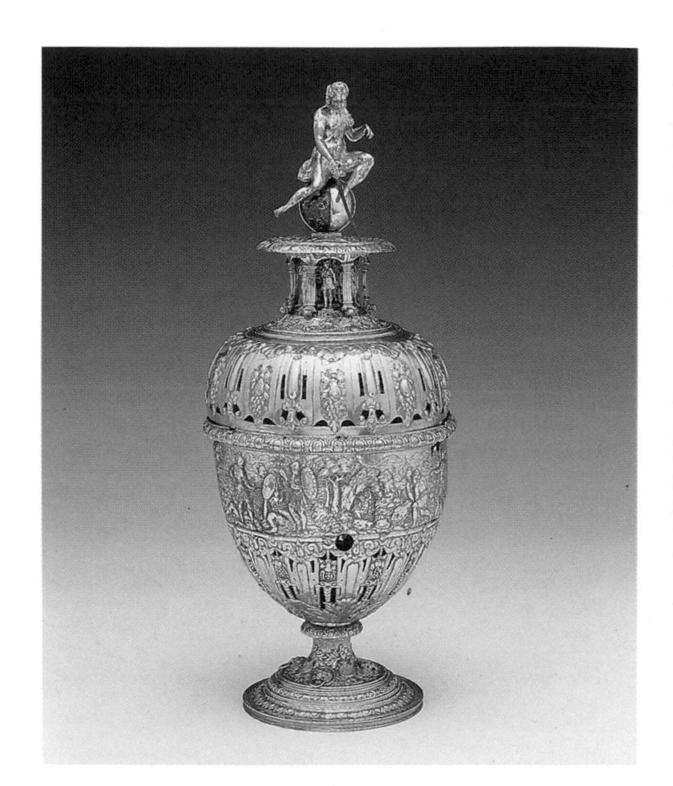

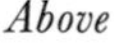

Above
A George III ormolu and enamel quarter striking musical automaton centrepiece table clock, commemorating the Treaty acknowledging the Independence of the United States in 1783, signed by the enamellist W.H. Craft, attributed to James Cox, 1796, height 40in (101.5cm)
London £330,000 ($656,700). 4.X.90

Above, right
A silver and silver-gilt musical clock, late sixteenth century, overall height 13⅜in (34cm)
London £385,000 ($766,150). 4.X.90

Right
A gold, silver-gilt, lapis lazuli and enamel exhibition clock by Gustave Baugrand, signed and dated *Paris 1867*, *circa* 1868, height 10¼in (26cm)
London £66,000 ($126,060). 28.II.91

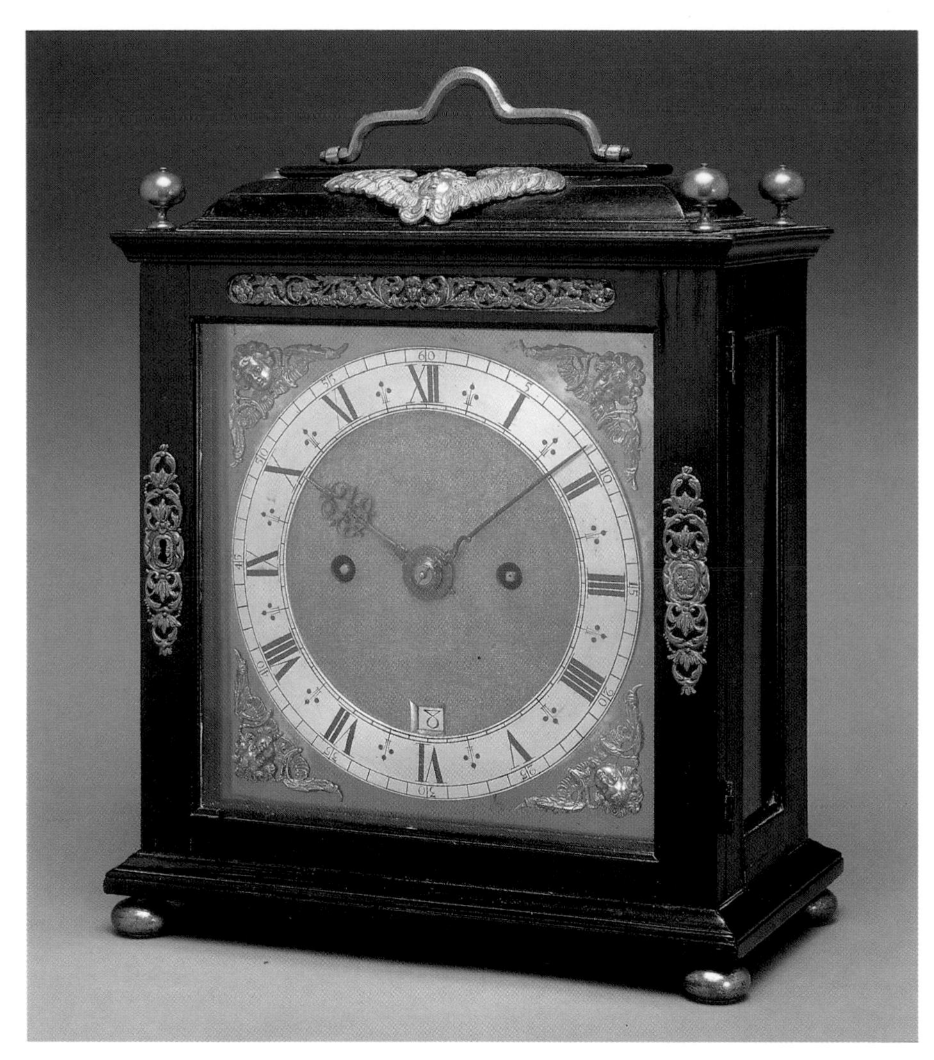

Above
A George III small mahogany long-duration perpetual calendar, astronomical and musical longcase clock by James Cole, signed, *circa* 1790, height 6ft 7¼in (201cm)
London £38,500 ($73,535). 28.II.91

Above, right
A Charles II ebony veneered bracket clock by Joseph Knibb, signed, *circa* 1670, height 13¾in (35cm)
London £38,500 ($76,615). 4.X.90

Right
A South German striking alarm table clock, sixteenth century, diameter 6¼in (16cm)
Zurich SF132,000 (£53,659:$105,600). 21.XI.90

Above, from left to right
A gold and enamel quarter repeating reversible pair case watch for the Turkish market by Breguet, No. 2955, *circa* 1816, diameter 2in (5.2cm)
Geneva SF82,500 (£33,537: $66,000). 13.XI.90

An enamel, gilt-metal and oxidised steel verge watch by Paul Bizot, *circa* 1665, 1⅜in (3.4cm)
Geneva SF154,000 (£61,600:$106,207). 14.V.91

A gold openface triple detent one minute tourbillon with constant force by Louis Richard, Locle, No.12, *circa* 1860, diameter 2⅛in (5.6cm)
New York $253,000 (£129,744). 30.X.90

A gold openface carillon minute repeating single button split second chronograph with perpetual calendar, moon phases, ages of the moon, double register and central alarm by Patek Philippe & Co., *circa* 1920, diameter 2½in (6.3cm)
New York $660,000 (£338,461). 30.X.90

Left
A rock crystal, obsidian and mother-of-pearl mystery timepiece by Cartier, No. 2929, *circa* 1925, height 5in (13cm)
London £99,000 ($197,010). 4.X.90

Top row, left to right
An eighteen carat gold 'Eclipse' wristwatch by Cartier, 1930, overall length $1\frac{3}{8}$in (3.5cm)
London £10,450 ($21,214)
18.XII.90

A white gold jump hour wristwatch by Breguet, *circa* 1930, width 1in (2.7cm)
New York $209,000 (£105,025). 8.II.91

A platinum and diamond wristwatch by Patek Philippe & Co., *circa* 1950, length $1\frac{5}{8}$in (4.3cm)
Geneva SF93,500 (£37,400: $64,483). 14.V.91

A platinum backwind 'Helm' bracelet watch by Cartier, inscribed *European Watch and Clock Co.*, *circa* 1940, diameter 1in (2.6cm)
New York $99,000 (£60,366). 21.VI.91

Bottom row, left to right
An eighteen carat gold moonphase calendar Oyster perpetual by Rolex, *circa* 1950, diameter $1\frac{1}{4}$in (3.3cm)
London £18,700 ($35,717). 28.II.91

A platinum and diamond minute repeating wristwatch by Vacheron & Constantin, *circa* 1955, diameter $1\frac{3}{8}$in (3.6cm)
New York $330,000 (£165,829). 8.II.91

A gold perpetual calendar wristwatch with moon phases by Patek Philippe & Co., *circa* 1961, diameter $1\frac{1}{2}$in (3.7cm)
Geneva SF231,000 (£93,902: $184,800). 13.XI.90

AMEN

The Spottiswoode Amen glass

R. J. Charleston

The 'Amen' glasses, some forty of which have now been identified, form a loosely-knit family with strong resemblances and occasional divergences.

For the most part they consist of plain drawn-stem trumpet-bowled glasses of medium size; but there are also drawn-stem glasses with air-twists (like the Spottiswoode), three-piece glasses with round-funnel bowls and air-twist or 'incised' twist stems, and a single example of a pedestal stem. If the shape varies, the formula of the decoration, however, is almost constant.

Engraved with a hardstone (probably diamond) point, this example consists of a crowned mirror-monogram comprising the letters 'JR' intertwined with the figure '8', (for 'Jacobus Rex VIII'–i.e. King James VIII of Scotland and III of England). Below this is the word 'Amen', the exact equivalent of the 'Fiat' of another well-known category of Jacobite glasses, both words signifying the consummation of a solemn pledge. The word 'Amen' is enclosed in a continuous scrolled border of intertwining loops, where the point has hardly been lifted from the glass, and similar but more elaborate borders run below the rim or delimit panels elsewhere on the bowl. The rest of the decoration consists of a written text: 'God Save the King I pray/God Blifs the King I pray/God Save the King:/Send Him Victorious/Happy and Glorious/Soon to Reign Over Us/God Save the King' – an unambiguous Jacobite variant of the National Anthem, which substitutes 'Soon' for 'Long' in the sixth line. 'Bliss' is a Scottish variant of 'bless': quite acceptable at this period. The second verse continues: 'God Blifs the Prince of Wales/The True-born Prince of Wales/Sent Us by Thee;/Grant us one favour more/The King for to Restore/As Thou hast done before/The Familie'.

The Spottiswoode Amen glass, engraved in hardstone-point with a crown surmounting the cypher *JR*, intertwined with the figure *8* above *AMEN* and inscribed with two verses of the Jacobite anthem, height 8¼in (20.8cm)
London £66,000 ($115,500). 25.III.91

The glass has descended through the family of Spottiswoode, of Spottiswoode in Berwickshire.

On some glasses the anthem is extended to four verses ('God Save the Church I pray . . .' and 'God bless the subjects all . . .') but this is far less common than the two-verse formula. The 'true-born Prince of Wales' was of course Prince Charles Edward, the 'Bonnie Prince Charlie' of Scottish song and legend, but the form of words probably harks back to the time of his father, the legitimacy of whose birth was impugned by the Whig party, with the allegation that he had been smuggled into the Palace in a warming pan.

A number of additional inscriptions are found on other individual glasses, such as 'Donald MacLeod of Gualtergil in the Isle of Skye. The Faithful Palinurus. Aet.69 anno 1747', commemorating the man who had piloted the boat which brought Prince Charles Edward from Borrodale through the Western Isles after the Battle of Culloden (1746), with the learned allusion to Palinurus, Aeneas's faithful pilot in Virgil's *Aeneid*. The Spottiswoode glass bears the more usual inscription: 'His Royal

Highnefs/Prince Henry/Duke of/Albany/and/York' – a reference to James's second son Henry, who became a Cardinal of the Roman Church in 1747, and is considered by some thereby to have excluded himself from the succession.

Such subsidiary inscriptions show by their wording that they were intended as toasts. A glass from Traquair House, seat of the Maxwell-Stuart family, is inscribed 'Prosperity to the family of Traquair'; it also contains a spirited variant of the second verse of the anthem, 'Send him soon over/And kick out hannover/And then we'll recover/Our old Libertie'.

A glass in the Royal Scottish Museum in Edinburgh makes it unequivocally clear that the formula on the Traquair glass implies a toast. It is inscribed 'A Bumper' and 'To the Prosperity of the Family of Lochiell'; (Cameron of Lochiel was the first important clan chief to rally to Prince Charles Edward's banner in July 1745). These toasts define the proper place of the Amen glasses within the Scottish society with which they have almost universally been associated, and in whose houses they have usually been preserved.

To understand this role, one has to turn back to the Scottish customs of the eighteenth century. Thomas Somerville wrote in his *My Life and Times, 1741 – 1814* (1861): 'To serve for the family, there was in many a household only one glass or tankard, which was handed on to the next person in succession as each finished his draft ...', and the *Statistical Account of Scotland* records that in Banff in 1748 a company might drink twelve bottles from one glass whereas in 1708 the ratio would have been reversed. This was clearly regarded as evidence of the degeneracy of the times. H.G. Graham in his *Social Life in Scotland in the 18th century* (1899) records that:

> When the table was cleared of viands, and the glasses once more were set on the shining mahogany, each person proposed the health of every other person present severally and thus if there were ten guests there were ninety healths drunk, with serious consequence to the health of all. There were also rounds of toasts, each gentleman naming an absent lady, each lady an absent gentleman. Next followed 'sentiments', as another excuse for further imbibing. Each person was called on in turn to propose a wish, called a 'sentiment' – it might be some crisp sentence, a poetic phrase, a jovial proverb, or, as generally a fatuous moral reflection . . .

It is evident that no opportunity was missed of drinking a toast, and some glasses survive which record in diamond-point the numerous toasts for which they commonly served. In this context the Amen glasses fit as relatively sober records of the 'Loyal' toasts current in the Scotland of their day. That so many have survived is testimony to the universal currency of such toasts and to the reverent regard in which they were held.

It seems likely that all these glasses were decorated by a single artist, whose sureness of touch developed as time went on. Up to the middle of the nineteenth century throughout Europe, remote areas were visited by packmen who specialised in supplying glass wares, and some of these men were qualified to engrave borders, commemorative inscriptions and so forth to their customers' requirements on the spot. Some even travelled with portable wheel-engraving equipment, but a diamond-point was a far handier tool. It may be that the engraver of the Amen glasses was such a travelling salesman, but it seems evident that whoever he was, his artistic training was in the field of calligraphy rather than in the decorative arts.

A St Louis magnum upright bouquet paperweight, diameter 4⅛in (10.5cm)
New York $77,000 (£39,691). 10.XII.90

Ceramics

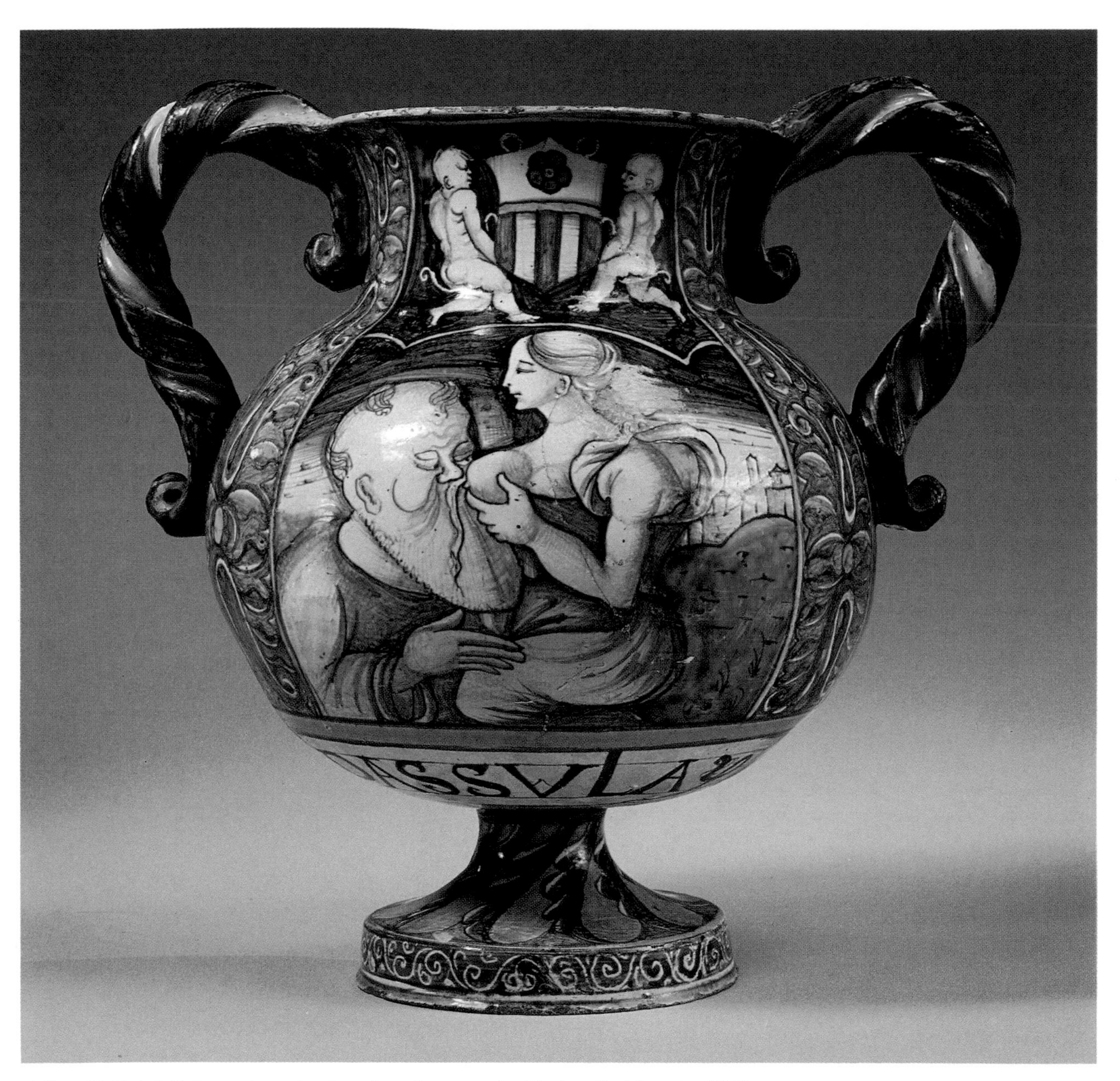

A Castelli Orsini-Colonna type tin-glazed earthenware double-handled jar, *circa* 1520,
height 12¼in (31cm)
New York $85,250 (£44,634). 12.I.91

This jar belongs to a group of apothecary vessels termed Orsini-Colonna pharmacy vases based on a large double-handled bottle painted with a bear, representing the Orsini family, embracing a column, representing the Colonna family, which may relate to the reconciliation of the two families in 1511 or 1517.

Right
A Sèvres green-ground tureen, cover and stand, painted by Jacques-François Micaud, *circa* 1760, width of stand 19⅞in (50.5cm)
London £22,000 ($35,860). 16.VII.91

Below
A creamware botanical dessert service, painted possibly by Thomas Pardoe or William Weston Young, early nineteenth century, diameter of dessert plates 8¼in (21cm)
London £11,550 ($23,562). 16.X.90

A Meissen group of Columbine and Pantaloon, modelled by Johann Joachim Kaendler, 1736–38, height 6⅜in (16.2cm)
New York $24,200 (£12,284). 9.X.90

A Chantilly potpourri figure of a Chinese lady mounted in Louis XV ormolu, 1735–49, length 12⅛in (30.8cm)
New York $29,700 (£15,076). 9.X.90

A pair of Flight, Barr and Barr cobalt blue-ground fruit coolers, covers and liners, painted possibly by Thomas Baxter, 1815–20, heights 11in (28.1cm)
New York $23,100 (£13,200). 18.IV.91

Opposite
A Meissen part tea and coffee service, *circa* 1735, the teapot height 4½in (11.4cm)
London £33,000 ($64,350). 19.II.91

Furniture

Above, left
One of a pair of George III inlaid mahogany pedestals with urns, attributed to Gillows of Lancaster, late eighteenth–early nineteenth century, overall heights 74in (188cm)
New York $35,750 (£20,429). 20.IV.91

Right
A Charles II tortoiseshell-mounted, silk-embroidered stump-work dressing mirror, *circa* 1665, height 30in (76cm)
New York $49,500 (£25,127). 13.X.90

Opposite
One of a pair of Queen Anne carved and inlaid walnut chairs, *circa* 1705
London £39,600 ($62,568). 5.VII.91

An identical pair of chairs, also formerly in the library of Arley Castle, Staffordshire, sold in London on 16 November 1990 for £29,700 ($61,182).

Opposite
An Anglo-Dutch walnut bureau cabinet, *circa* 1700, height 7ft 4in (223cm) London £71,500 ($138,710). 22.II.91

Right
One of a pair of George III painted and parcel-gilt armchairs, *circa* 1755 New York $286,000 (£146,666). 26.I.91 From the estate of Henry Ford II

Far right
One of a pair of Regency painted and parcel-gilt page's stools, *circa* 1810, heights 18in (46cm) London £44,000 ($85,360). 22.II.91 From the collection of His Grace the Duke of Wellington

A George II marble-topped carved pine side table, *circa* 1730, length 6ft 7½in (202cm) London £68,200 ($132,308). 22.II.91

A German Rococo ormolu and gilt-brass mounted walnut, fruitwood parquetry and parcel-gilt writing cabinet attributed to Peter Schuß, Mainz, *circa* 1763,
height 8ft 4¾in (256cm)
New York $1,017,000 (£518,878). 27.X.90

Opposite
A Venetian painted and *lacca povera* bureau cabinet, *circa* 1730, height 7ft 9in (236cm)
London £159,500 ($330,165). 30.XI.90
From the collection of the late Eva, Countess of Rosebery

A Louis XV ormolu-mounted lacquer commode by Jacques Dubois, signed, the mounts inscribed with the crowned *C*, mid eighteenth century, height 34in (86.5cm)
New York $275,000 (£140,306). 27.X.90

Opposite
One of a pair of Neapolitan ebony and tortoiseshell cabinets-on-stands, mounted with painted panels under glass, late seventeenth century, widths 8ft 2in (249cm)
London £286,000 ($592,020). 30.XI.90

Far left
One of six armchairs from a suite of Louis XV/XVI transitional seat furniture by Nicolas Heurtaut, further comprising a sofa, *circa* 1768
Monte Carlo FF14,430,000 (£1,450,251: $2,346,341).
22.VI.91

Left
One of six armchairs from a suite of Louis XVI seat furniture, further comprising two chairs, all pieces bearing the mark of Garde-Meuble de la Reine, by Georges Jacob
Monte Carlo FF1,665,000 (£168,182: $326,471).
8.XII.90

Left
A Louis XVI mahogany commode by Jean-Henri Riesener, bearing the mark of the Journal du Garde-Meuble, 1784, length 4ft 6⅜in (138cm)
Monte Carlo FF9,213,000 (£925,930: $1,498,049).
22.VI.91

This commode was made for the bedroom of Marie-Antoinette in her private apartments at Versailles.

An English needlepoint carpet with the arms of Queen Victoria, mid nineteenth century, approximately 13ft 10in by 11ft 9in (421cm by 358cm)
New York $148,500 (£83,898). 10.IV.91

A Beauvais tapestry depicting *L'Audience du Prince d'après l'Histoire du Roi de Chine*, *circa* 1725, approximately 11ft 6in by 16ft 5in (350cm by 500cm)
Monte Carlo FF1,887,000 (£189,648:$306,829). 22.VI.91

A Franco-Flemish mille-fleur tapestry, *circa* 1520, approximately 9ft 2in by 9ft (280cm by 275cm)
New York $209,000 (£122,941). 1.VI.91
From the estate of Mrs Lucy Goldschmidt Moses

A château in Burgundy

Ronald Varney

Opposite, above
Fig. 1
Château de Menou (1672), West Front.

Below
Fig. 2
Château de Menou, West Front, with moat and South Pavilion.

Above
Fig. 3
Postcard photograph of the Château de Menou, early 1900s.

On a recent summer evening in Burgundy, the imposing seventeenth-century château which straddles the tiny village of Menou behind a sombre stone wall was abuzz with activity in anticipation of house guests arriving from Paris. When the guests finally passed through the front gate around midnight, after a zig-zagging journey through medieval towns shuttered for the night and along narrow country roads, the château had about it a magical aura. It was wreathed in a light mist, smoke rose from its chimneys and candles flickered in the big front windows. It was like a scene out of Proust.

As recently as 1987, however, the Château de Menou (Figs 1, 2 and 3) presented an altogether different picture to visitors. Owned since the reign of Louis XIV by the same family, the château had been occupied during the Second World War and all but abandoned thereafter. Since the family already owned the beautiful and famous Château d'Usse in the Loire Valley, they had little inclination to restore Menou as a residence. The house was put on the market.

In 1987 Jacques Garcia, the renowned French interior designer, received a photocopied picture of the château in the mail. He and a friend had been looking at châteaux for some time, hoping to find one they could divide evenly into two separate but unified living quarters. They had agreed that Jacques would have complete freedom to supervise restoration of the house and grounds to his own taste. At the time Mr Garcia was in the middle of an extensive redecoration of his house in the Marais area of Paris. Jules-Hardouin Mansart (1646–1708), principal architect to Louis XIV, had built the house for himself, and Mr Garcia recreated and

Fig. 4
Louis XIV Salon, Château de Menou, looking through the Entrance Hall towards the Salon Restauration.

furnished the rooms there in splendid period style. That project completed, he turned his attention to visiting Menou. As he recalls:

The light was just right when we arrived and began looking about the front of the house, and we became excited. But then there was the shock of seeing the inside of the house, which was completely devastated. We began having second thoughts. Suddenly, however, the shutters along the back of the house were thrown open, revealing the most beautiful landscape. I have seen many châteaux in France and I can't think of one that has such a magnificent spread of fields and woods as the one at Menou. That did it.

In approaching the Olympian task of bringing the château back to life Mr Garcia was faced with several considerations. What appealed to him most about the house was that it was a beautiful empty shell, one that had to be recreated rather than simply restored. Except for the so-called King's Bedroom on the second floor (Fig. 10), there was virtually nothing left of what might have been the original decor. While Mr Garcia is the acknowledged master of Louis XIV period rooms, he had something altogether different in mind for the château. This was one reason why he took the major step of dispersing the collection in his Paris apartment at Sotheby's and devoting all his energies to Menou. He would design the house around the history of the family who had inhabited it since its construction in 1672,

Right
Fig. 5
Louis XIV Salon, Château de Menou, with Menou family portraits.

Far right
Fig. 6
Louis XIV Salon, Château de Menou, with an eighteenth-century bureau plat, and Menou family portraits.

making it look as though the succeeding generations of the family had, over a period of 300 years, imposed their own tastes and styles on the various rooms.

This particular family had enjoyed a distinguished, if undramatic, history. The first inhabitants of the house were Armand-François de Menou, the Marquis de Charnisay, and his wife Françoise de Clere. Menou served as a captain in the army of Louis XIV and distinguished himself at the Battle of Lens in 1648. For his service to the crown he was made Marquis de Menou in 1697, which allowed the family to change the name of the village adjoining the château, previously called Nanvignes. When Armand's son François-Charles inherited the title and lands, they comprised 2,500 acres. In 1734 François-Charles's daughter and heir, Marie-Louise, married the Count Louis-Alexandre de Damas Cruz. She was widowed in 1763, and, left alone in the château throughout the violent upheavals of the French Revolution, died there in 1796, the last Dame de Menou. In 1814 her granddaughter, Henriette de Montsoreau, married the 1st Duke of Blacas, bringing the château in her dowry. The house remained in the Blacas family until 1987, when it was sold to Mr Garcia and his partner.

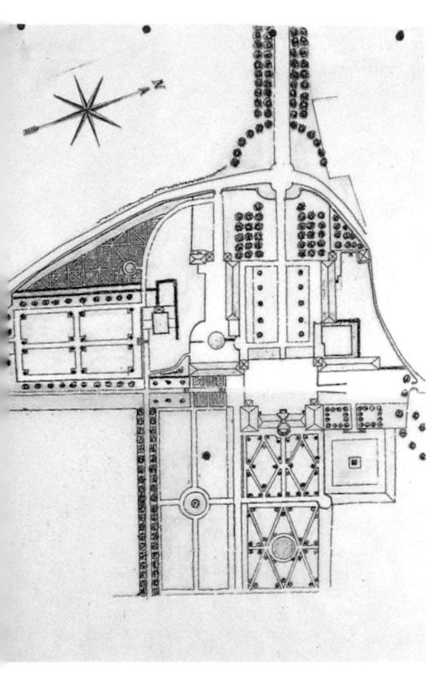

Fig. 7
Plan of the gardens, outbuildings and Château at Menou, from the archives of the Hôtel de Ville, Menou.

The Château de Menou was designed by the architect Barthélémy le Blanc along traditional lines, with a main three storey building flanked by symmetrical pavilions. The pavilions house a private chapel, dining room and an extensive kitchen on the north side of the house, and on the south a library and a sun room. A grand staircase in each pavilion leads to bedrooms on the first and second floors.

The most impressive rooms in the house are the two enormous ground floor drawing rooms, which are joined by a soaring Entrance Hall to which Mr Garcia restored its original seventeenth-century proportions by inserting a Louis XIV painted ceiling (see Fig. 9). One of the drawing rooms, the Louis XIV Salon (Figs 4 and 6), prominently features on its walls paintings of the 1st Marquis de Menou, his wife and various descendants (see Fig. 5). The room is decorated primarily with Louis XIV and Louis XV commodes, chairs, tables, mirrors, vases and tapestries.

Fig. 8
Salon Restauration, Château de Menou, with a suite of chairs stamped by Jacob-Desmalter, and Blacas family portraits.

Below, left
Fig. 9
Upper level of the Entrance Hall, Château de Menou, with the Louis XIV painted ceiling.

Right
Fig. 10
The King's Bedroom, Château de Menou, (unrestored).

Here and there one finds books, photographs and decorations from the late nineteenth and early twentieth centuries which help to soften the room's period atmosphere.

Across the Entrance Hall one encounters the Salon Restauration (Fig. 8). Mr Garcia has decorated the room in the style of the second quarter of the nineteenth century when the Duke of Blacas was given his title. Appropriately, Mr Garcia has graced the walls with paintings of various Blacas family members. Much of the furniture dates from the Empire period and is highlighted by a suite of chairs stamped by Jacob-Desmalter, a great cabinet-maker of the late eighteenth and early nineteenth centuries. The room has a fascinating atmosphere of relaxed self-importance. Chairs bearing inventory marks from Versailles and from King Louis Philippe's Château de Neuilly share the room with more casual pieces and furniture of no importance – such as a red tufted chaise longue – which would have been added by the family in the nineteenth century for comfort.

Containing objects from many different periods, the upstairs bedrooms follow a similarly eclectic scheme. Beds are set into alcoves and enclosed in curtains, family portraits from various periods grace the walls, and small personal effects of sentimental value are artfully arranged. Mr Garcia is a relentless collector, and nearly all of these objects have been acquired by him through visits to the shops of dealers as well as to auctions, not only throughout the provinces but in Paris and abroad. 'There would be no way to tell that these furnishings had not been in these rooms forever and were not there originally,' comments Thierry Millerand of Sotheby's New York, and a visitor at Menou. 'This sense of originality greatly adds to the atmosphere of the house and it is one of Jacques' most brilliant achievements. Of course, there is no modern plumbing in the house. The bathroom fixtures and wooden lavatory seats are just as you would expect them to be in a period château.'

He continues, 'Overall, the house evokes a marvellous sense of permanence and continuity of family tradition. One feels that the furniture has stood in the same exact location for generations. Some of the furniture looks frayed, and there are many pieces which one might describe as junk. This is what gives Menou its warmth and character. In every French château lampshades will be slightly falling apart. Nothing is too perfect. The atmosphere, the softness, the slowness of life – that's what every château is about, and Jacques has captured that quality of mellowness here.'

On a walk around the grounds of the château one day with the energetic Mr Garcia as he busily supervises the extensive work being done on various follies, outbuildings and gardens which comprise his master plan for Menou, one senses a lifetime of tasks yet to be done. In wellington boots and raincoat, he peers at the back range of the château and its several hundred acres of nearly virgin land. This is where Mr Garcia's next challenge lies. In the local town hall he uncovered the original plans for Menou's terraced gardens (see Fig. 7), whose star-shaped axis points are still visible. Mr Garcia has bought an entire garden from another château, and this will provide fully-grown yews and boxwoods for replanting in the restored gardens.

Looking across the grounds of the château as a light rain begins to fall, Mr Garcia remarks with his customary enthusiasm, 'This may take many years. But I am patient.'

Nineteenth-century decorative arts

A pair of English fruitwood and ivory recamiers, *circa* 1870, lengths 7ft (213cm)
New York $28,600 (£14,592). 21.II.91

Opposite
An American parcel-gilt side cabinet, with a French marquetry panel by Joseph Cremer of Paris, made or retailed by Sypher, New York, *circa* 1860, height 4ft 7in (140cm)
London £20,900 ($35,321). 31.V.91

One of a pair of French Napoleon III ebony and gilt-bronze mounted side cabinets by Charles-Guillaume Winckelsen of Paris, dated *1865*, widths 4ft (122cm)
London £71,500 ($146,575). 2.XI.90

One of a pair of English cut-brass and tortoiseshell 'Boulle' commodes, by Blake of London, *circa* 1850, widths 49¼in (125cm)
London £135,000 ($276,750)

Opposite
A French Napoleon III parcel-gilt bronze sculptural band clock, Paris, *circa* 1870, with contemporary marble pedestal, overall height 7ft 3in (221cm)
London £110,000 ($209,000). 1.III.91

GRAND
OU

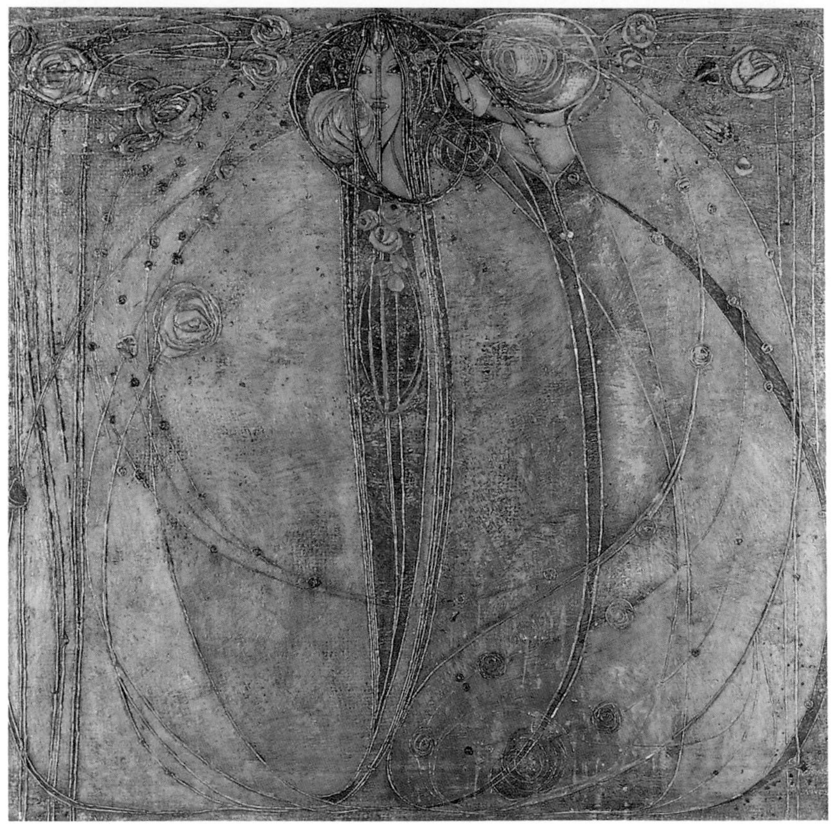

'Glasgow girls': women in art and design

Jude Burkhauser

Fig. 1
Margaret Macdonald Mackintosh (1864–1933).

Opposite, above
Fig. 2
Margaret Macdonald Mackintosh
THE HEART OF THE ROSE
Gesso over burlap, 38½in by 39½in (97.8cm by 100.3cm)
New York $132,000 (£80,488). 14.VI.91

Below
Fig. 3
Margaret Macdonald Mackintosh
THE WHITE ROSE and THE RED ROSE
Gesso over burlap, 38½in by 39½in (97.8cm by 100.3cm)
New York $88,000 (£53,659). 14.VI.91

At the turn of the last century Glasgow was the centre for an avant-garde movement of art and design now known as the Glasgow Style. This unique Scottish version of Art Nouveau was applied in a variety of forms, including architecture, furniture design, stencilling, posterwork, embroidery, gesso, metalwork and stained glass. Although the Style found little acceptance in Britain, its influence quickly spread to the Continent, particularly to Austria and Germany where it received enthusiastic endorsement.

The reputation Glasgow's Art Nouveau enjoys today stems largely from the rediscovery and recognition of the work of its principle figure, Charles Rennie Mackintosh (1868–1928), however the same style can be found in the work of a large number of talented designers, craftsmen and particularly craftswomen (see Fig. 6) who emerged from the Glasgow School of Art at that time.

The recent major retrospective at the Glasgow Museum and Art Gallery, *'Glasgow Girls': Women in Art and Design 1880–1920*, brought to light the extensive contribution of the Glaswegian women of the period, whose work had been largely forgotten. Although stereotypes surrounding the arts had traditionally placed women in the so-called 'minor arts', it is clear that some women artists involved in the decorative arts in the early twentieth century were making a very real contribution to the social and aesthetic revolutions of their times.

Of the many talented female personalities who played a role in the Glasgow phenomenon, Margaret Macdonald (1864–1933) (Fig. 1) and her sister Frances Macdonald (1873–1921) are the two most widely recognised contributors to the development of the Glasgow Style. Based on stylised elongated organic motifs, the Style incorporated skeletal plant forms, a geometricised 'Glasgow rose', birds in flight and the use of a distorted and attenuated human form so grotesquely unfamiliar that it earned the artists the sobriquet 'the Spook School'. The epithet was directed primarily at the Macdonald sisters for their early posterwork and watercolours. Their startling visual iconography of a spectral female persona introduced a 'new woman' into art – a radical departure from the Pre-Raphaelite or Arts and Crafts ideal of the feminine.

Recent re-evaluation of the Glasgow Style has demonstrated that Charles Rennie Mackintosh's undisputed 'genius' was fed by and infused with the creative spirit of what was known as the 'Mackintosh Group', which then became the 'Glasgow Four'. These were Mackintosh and his wife and partner Margaret Macdonald (the only designer with whom he ever worked), her sister, designer Frances Macdonald, and Frances's husband, the architect and designer Herbert MacNair. In their collaborative work on art and architecture projects the 'Four' epitomised the ideal of creative interaction between architect and designer, elevating the arts of design to the level of fine art. In a stunning series of interiors they demonstrated the concept of *gesamtkunstwerk*: the concern for the design of an interior as an aesthetic whole, resulting in a totally designed environment.

The reputation of Mackintosh and the Four was spread internationally through the pages of contemporary art journals such as *Die Kunst*, *Deutsche Kunst und Dekoration*, and illustrated articles in *The Studio*. The Four's rejection of easel painting in favour of dedication to applied arts was considered to be a revolutionary challenge to established ideology, and Mackintosh was hailed by the Vienna Secessionists as the herald of a new movement.

After seeing work by the Four illustrated, the Secessionists invited Mackintosh and 'Monsieur M. Macdonald' (!) to take part in the VIIIth Secession exhibition in 1900. At the request of Josef Hoffmann, who was responsible for organising the exhibition, Herr Fritz Wärndorfer, an enthusiastic patron of the Secession group, travelled to Scotland to meet the young Glaswegian designers. The Four agreed to participate in the exhibition, the first to be devoted primarily to the applied arts (Fig. 4). Mackintosh and Margaret Macdonald spent six weeks in Vienna, where they were carried through the streets with flowers strewn at their feet by admiring art students. The pair sold all of their work, and received important commissions. Wärndorfer purchased a silver brooch by Macdonald, a drawing and two prints, and subsequently commissioned a music salon from the Glasgow pair for his home at

Below, left
Fig. 4
The VIIIth Vienna Secession Exhibition, 1900, showing *The May Queen*, by Margaret Macdonald and Charles Rennie Mackintosh.

Right
Fig. 5
The 'Rose Boudoir' installation by Margaret Macdonald and Charles Rennie Mackintosh, at the Turin International Exhibition of Decorative Art, 1902.

Fig. 6
Women students at the Glasgow School of Art, *circa* 1900.

Carl-Ludwigstrasse 45 in Vienna. (At the same time he commissioned a dining room from Josef Hoffmann.)

Completed – except for the piano – by around Christmas 1902, the two distinctive room additions to the Wärndorfer house soon became a Mecca for those interested in the modern design movement. The Music Room, based on a square plan with two rectangular bays, was designed by Mackintosh in collaboration with Macdonald. The interior was seen as a 'composition [which] forms an organic whole, each part fitting into the rest with the same concord as do the passages in a grand symphony' (Ludwig Hevesi, 1905). The colour scheme of the room was muted white and grey, with characteristic jewel-like insets of lavender and red realised in varied design punctuations of inset glass, gesso, stencilled fabric and embroidery. The concept for the room was inspired by the Belgian playwright Maurice Maeterlinck's *Seven Princesses*. Scenes from the story appeared in a wall frieze of at least six large gesso and mixed media panels, forming the room's main feature, and two small gesso panels, set into the case of the grand piano.

The gesso was inset with mother-of-pearl, and a textured, three-dimensional effect was achieved by the insertion of semi-precious stones which projected from the plaster surface and adorned the robes of the Princesses. The case for the grand piano, the largest piece of furniture Mackintosh was to design, was surrounded by carved wooden panels in both cut-out and relief. Stylised birds in flight were repeated in a vertical stack to form the composition similar to one of his early watercolours *The Descent of Night* (1893) and a frequent motif in his earliest Glasgow Style designs. Two small gesso panels which fitted in to the front of the piano were designed and made by Margaret Macdonald. These two works, *The Opera of the Wind* and *The Opera of the Sea* (Fig. 7), may be considered two of Macdonald's most innovative and well-realised designs in gesso. Comparisons may be made between these works and certain segments of the *Beethoven Frieze* by Gustav Klimt, designed at around the same time. Scholars now agree that Klimt's *Beethoven Frieze* was almost certainly a response to two gesso panels, *The May Queen* (see Fig. 4) and *The Wassail*, designed by Macdonald and Mackintosh and exhibited in the 1900 Vienna Secession exhibition. Klimt's work and the work of the Glasgow artists certainly appear to have been an influence upon each other from their Vienna connection.

In 1902, Wärndorfer met the Glasgow artists for a second time, at the Turin International Exhibition of Decorative Art, an international array of the best examples of contemporary design. Three special rooms had been set aside for the Glasgow Style. The first room, the 'Rose Boudoir' installation (Fig. 5), designed and executed by Mackintosh and Margaret Macdonald, was considered the main attraction of the Scottish section. A harmony of white, silver and rose, the room demonstrated a fully integrated effort between architect and designer, where every element of form and colour acted to create a unity of design.

Wärndorfer was later to purchase a set of chairs very similar to those made for this room. He also bought two of four very fine large-scale gesso panels designed and executed by Margaret Macdonald for inclusion in the Turin room setting, *The Heart of the Rose* (Fig. 2) and *The White Rose and the Red Rose* (Fig. 3; see also Fig. 5). These panels are perhaps two of the best examples of Macdonald's familiar symbolic theme, the motif of women and roses expressing, according to one contemporary critic, 'holy ideals where the spirit of love hovers over all and crowns all'. This theme was employed in many metalwork, watercolour, gesso and inset furniture designs.

The second of the Turin installations, a writing room, was designed and executed by Margaret's sister, Frances Macdonald and her husband Herbert MacNair. In addition to the rooms set aside for the Four, a number of women designers from Glasgow were represented in the third room, where Glasgow School of Art embroidery, enamels, metalwork, glass, and small works of art were presented, including work by Ann Macbeth, Jessie M. King, and De Courcy Dewar. Turin was the highpoint of the Glasgow Style, which by around 1908 would begin a steady decline.

Until the recent location and documentation of Mackintosh's grand piano, and four important gesso panels by Margaret Macdonald, no trace of any works from the Wärndorfer Music Salon were thought to have survived. Wärndorfer emigrated to America in 1914 and the house on Carl-Ludwigstrasse was signed over to his wife, Lili Wärndorfer, who arranged for its sale and all trace of its contents was lost from around April 1916 until today. Writing in 1983 Peter Vergo, the noted Vienna scholar, speculated on the fate of Wärndorfer's music room:

> . . . by 1916 art nouveau was too old-fashioned to be considered modern and not old enough to be of historical interest. One can well imagine that the new occupants of the house in Carl-Ludwigstrasse found the decor hideous, and simply removed it. If this was indeed the case, the destruction of the Wärndorfer interiors must rank . . . as one of the most serious acts of vandalism perpetrated in our century.

The recent discovery of Margaret Macdonald's gesso panels from the music room and Wärndorfer's two 'Rose Boudoir' panels from Turin makes this major loss to design history somewhat less painful.

Fig. 7
Margaret Macdonald Mackintosh
THE OPERA OF THE WIND
and THE OPERA OF THE SEA
Two panels, gesso on panel, both signed with monograms, one dated *1903*, each panel 8in by 8in (20.5cm by 20.5cm)
New York $71,500 (£43,598). 14.VI.91

A Morris & Co. Hammersmith carpet designed by John Henry Dearle, *circa* 1900, approximately 20ft 9¼in by 13ft 6¼in (633cm by 412cm)
London £220,000 ($455,400). 19.X.90

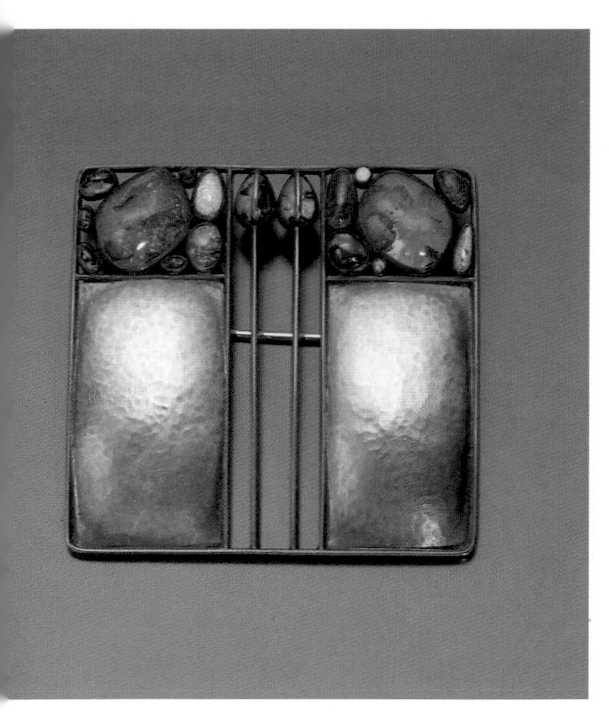

A Wiener Werkstätte silver, gold and opal brooch designed by Josef Hoffmann and executed by Karl Ponocny for Mathilde Flögel, stamped *WW*, *circa* 1905, 2in (5.1cm)
London £79,200 ($163,944). 19.X.90

Right
As important members of Vienna's avant-garde, the Flögel sisters were closely involved in the founding of the Werkstätte. Here Mathilde Flögel is shown in a contemporary photograph wearing the above brooch on a dress probably designed in collaboration with Gustav Klimt. The cabinet in the background is by Koloman Moser.

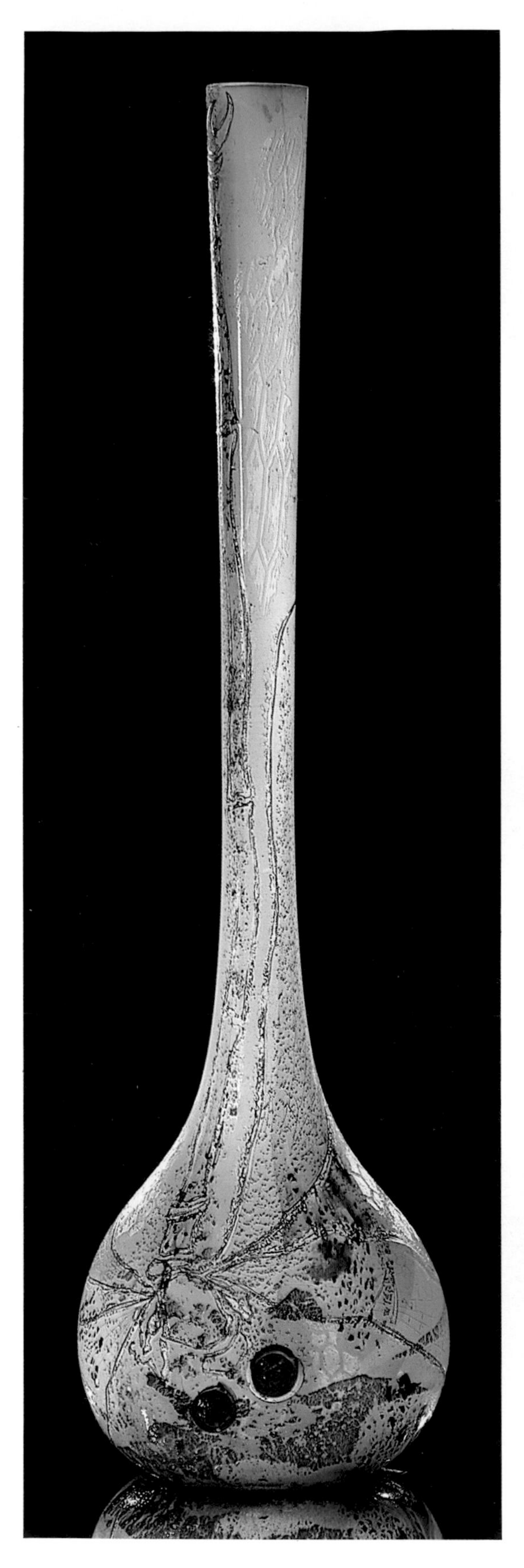

Far left
A Gallé cameo and gold leaf 'parlant' vase, engraved with dragonfly motif, signed and inscribed *Dans les suprêmes symphonies Cherchez la note humaine, allez! Hugo / au Maître Ysaye Gallé, circa* 1900, height 33in (84cm)
Monte Carlo FF2,830,500 (£283,050:$555,000). 14.X.90

Left
A Tiffany favrile glass and French gilt-metal mounted hall lantern, *circa* 1900, height 40in (101.6cm)
New York $23,100 (£14,085). 14.VI.91

A Tiffany favrile glass and bronze nasturtium lamp, the shade and the base impressed with the mark of Tiffany Studios, New York, 1899–1920, height 31½in (80cm)
New York $115,500 (£59,536). 1.XII.90

An engraved glass bottle and stopper by Maurice Marinot, the base inscribed with the maker's mark and number, *circa* 1925, height $4\frac{3}{4}$in (12cm)
Monte Carlo FF266,400 (£26,640:$52,235). 14.X.90

An ebony and ivory *secrétaire à cylindre* by Emile-Jacques Ruhlmann, stamped *Ruhlmann A*, 1928, width 3ft $2\frac{3}{8}$in (100cm)
Monte Carlo FF1,776,000 (£177,600:$348,235). 14.X.90

American decorative arts

A Chippendale carved and figured mahogany china table, attributed to the Anthony Hay Shop, Williamsburg, Virginia, *circa* 1765, length 34¼in (87cm)
New York $110,000 (£67,073). 27.VI.91

Opposite, left
A Queen Anne carved mahogany bonnet top highboy, North Shore, Massachusetts, *circa* 1760, height 7ft (213cm)
New York $247,500 (£125,000). 1.II.91
From the Rosen Family Collection

This piece descended through the Kittredge family along with a mahogany block-front chest of drawers of similar date.

Right
A Queen Anne japanned pine tall-case clock by John Doane, Scituate, Massachusetts, the case signed by Peter Stelling, Boston, Massachusetts, *circa* 1740, height 7ft 11in (241cm)
New York $319,000 (£194,512). 27.VI.91

A Chippendale carved mahogany card table attributed to the Garvan Carver, Philadelphia, *circa* 1765, width 35in (89cm)
New York $1,045,000 (£533,163). 2.II.91

Thomas Willing's card table

Wendell Garrett

Mid eighteenth-century Philadelphia was a prosperous urban centre: its strategic location at the mouth of the Schuylkill and Delaware Rivers, its vigorous industrial and commercial activity, and its large and cosmopolitan population combined to make the city the economic, cultural and political capital of the American colonies. Excellent print shops and the city's seven newspapers gave wide access to cultural and political information. Philadelphia was also a centre of fashion and luxury, a haven for middle-class artisans and craftsmen who were patronised by the city's wealthy merchants.

This was the world in which Thomas Willing – legislator, statesman and entrepreneur – moved and lived. He was elected mayor of Philadelphia in 1763 and served as Justice of the Supreme Court of Pennsylvania from 1767 to 1777. More significantly, he was a partner of Willing, Morris and Co., Philadelphia's leading mercantile firm.

By 1774 the Chippendale rococo style was fully developed in America, finding expression throughout the decorative arts, particularly in richly carved furniture. According to Hornor's *Blue Book*, the definitive guide to eighteenth-century Philadelphia furniture, 'Colonials were persistent tea drinkers and card players . . . [and] every well-equipped parlour had at least one [table] for each purpose'.

Made in the late 1760s, Willing's card table is a richly sculpted example of early rococo. A crisp control of the sinuous curves and an unusual combination of design elements places this table within an identifiable group of pieces that can be attributed to the Garvan Carver. This anonymous craftsman is believed to have been responsible for the matching high-chest and dressing-table in the Mabel Brady Garvan Collection at Yale University. The same hand also carved a pair of card tables, one now in the Kaufman Collection, and one at the Colonial Williamsburg Foundation, both in Virginia. Through their integration of design and ornament, the Thomas Willing card table and its companion pieces can be considered among the best examples of high-style Philadelphia furniture.

After Willing's death in 1821, his inventory of 'Plate, Wine, Horses, Carriage, Houshold furniture &c.' listed '1 Mahogany Card Table' valued at fifty cents. Thomas Willing's son George inherited the table and passed it on to his own son Charles. In the 1890s Charles Willing's estate – consisting of portraits, paintings, furniture, silver and pewter – went into storage and was forgotten until 1964, when the property was accidently discovered by a descendant, who consigned it for auction. The table was purchased by the Chipstone Foundation for American Decorative Arts of Milwaukee, Wisconsin.

An incised and cobalt-blue decorated salt-glazed stoneware presentation inkwell, signed by William Crolius, New York, dated *July 12 1773*, width $5\frac{1}{2}$in (14cm)
New York $148,500 (£90,549). 27.VI.91

The American gold freedom box presented by the corporation of the City of New York to John Jay, with the original document with ribbon and seal, engraved and signed by Peter Rushton Maverick, maker's mark of Samuel Johnson, New York, 1784, length $3\frac{3}{8}$in (8.6cm)
New York $506,000 (£308,537). 26.VI.91

The Washington-Sussel Artist

LAEDY WASCHINGTON: A WATERCOLOUR FRAKTUR DRAWING

Watercolour and pen and ink, *circa* 1780, 8in by 6½in (20cm by 16.5cm)

New York $110,000 (£56,122). 20.X.90

This rare fraktur is one of a small distinctive group executed in Bethel Township, Berks County, Pennsylvania. They are decorated with figures of elaborately and colourfully clad gentlemen, often with hunting horns, and ladies with 'beehive' headdresses; a small number illustrate notable personages such as this one captioned 'Laedy Waschington'.

Musical instruments

Far left
A violin by Giuseppe filius Andrea Guarneri, Cremona, *circa* 1705, length of back 14in (35.6cm)
London £180,400 ($373,428). 22.XI.90

Left
A violin by Giovanni Battista Guadagnini, Turin, 1772, length of back 13⅞in (35.3cm)
London £176,000 ($364,320). 22.XI.90

A grand pianoforte by Manuel Antunes, Portugal, last quarter eighteenth century, length 7ft 7in (231cm)
London £68,200 ($141,174). 22.XI.90

Sporting guns, arms and medals

A pair of 16-bore self-opening sidelock ejector guns built for H.R.H. Edward, Prince of Wales, by J. Purdey & Sons, *circa* 1909–13, length of stocks 14in (35.6cm)
Geneva SF302,500 (£120,518:$196,429). 18.VI.91

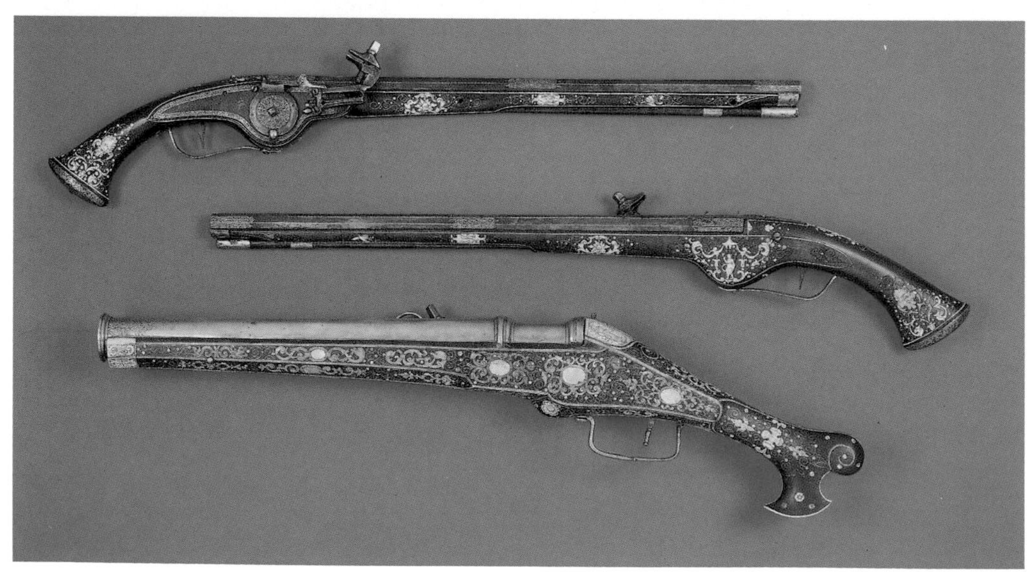

Top and centre
A pair of long wheel-lock holster pistols, probably Dutch, *circa* 1650, lengths $27\frac{5}{8}$in (70.2cm)
New York $82,500 (£42,526). 15.I.91
Bottom
A wheel-lock hand mortar, Nuremberg, *circa* 1595, length $27\frac{1}{2}$in (69.9cm)
New York $38,500 (£19,845). 15.I.91

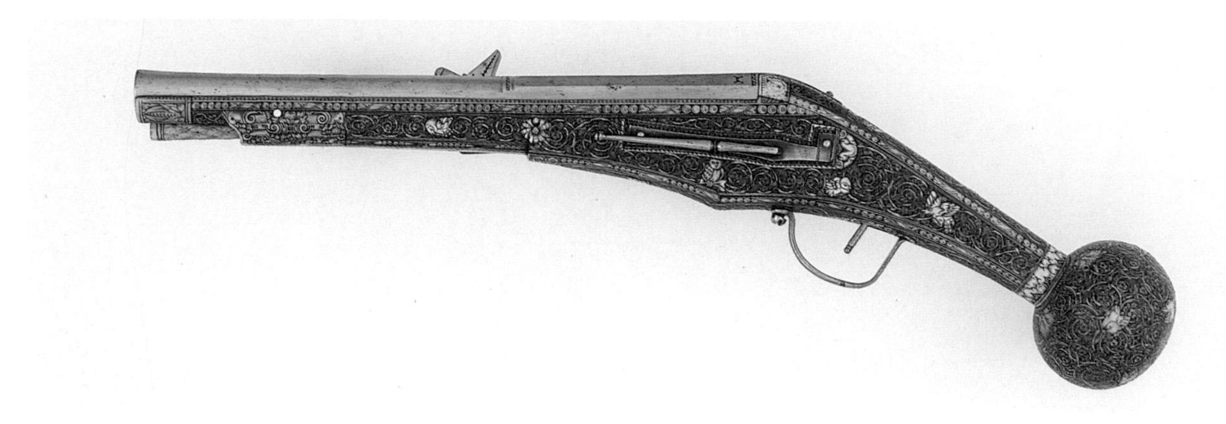

A wheel-lock belt pistol, probably Thuringian, *circa* 1585, length 21½in (54.6cm)
London £24,750 ($41,828). 3.VI.91
From the Visser Collection

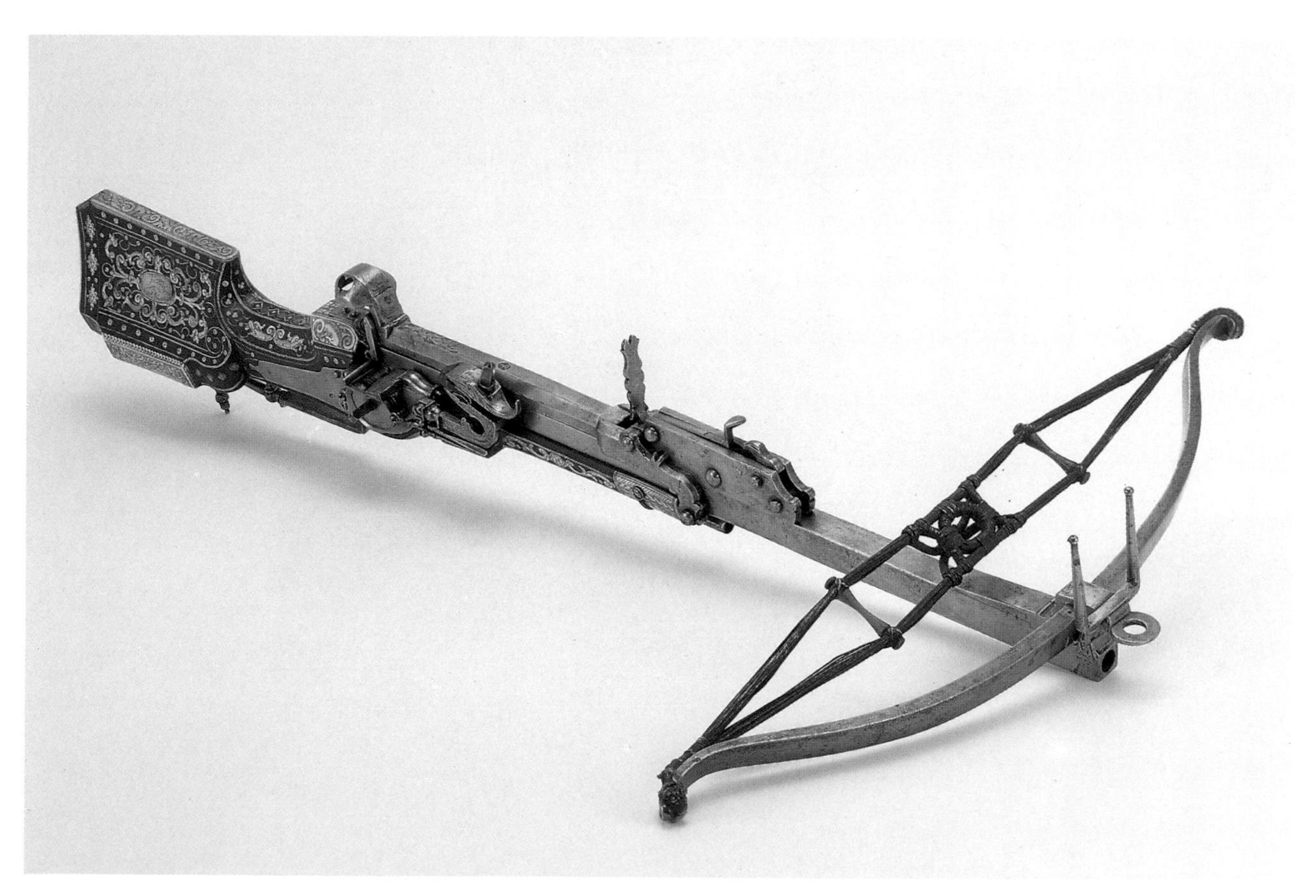

A combined stone-bow and wheel-lock pistol, Nuremberg, *circa* 1620, length 29⅛in (74cm)
London £63,800 ($107,822). 3.VI.91
From the Visser Collection

This is the safety pin
the 100lb bomb just before your
father started
for Courtrai on April 25th
which was handed to him just as he
was going to
It was in this pocket
when he came
M.B.B.
1914-15
GEORGIVS V BRITT: OMN: REX ET IND: IMP:
LOG
Name W B Rhodes Moorhouse
Rank 2nd Lt.
Royal Flying Corps.

Opposite
Victoria Cross Group, awarded to W.B.R. Rhodes-Moorhouse, of the No. 2 Squadron, Royal Flying Corps, 1915, with his flying log book and a bomb pin
Hendon £126,500 ($247,940). 15.IX.90

This V.C. was the first ever awarded to an airman. In the words of his official citation, Lt. Rhodes-Moorhouse showed 'conspicuous bravery. . . in flying to Courtrai and dropping bombs on the railway line near that station. On starting his return journey he was mortally wounded but succeeded in flying thirty-five miles to his destination at a very low altitude, and reported the successful accomplishment of his objective. He has since died of his wounds.'

A collar and sash badge from the Imperial Russian Order of St Andrew, 1835
Geneva SF64,900 (£25,960:$44,759). 16.V.91

The Order of St Andrew was founded by Peter the Great in 1698 and was the highest ranking Imperial Order. Grand Dukes were decorated at baptism and Princes of the Blood on coming of age. Upon admission to the Order, a Knight paid a fee of 500 roubles, but needy recipients could apply for a pension of between 800 and 1,000 roubles per annum. This example was issued in 1835; each of the twenty-three links of the collar chain being hallmarked. Emanual Pannasch, the maker, was the official manufacturer of Russian insignia between 1821 and 1836.

Postage stamps

China, 1941 $2 black and blue with the central portrait of Dr Sun Yat Sen inverted
London £6,325 ($13,093). 8.XI.90

This variety was discovered in 1945 by a schoolboy who had bought a complete sheet of $2 stamps at the Chungking Post Office. He was surprised to find later that the centre of the stamps had been printed upside down.

Cyprus, 1867–83 Austrian Post Office in Cyprus, 3 soldi, 5 soldi and 15 soldi together on small piece, cancelled LARNACCA DI CIPRO
London £352 ($609). 22.V.91

Cyprus, 1882–86 ½ piastre emerald green from die I
London £2,530 ($4,377). 22.V.91

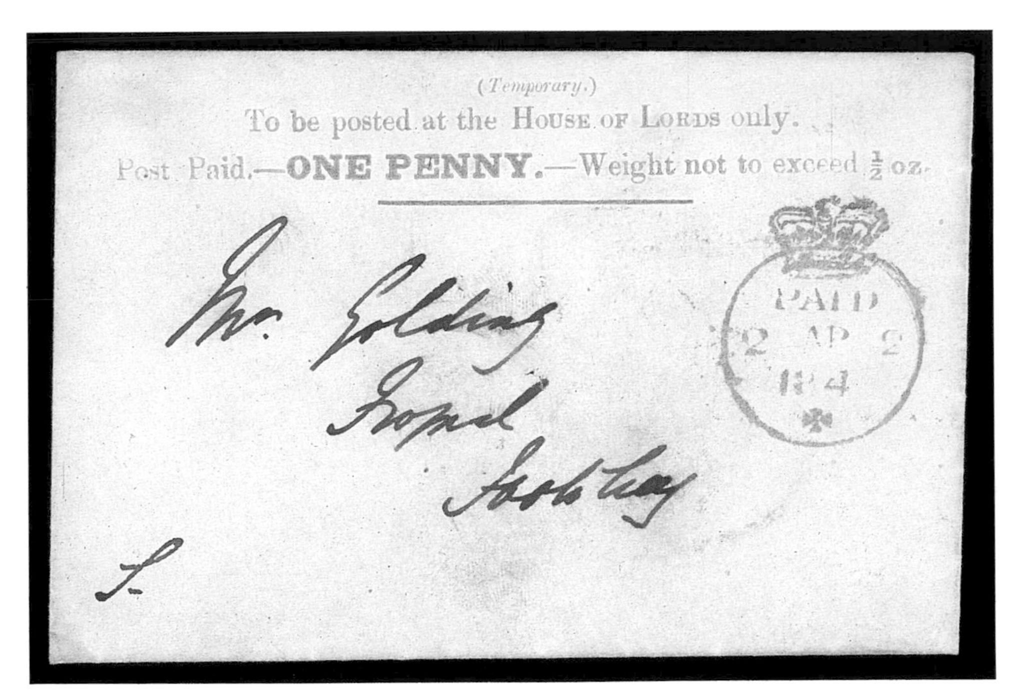

Great Britain, 1840 special envelope printed for use at the House of Lords only
London £3,300 ($6,831). 8.XI.90

Netherlands, 1852–63 5 cent deep blue horizontal pair from Plate I
London £418 ($723). 22.V.91

Rhodesia, 1910–13 £1 red and black perforated 15
London £5,775 ($9,991). 22.V.91

MICKEY MANTLE
Mickey Mantle
PITTSBURG
WAGNER, PITTSBURG

A
PLANK, PHILA. AMER.
C
NAPS
YOUNG CLEVELAND AMER.
LOU GEHRIG
NEW YORK YANKEES

The old ball game

Opposite, top, from left to right
Mickey Mantle baseball card, 1952
$49,500 (£27,654)
T206 Honus Wagner Piedmont cigarette card, *circa* 1910
$451,000 (£251,955)
Bottom, from left to right
T206 Eddie Plank Sweet Caporal cigarette card, *circa* 1910
$26,400 (£14,749)
T205 gold border baseball card set, 1911
$41,250 (£23,045)
R333 Lou Gehrig Delong gum card
$17,600 (£9,832)
These baseball cards, from the Copeland Collection, were sold in New York on 22 and 23 March 1991.

The game of baseball seems to possess a universal charm, linking the small boy who grins under his pristine cap (listing slightly with the weight of his oversized mitt) to millions of fans of all ages right across America. The word baseball first appeared in print in England in 1744, but it is Abner Doubleday who is usually credited with inventing the game in Cooperstown, New York, in 1839. Today it is generally agreed that the first 'organised' game was played by the New York Knickerbockers and the New York Nine in 1846 near Hoboken, New Jersey, known appropriately enough as Elysian Fields.

To many Americans baseball has a mythic quality, a spirit associated with youth and renewal, with potential and victory: 'It is youth, springtime, a trip to the country, part of our past. It is the roaring excitement of huge urban crowds and the sleepy green afternoon silences of midsummer. Without effort, it engenders and thrives on heroes, legends, self-identification and hometown pride', as Roger Angell has written. By the 1880s, these sorts of feelings were sufficiently ingrained as to encourage a souvenir industry to grow up around the players and their achievements, providing the fans with images and statistical records of their heroes. Then, as today, these cards, photographs, pins and other ephemera accompanied gum, tobacco, candy and other inexpensive products. From the beginning they were eagerly collected, traded, and preserved, but never with quite the zeal evident in the Copeland Collection, a collection that vividly captured the events and personalities of the sport over the past century.

Here in this collection was the jewelled pendant presented to Doc Bushong, catcher of the 'World Beater' St Louis Browns, who was at bat as Curt Welch stole home to score the winning run in the 1886 championship. Here, too, were the images of the famous pitchers and fielders of the turn of the century – the immortal Cy Young, a giant from the cornfields of Ohio; Eddie Plank, the 325-game winning southpaw of the Philadelphia Athletics; his teammate at second base Napoleon 'King Larry' Lajoie; and, of course, the game's greatest shortstop, Honus Wagner of the Pittsburgh Pirates. For all his glory, Wagner's image is extremely rare. In 1909 he objected to being associated with cigarettes, and the Piedmont Tobacco Company was forced to withdraw his card from the set. Fewer than forty are known, and the Copeland T206 is considered the finest in existence.

The roster continued with Babe Ruth, Lou Gehrig, Jimmy Foxx, Joe DiMaggio, the great Yankee triumverate Mantle, Maris and Ford, Ted Williams, Hank Aaron, Willie Mays, Sandy Koufax, Reggie Jackson, and a host of other stars. There were thousands of items in this collection, and together they created a vivid portrait of the sport that has enlivened the American summer for more than a hundred years.

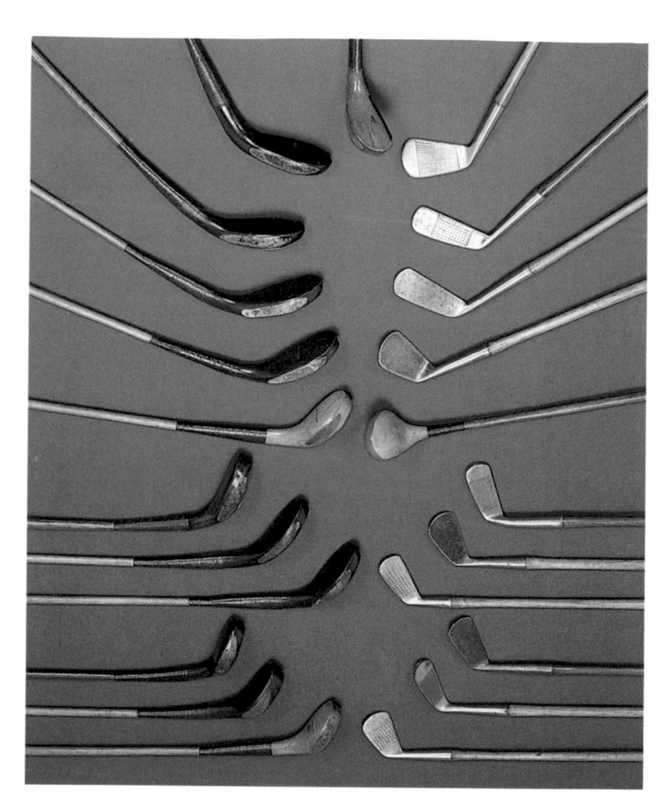

A collection of twenty-three golf clubs renowned as the Auchterlonie Open Champions Collection, collected by Willie and Laurie Auchterlonie from winners of the Open Championships between 1860 and 1930
Chester £627,000 ($1,003,200). 15.VII.91

Many individuals made significant contributions to the development of golf down the ages, but it is difficult to nominate a family to challenge the Auchterlonies of St Andrews in the scope of their influence on the game.

Willie Auchterlonie was the first to achieve prominence when he won the Open Championship of 1893 at Prestwick at the age of twenty. At that time he was working for Robert Forgan but as the champion golfer he set up in business as D. and W. Auchterlonie. Willie's brother Lawrence was also a player of considerable accomplishment and he won the United States Open Championship of 1902 at Garden City Golf Club. Playing with the new rubber core ball he improved on the previous year's winning total by twenty-four strokes and he was the first to break eighty in every round.

Their workshop in North Street became a mecca for collectors and golfers who appreciated the unique feel of a bespoke putter. Customers had a long wait because Auchterlonie insisted that every stage of the process of converting a seasoned block of hornbeam into a delicately crafted club must be performed by his hands alone. To many people his clubs had a sculptural quality which qualified them as works of art, yet the Auchterlonies insisted that their sole purpose was to create an implement which was as well suited to its golfing purpose as he could achieve. To those who were privileged to spend hours beside his bench, watching him hollow a head or shave a scared joint, it was clear, however, that an artist's instinct shaped the heads and brought up the grain of the wood.

The Auchterlonie Collection was certainly unique; to the collector these clubs of golf's founding father represent a window to the past.

PETER DOBEREINER

Left
Willie Auchterlonie (1872–1963).

An English admiralty dockyard model of a 60-gun ship-of-the-line, 1702–1704, length 48in (122cm)
London £137,500 ($237,875). 22.V.91

The Little Mermaid

In 1985, after completing work on the Disney animated feature *The Great Mouse Detective*, director Ron Clements began searching for a new project. A visit to a bookshop resulted in his finding a copy of Hans Christian Andersen's fairy tales and he quickly saw the cinematic possibilities of an underwater fantasy based on *The Little Mermaid*. 'I thought it was a beautiful and poetic story with really exciting visual opportunities,' Clements recalls, 'but it was also one of the saddest stories ever written. Our ending retained the bittersweet quality of the original story, yet is uplifting at the same time.'

In a departure from the tradition of most animated features, *The Little Mermaid* was launched with a full script. Written by Clements and John Musker, the script created new characters like Sebastian, Flounder and Scuttle, all very comical and endearing; gave a prominent role to the evil seawitch Ursula, a vampish villain of exquisite nastiness; and shaped the central character Ariel, the rebellious teenage mermaid, into a romantic heroine with allure and spunk.

With script in hand, composer Alan Menken and lyricist Howard Ashman began writing the music. The seven songs they composed for the film, including the hip, reggae-inspired 'Under the Sea' and the enchanting ballad 'Kiss the Girl', created tremendous enthusiasm among the animators, particularly since the music was so successful at keeping the action moving forward.

Once the voices for the film had been cast, the actors – notably Pat Carroll as Ursula, Sam Wright as Sebastian and Buddy Hackett as Scuttle – proved to be unusually helpful in providing 'live-action reference' for the animators. Buddy Hackett's habit of talking out of the side of his face, for example, and his rolling eyeball movements were hilariously translated into Scuttle. During the recording session for the musical number 'Under the Sea', Sam Wright delivered a medley of barrel turns and jumps. The animators sketched away, and Sebastian came to life.

The Little Mermaid has the distinction of being the highest-grossing animated film of all time for a first release, and much of the credit for this must go to the heroic efforts of the Disney artists. Some 450 of them worked on the film over a four year period, painting 150,000 cels and 1,100 backgrounds from a palette of 1,000 colours. There were 37 colour models for Ariel alone, with numerous costume changes (from mermaid fin to rag dress to wedding gown). The Disney paint laboratory even invented a new colour, 'Ariel', for the blue-green of her fin. In addition, nearly eighty percent of *The Little Mermaid* required some sort of effects work, such as billowing sails, raging fire, ripples and bubbles and schools of fish.

The backgrounds offered at Sotheby's were all original Disney production pieces. Combined with their corresponding cels, they represent the very best in classic hand-drawn animation.

Opposite, above
Ariel, Eric and Grimsby, a Disney three cel set-up applied to a matching watercolour background of the interior of the dining room, from *The Little Mermaid*, 1989, each cel 12½in by 19¼in (31.8cm by 49cm)
New York $25,300 (£13,041). 15.XII.90

Below
Flounder and Ariel, a Disney two cel set-up applied to a matching watercolour background of the interior of the ship, from *The Little Mermaid*, 1989, each cel 10½in by 13in (26.6cm by 33cm)
New York $11,550 (£5,954). 15.XII.90

A Walt Disney celluloid from *Alice in Wonderland*, 1951, 10¾in by 14½in (27.3cm by 36.8cm)
New York $47,300 (£29,379). 18.VI.91

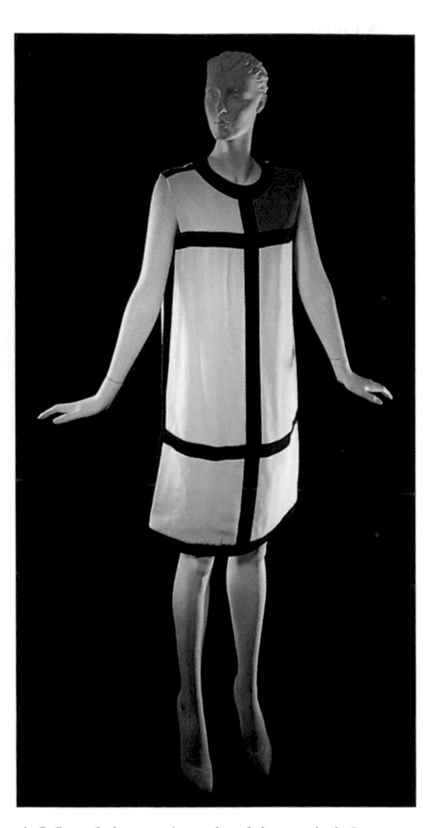

A Mondrian crêpe de chine mini dress by Yves Saint Laurent, labelled and numbered *10494*, 1965
London £2,860 ($4,891). 9.V.91

An Ives cast-iron horse-drawn sleigh, 1890s, length 20in (50.8cm)
New York $25,300 (£13,109). 18.XII.90

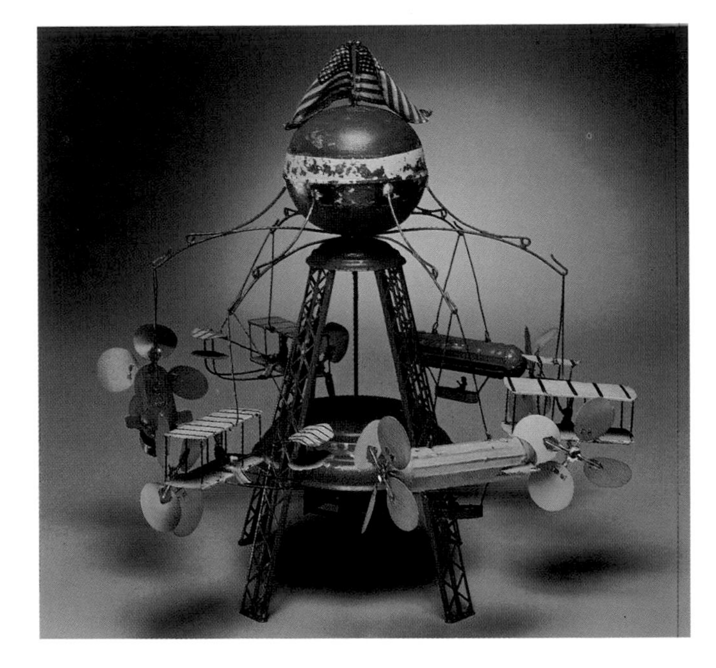

A German clockwork painted tin carousel toy, by Muller & Kadeder, late nineteenth century, height 17in (43.2cm)
New York $7,700 (£3,990). 18.XII.90
From the collection of Anthony Koveleski

A 121 key 'De Kempenaer' dance organ, Antwerp, 1938, length 26ft (792.5cm)
London £82,500 ($141,075). 9.V.91

A French musical automaton of a Turkish smoker by Leopold Lambert, *circa* 1890,
height 22in (56cm)
London £19,800 ($33,858). 9.V.91

Above
A French bisque doll, impressed *A.7.T.BIS*, probably by A. Thuillier, *circa* 1880, height 16in (41cm)
London £17,600 ($34,848). 4.IX.90

Above, right
A French bisque doll, impressed *9 E.J.*, by Jumeau, *circa* 1875, height 24in (61cm)
London £12,100 ($23,958). 4.IX.90

A French bisque swivel-head bebe, impressed *Bru Jne / /10*, by Bru, height 22in (55.8cm)
New York $19,800 (£10,259). 17.XII.90

The Norman Ball Collection

Stewart Skilbeck

Opposite, above
Fig. 1
A 1915 Vauxhall D type 25hp army staff car
Isle of Wight £37,950 ($67,172). 13.IV.91
From the Norman Ball Collection

Below
Fig. 2
A 1925 Hispano-Suiza H6 32CV dual cowl seven seat tourer
Isle of Wight £110,000 ($194,700). 13.IV.91

Bill and Ben, the majestic pair of 1921 Fowler ploughing engines, steamed quietly on the hillside as bidders fought eagerly to acquire items of road transport history at the dispersal sale of the Norman Ball Collection on the Isle of Wight.

One of England's finest and most broad ranging collections of vehicles had started from modest beginnings in 1965 when schoolboys Norman and Robert Ball spotted an advertisement for a humble Morris 8 tourer. An investment of £75 and many hours of labour saw what started as something of a wreck become a smart and serviceable two seat car, and there is no doubt that the boys' enthusiasm rubbed off on their father, Norman Ball, Sr. The collection was built up over a period of twenty-five years and had been a popular tourist attraction on the island.

Early cycles included a *circa* 1880 Salvo quad tricycle (£7,150) of a type once favoured by Queen Victoria on her visits to her beloved Osborne House, reflecting the island connection. Four Victorian bicycles had been found in the cellar of a local bank, and the *circa* 1860 Landau by Woodall & Son of London (£6,270) had once graced the coach house of Squire Carter, High Sheriff of Hampshire. Several motorcycles had been dug out of hedge bottoms on the island and meticulously restored, a *circa* 1918 Royal Enfield 6hp combination justifying a top bid of £7,700 from a Japanese collector (Fig. 3).

Prince Gypsy Lee 'Petulengro' had operated in Portobello market in the traditional horsedrawn caravan, but even he could not have foretold the price of £5,060 paid for it by a New York bidder.

The humble Morris 8 tourer, once the pride of the two schoolboys, found a new enthusiast owner at £5,830. A macabre history surrounded the 1954 Emperor HRG once owned by David Blakely, who was shot by jealous lover Ruth Ellis, the last woman to be hanged in 1955. Nevertheless the car sold for £12,100.

The oldest car offered was the Scottish built 1902 Arrol-Johnston 12hp dog cart (£31,625), once used as a station taxi on the Isle of Skye during the First World War, while the 1915 Vauxhall D type staff car (Fig. 1) may have been used by King George V to review his troops, and certainly in more recent years had carried various members of the Royal family on official visits.

A 1925 Hispano-Suiza H6 tourer with Parisian coachwork (Fig. 2), the property of a European collector but housed in the museum, brought top price of the day, £110,000, the ultimate birthday present for an English collector.

As Bill and Ben, the 1921 Fowler ploughing engines (£42,350) steamed to the ferry at Fishbourne heading for the mainland, the disposal of the Norman Ball Collection had itself earned a place in the history books, a memorable day for the enthusiasts and collectors who had packed the Isle of Wight ferries.

Below
Fig. 3
A *circa* 1918 Royal Enfield 6hp 770cc motorcycle combination
Isle of Wight £7,700 ($13,629). 13.IV.91
From the Norman Ball Collection

A 1934 Rolls-Royce 20/25hp three position drophead coupé, coachwork by Mulliner
Hendon £68,200 ($139,128). 3.XII.90

A 1928 Bugatti type 37A Grand Prix two seater
Hendon £192,500 ($309,925). 1.VII.91

Opposite, above
A 1934 Invicta $4\frac{1}{2}$ litre type S low chassis tourer
Hendon £154,000 ($281,820). 16.III.91

Below
A 1930 Bentley $4\frac{1}{2}$ litre supercharged two seater, coachwork by J. Gurney Nutting
Hendon £1,210,000 ($2,468,400). 3.XII.90
From the collection of Captain Woolf Barnato

GK 6661

Garden statuary

Above
One of a pair of lead Egyptian busts, in the style of Thomas Hope, England, *circa* 1810, heights 22in (56cm)
Billingshurst £14,850 ($29,255). 25.IX.90

Left
A bronze group of a naked Bacchante, foundry mark *F^{lli} G*lli, Firenze*, by Cesare Fantacchiotti, Italy, signed and dated *1898*, height 60in (153cm)
Billingshurst £34,100 ($58,311). 30.V.91

Opposite
A cast iron figure of Diana the Huntress, France, late nineteenth century, height including base 82$\frac{5}{8}$in (210cm)
Billingshurst £44,000 ($86,680). 25.IX.90

Fig. 1
Belle Isle, Windermere. A Romantic island retreat sold by Sotheby's for an undisclosed sum.

'Give me six hundred pounds a year and Curwen's house on Windermere'

In as idyllic a setting as anyone could wish for, Belle Isle House stands on the largest island on Windermere, at the heart of the Lake District (Fig. 1). There are spectacular views across the tranquil water, towards Wordsworth's homes at Rydal and Ambleside. Nearer, there rise the wooded banks of Claife Heights, protected by the National Trust and planted with every shade of summer foliage, larch, oak, ash, scots pine, elder, elm and beech, by the former owner of the house, John Christian Curwen the pioneer agriculturist and forester. No wonder that his Lakeland retreat struck a contemporary as Paradise: 'Give me six hundred pounds a year and Curwen's house on Windermere'.

Belle Isle has been inhabited at least since Roman times. An elaborate mosaic pavement, found when the present house was built, formed part of the luxurious home of the commander of the garrison at Ambleside. Up to the eighteenth century the island was known as Long Holme. During the Civil War it was the site of a siege by Colonel Briggs of his Royalist kinsman, Colonel Huddleston Philipson, who was saved in the nick of time by the arrival of his brother's forces. The island then passed through the Braithwaite, Floyer and Barlow families, before being acquired by Thomas English in 1774. Wordsworth credits English with being the first man to come to the Lake District for its scenery.

English commissioned the architect John Plaw (later famous for Paddington church and Montagu House) to construct the handsome house on Belle Isle. A perfect circle 54 feet in diameter, it was the first truly circular house in Britain, a porticoed neoclassical structure inspired by Palladio's Veneto villas. A formal garden surrounded the house, to the annoyance of neighbours whose taste was already turning towards the Romantic. English spent £6,000 on Belle Isle but sold the island for only £1,720 in 1781 to Isabella, heir to the Curwens of Workington Hall, West Cumberland. She soon swept away English's formal garden and commissioned the well-known landscapist Thomas White to plant an informal *jardin anglais*, delightfully in keeping with the surrounding lake and hills.

Dazzlingly pretty Isabella, only sixteen at the time that Belle Isle was bought, was naturally besieged by suitors. Among them was her unsuitable young cousin John Christian. He applied to the Lord Chancellor for permission to marry Isabella, but was refused. As his sister Jane's diary reveals events then moved quickly: 'October 7th 1782. My brother to be married to Miss Curwen prevented by the banns being forbid. October 9th. Married at Edinburgh.' The Lord Chancellor forgave Christian and the marriage proved a very happy one. John Christian took the surname of Curwen and the family arms, so that the ancient family name could continue.

Fig. 2
George Romney
PORTRAIT OF ISABELLA CURWEN

The Curwens divided their time between Workington Hall and Belle Isle House, which was used as a summer retreat. They owned the house right up until its recent sale by Sotheby's.

Built of hard stone quarried at nearby Ecclerigg, Belle Isle House withstood well the northern winters, and has altered little in 216 years. The interior of the house was decorated by Carr of York, who also made additions to Workington Hall. The rooms on every floor are carved neatly from sections of the circular plan and command superb views over the gardens to the lake beyond.

The house is approached from an imposing classical entrance portico, which leads into the hall, where an elegant pine staircase rises the full height of the house. John Christian Curwen was a keen Master of Hounds and his enthusiasm is celebrated in the drawing and dining rooms at Belle Isle: the dining room plasterwork has foxes' masks and plaques of hunting dogs, while the drawing room bears the motif of the bugle. The house retains most of its original mouldings, window shutters and mahogany doors, perfectly in keeping with the neoclassical proportions of John Plaw's design.

Fig. 3
John Warwick Smith
VIEW OF BELLE ISLE
Watercolour, *circa* 1780–90

John Christian Curwen was a patron of artists, among them George Romney (1734–1802), who painted Isabella on more than one occasion, with Belle Isle in the background (Fig. 2). Belle Isle and Windermere itself were painted in many moods. John Warwick Smith (1749–1831) did a series of 100 watercolours of the house and its environs between 1780 and 1791, showing the beauty of the lakeland scenery (Fig. 3). The house, as it still is today, was partly screened by trees. Approached by boat from the private mooring at Bowness, Belle Isle House is glimpsed, then disappears, in a screen of green, grey-green and copper foliage from the myriad different species planted on the island by John Christian Curwen. He also built a gothic banqueting house on the shore opposite Belle Isle, which became one of Thomas West's 'Stations' at which visitors stood, guide book in hand, to admire the scenery. No longer dismissed, Belle Isle House took its place as one of the attractions of the lake, praised as a dwelling of 'tasteful and elegant seclusion'. Wordsworth never went there, but his grandson the Rev. John Wordsworth married Isabella's granddaughter and there are charming portraits of the Curwen and Wordsworth children among the Belle Isle pictures.

Built as an eighteenth-century gentleman's answer to a classical villa, and set in the most Romantic of English scenery, Belle Isle House remains, as it was for John and Isabella, a little island Paradise.

BOLLINGER
150ème
1829 Anniversaire 1979

Champagne
R.D.
BOLLINGER
TRADITION
1970
AY - MARNE
PRODUCE OF FRANCE
N.M. 2.433.362
CHAMPAGNE
BOLLINGER
AY-FRANCE
R.D. 1961
DÉGORGÉ LE 23 FÉVRIER 1973
PRODUCE OF FRANCE
NM. 2.433.362

‘Madame Jacques’

Madame Lily Bollinger, (1899–1979).

When Madame Lily Bollinger took over the running of that famous Champagne house in 1941, she could regularly be seen bicycling many miles every day around the Marne valley on her inspections of the Bollinger vineyards. In the thirty years of her stewardship that were to follow, she never lost that energy and dedication, and was to earn a unique reputation as one of Champagne’s most famous characters.

It was a reputation that was based on an unstinting addiction to quality. She was not always easy – Guy Adam who worked with her for thirty years remembered that ‘she was a perfectionist: if I forgot something she had told me to do she had a voice and a face like iron’. But she was generous too, and always an immaculate hostess. A legend in the tasting-room, she relied as much on intuition as experience, and was very rarely proved to be wrong. The finer skills of tasting had been learned from her husband Jacques, head of the business and the family until his sad and early death in 1941. Left a widow at the age of forty-two, ‘Madame Jacques’, as the staff were always to call her, dedicated the rest of her life to maintaining the unassailable reputation of Champagne’s most envied house.

Within the district, Bollinger is quite unique for still being very much a family house. It has remained faithful to the traditional methods used in the region, even fermenting all its vintage Champagne in small casks, maintained by the firm’s own cooper.

There was consequently a great deal of excitement when some of the contents of Madame Bollinger’s personal cellar appeared at Sotheby’s in London on 17 July this year. Her own rigorous standards had made certain that this selection of mature Champagne had been kept in perfect conditions in Bollinger’s notoriously cold cellars. Some great years were represented – 1953, 1961, 1964, 1969, 1970 and 1973 – and much of the wine was in Magnums and Jeroboams. The fact that Bollinger still make the Champagne in these large bottles (rather than making it in normal bottles and then transferring it as most other houses do) guaranteed an extraordinary freshness. The sale provided a rare chance to discover the elegance and power of aged, recently disgorged, Bollinger, and all the lots made more than their estimates.

Once, when asked how she enjoyed her own champagne, Madame Bollinger replied ‘I drink it when I’m happy and when I’m sad. Sometimes I drink it when I’m alone. When I have company I consider it obligatory. I trifle with it if I’m not hungry and I drink it when I am. Otherwise I never touch it – unless I’m thirsty.’ Although a life of extraordinary achievements, hers was clearly also one of unparalleled rewards.

Opposite, left
A Jeroboam of Bollinger RD 1970 OB £264 ($433)
Right
One of two Magnums of Bollinger RD 1961 OB (disgorged on 23 February 1973) £264 ($433)
These two bottles from the personal cellar of Madame Lily Bollinger were sold in London on 17 July 1991.

Principal officers and experts

Michael Ainslie
President and Chief Executive, Sotheby's Holdings, Inc.
The Rt.Hon. The Earl of Gowrie
Chairman, Sotheby's UK & International
John L. Marion
Chairman, Sotheby's North America
Diana D. Brooks
President and Chief Executive Officer, Sotheby's North America
Timothy Llewellyn
Managing Director, Sotheby's UK & International
Julian Thompson
Deputy Chairman, Sotheby's UK & International (Asia)
Simon de Pury
Deputy Chairman, Sotheby's UK & International (Europe)

American decorative arts and furniture
Leslie B. Keno *New York, 606 7130*
William W. Stahl, Jr *606 7110*
Wendell Garrett *606 7137*

American folk art
Nancy Druckman *New York, 606 7225*

American Indian art
Dr Bernard de Grunne *New York, 606 7325*

American paintings, drawings and sculpture
Peter B. Rathbone *New York, 606 7280*

Antiquities and Asian art
Richard M. Keresey (Antiquities) *New York, 606 7328*
Carlton Rochell (Asian) *606 7328*
Felicity Nicholson (Antiquities) *London, 408 5111*
Brendan Lynch (Asian) *408 5112*

Arms and armour and medals
David Erskine-Hill *London, 408 5315*
Margie Schwartz *New York, 606 7250*

Books and manuscripts
Roy Davids *London, 408 5287*
David N. Redden *New York, 606 7386*
Paul Needham *606 7385*

British paintings 1500-1850
James Miller *London, 408 5405*
David Moore-Gwyn *London, 408 5406*
Henry Wemyss (watercolours) *408 5409*

British paintings from 1850
Simon Taylor (Victorian) *London, 408 5385*
Janet Green (twentieth-century) *408 5387*

Ceramics
Peter Arney *London, 408 5134*
Letitia Roberts *New York, 606 7180*

Chinese art
Carol Conover *New York, 606 7332*
Arnold Chang (paintings) *606 7334*
Julian Thompson *London, 408 5371*
Colin Mackay *408 5145*
Mee Seen Loong *Hong Kong, (852) 524 8121*

Clocks and watches
Tina Millar (watches) *London, 408 5328*
Michael Turner (clocks) *408 5329*
Daryn Schnipper *New York, 606 7162*

Coins
Tom Eden (Ancient and Islamic) *London, 408 5315*
James Morton
(English and paper money) *408 5314*
Gerard Hill *New York, 606 7150*

Collectables
Dana Hawkes *New York, 606 7424*
Hilary Kay *London, 408 5205*

Contemporary art
Hugues Joffre *London, 408 5400*
Lucy Mitchell-Innes *New York, 606 7254*

European works of art
Margie Schwartz *New York, 606 7250*
Elizabeth Wilson *London, 408 5321*

Furniture
Graham Child (English) *London, 408 5347*
William W. Stahl, Jr. *New York, 606 7110*
Thierry Millerand (French and Continental) *New York, 606 7213*
Jonathan Bourne *London, 408 5349*
Alexandre Pradère *Paris, 33 (1) 42 66 40 60*

Garden statuary
James Rylands *Sussex, (0403) 783933*
Jennifer Cox *London, 408 5217*
Elaine Whitmire *New York, 606 7285*

Glass and paperweights
Lauren K. Tarshis *New York, 606 7180*
Simon Cottle *London, 408 5135*

Impressionist and modern paintings
David J. Nash *New York, 606 7351*
Alexander Apsis *606 7360*
Sharon Schultz Simpson *606 7360*
John L. Tancock *606 7360*
Marc E. Rosen (drawings) *606 7154*
Simon de Pury *London, 408 5222*
Michel Strauss *408 5389*

Islamic art and carpets
Richard M. Keresey (works of art) *New York, 606 7328*
William F. Ruprecht (carpets) *606 7996*
Professor John Carswell (works of art) *London, 408 5153*
Jacqueline Bing (carpets) *408 5152*

Japanese art
Neil Davey *London, 408 5141*
Suzanne Mitchell
Nyr Indictor *New York, 606 7338*

Jewellery
David Bennett *Geneva, 41 (22) 732 85 85*
John D. Block *New York, 606 7392*
Alexandra Rhodes *London, 408 5306*

Judaica
David Breuer-Weil *Tel Aviv, 972 (3) 22 38 22*
Camilla Previté *London, 408 5334*

Latin American paintings
August Uribe,
Sharon Schultz Simpson *New York, 606 7290*

Musical instruments
Leah Ramirez *New York, 606 7190*
Graham Wells *London, 408 5341*

Nineteenth-century European furniture and works of art
Christopher Payne *London, 408 5350*
Elaine Whitmire *New York, 606 7285*

Nineteenth-century European paintings and drawings
Michael Bing *London, 408 5380*
Nancy Harrison *New York, 606 7140*
Pascale Pavageau *Paris, 33 (1) 42 66 40 60*

Old master paintings and drawings
Julien Stock *London, 408 5413*
Elizabeth Llewellyn (drawings) *408 5416*
George Wachter *New York, 606 7230*
Scott Schaefer (drawings) *606 7222*
Nancy Ward-Neilson *Milan, 39 (2) 78 39 11*
Etienne Breton *Paris, 33 (1) 42 66 40 60*

Oriental manuscripts
Nabil Saidi *London, 408 5332*

Photographs
Philippe Garner *London, 408 5138*
Beth Gates-Warren *New York, 606 7240*

Portrait miniatures, objects of vertu, icons and Russian works of art
Julia Clarke (vertu) *London, 408 5324*
Haydn Williams (miniatures) *408 5326*
Heinrich Graf von Spreti
Munich, 49 (89) 291 31 51
Gerard Hill *New York, 606 7150*

Postage stamps
Richard Ashton *London, 408 5224*

Pre-Columbian art
Stacy Goodman *New York, 606 7330*

Prints
Susan Pinsky *New York, 606 7117*
Ian Mackenzie *London, 408 5210*
Ruth M. Ziegler *Tokyo, (212) 606 7112*

Silver
Kevin L. Tierney *New York, 606 7160*
Peter Waldron (English) *London, 408 5104*
Harold Charteris (Continental) *408 5106*
Dr Christoph Graf Douglas
Frankfurt, 49 (69) 74 07 87

Sporting Guns
Adrian Weller *London, 408 5319, Sussex (0403) 783 933*
Windy Phillips *New York, 606 7261*

Tribal art
Dr Bernard de Grunne *New York, 606 7325*
Sabine Dauwe *London, 408 5115*

Trusts and estates
Timothy Sammons *London, 408 5335*
Warren P. Weitman *New York, 606 7198*

Twentieth-century applied arts
Barbara E. Deisroth *New York, 606 7170*
Philippe Garner *London, 408 5138*

Vintage cars
Malcolm Barber *London, 408 5320*
David Patridge *Rumney NH, (603) 786 2338*

Western manuscripts
Dr Christopher de Hamel, FSA, *London, 408 5330*

Wine
Serena Sutcliffe, MW, *London, 924 3287*

Contributors

Ian Bennett worked at Sotheby's London for ten years, and is now senior contributing editor of *Hali International Magazine of Fine Carpets and Textiles*. He has published four books on oriental carpets, including *Rugs and Carpets of the World* (1978).

Denise Bethel, a graduate of the Courtauld Institute of Art, was formerly Director of the Photographs department of the rare book auction house, Swann Galleries, Inc. She is now a Vice President of Sotheby's New York and an expert in the photographs department.

Hugh Brigstocke is a Director in the old master paintings department at Sotheby's London and was formerly Curator of Italian and French paintings at the National Gallery of Scotland. He organised the 1981 Edinburgh exhibition *Poussin Sacraments and Bacchanals* as well as the recent *Drawings by Nicolas Poussin* exhibition at the Ashmolean Museum, Oxford.

Jude Burkhauser is both artist and curator, specialising in art and architecture, exhibition design, and research into women in the arts. A Rotary Scholarship at Glasgow School of Art led to the 1990 exhibition *'Glasgow Girls': Women in Art and Design 1880–1920* which she organised, designed and curated. She has also recently completed two large scale commissions for British Rail.

John Carswell is Director of the Islamic art department at Sotheby's London, and was formerly Director of the Smart Museum at the University of Chicago. His books include *Kutalya Tiles and Pottery* (1972), *Islamic Bookbindings and Bookmaking* (1981) and *Blue and White: Chinese Porcelain and its Impact on the West* (1985).

R. J. Charleston, former Keeper of the Department of Ceramics and Glass at the Victoria & Albert Museum, is President of the Glass Circle and former President of the Fellows of the Corning Museum of Glass. His publications include the catalogue of *Glass & Enamels at Waddesdon Manor* (1977) and *English Glass and the Glass used in England c.400–1940* (1984).

Peter Dobereiner recently retired after twenty-five years as golf correspondent to *The Observer*. He remains active in golf journalism as contributing editor of *Golf Digest* and consultant editor of *Golf World*.

Ian Fleming-Williams trained at the Royal Academy Schools and followed a career in teaching before devoting his time to research, with Constable his special field of study. He has published *Constable Landscape Watercolours and Drawings* (1976), *The Discovery of Constable* (1984, with Leslie Parris) and *Constable and his Drawings* (1990). He was co-organiser of the 1991 Constable exhibition at the Tate.

Wendell Garrett is a Senior Vice President of the American furniture and decorative arts department at Sotheby's New York. He is also Director of the museums services department. He was editor and publisher of *The Magazine Antiques* from 1972 until 1990 and his books include *Arts in Early American History* (1965) and *The Arts in America: the nineteenth century* (1969).

Philippa Glanville is Curator of Metalwork at the Victoria & Albert Museum. Her publications include *Silver in England* (1987), *Women Silversmiths* (1990, with Jennifer Goldsborough) and most recently, a catalogue of the national collection of silver 1480–1660, *Silver in Tudor and Early Stuart England* (1990).

Jack Hillier is a wood engraver and collector and connoisseur of the Japanese book. He has been a consultant in Oriental art to Sotheby's for twenty-five years, and is the author of numerous books. Recent publications include *Japanese Prints and Drawings from the Vever Collection* (1976), *The Art of Hokusai in Book Illustration* (1980) and *The Art of the Japanese Book* (1987).

Nyr Indictor joined Sotheby's in 1986, as a member of the Chinese department. He has been Director of the Japanese department in New York since 1989.

Selby Kiffer studied literature and bibliography at Pennsylvania State and Columbia University before joining Sotheby's New York in 1984 where he is now a Vice President in the department of books and manuscripts. He has since participated in the sale of many famous collections and supervised the cataloguing of the library of H. Bradley Martin.

Simon Maguire joined Sotheby's in April 1990 having taught music at Oxford for about ten years. Besides cataloguing manuscripts for Sotheby's, he writes regularly about Italian opera and is author of *Vincenzo Bellini and the Aesthetics of Nineteenth-Century Italian Opera* (1989).

Marsha Malinowski is an Assistant Vice President in the department of books and manuscripts at Sotheby's New York where she specialises in European and American literary manuscripts. She has been responsible for the important sales of Kafka's letters to Felice, Conan Doyle's *The Valley of Fear*, the amended typescript of *The War of the Worlds* and the literary archive of Alan Paton.

Ann Payne is a Curator of Manuscripts at the British Library. Her publications include *Medieval Beasts* (1990), a book based on bestiaries in the British Library. She has also organised a number of exhibitions, including *British Heraldry* in 1978 for the British Library.

John Russell is the former chief art critic for *The New York Times*. He is the author of many books of travel and art, including *Jennifer Bartlett: In the Garden* (1982) and *Paris* (1983).

Timothy Sammons is a Director of Sotheby's London, heading the trusts and estates department, which assists clients and their advisors in the management of works of art and collections. He is also an expert in Chinese art, and acts as a consultant to the Chinese departments worldwide.

Diana Scarisbrick, FSA is a freelance writer and lecturer specialising in the history of jewellery and engraved gems. She contributes regularly to *Country Life*, *Apollo* and *The Burlington Magazine*, and is jewellery editor of *Harpers and Queen*. She is author of *Ancestral Jewels* (1989) and the forthcoming *Jewels in Britain 1066–1837*.

Stewart Skilbeck has been a consultant with Sotheby's collectors' vehicles department since 1984. He campaigns his own collection of cars in club events and rallies and serves on the executive committee of the Veteran Car Club of Great Britain.

Lynn Stowell Pearson was an editor at the International Foundation for Art Research before joining Sotheby's New York in 1987 where she is an Assistant Vice President in the publications department. She recently published a paper on 'Ancient Stones: Quarrying, Trade and Provenance', *Acta Archaeologica Lovaniensa* (1991).

John L. Tancock is a Senior Vice President and Director of the department of Impressionist and modern paintings at Sotheby's New York. His publications include *The Sculpture of Auguste Rodin* (1976) and *Multiples: The First Decade* (1971).

Ronald Varney is a Vice President in the marketing department at Sotheby's New York. He has written widely on the arts for *Esquire*, *Smithsonian* and *Connoisseur* magazines, and *The Wall Street Journal*.

John Wilton-Ely is Director of Sotheby's educational studies in London, and Professor Emeritus of Art History at the University of Hull. He organised the Piranesi Bicentenary exhibition in 1978 at the Hayward Gallery, London and his publications include *The Mind and Art of Piranesi* (1978). He is currently organising an exhibition on the Adam Brothers.

Index

Previous page
A pair of Regency chinoiserie painted plaster nodding-head figures, early nineteenth century, height 28½in (72cm)
New York $71,500 (£36,294). 13.X.90

Above
An Irish gilt-bronze mount found in Markyate, Hertfordshire, eighth–ninth century AD, 2⅜in (6.1cm)
London £60,500 ($98,615). 8.VII.91